GERRY BIRRELL
Lost Before His Time

Kevin Guthrie archive

Dedication

To my sister Susan, who in the past couple of years has endured the passing of our parents, a serious illness to a dearly loved son and made a life-changing decision. While there have been the inevitable lows and many tears, she still managed to face the world every day and never chose the easy option. Her strength and fortitude is inspirational on a daily basis and has influenced me on how I look at life. Carpe diem!

And, to the equally strong group of women - the wives/girlfriends of racing drivers – particularly those from that most dangerous of eras, the '70s – who had to face unimaginable anxieties whether at home or the circuit. They were a close-knit group who never sought the limelight but when called upon to undertake that most sorrowful of tasks, the clearing of the personal effects of a fallen comrade, did so with great dignity and compassion and still offered the strength and support to the man in their life who had also lost someone close. The role played by those remarkable women should never be forgotten.

First Published: February 2023

ISBN 978-1-7391249-1-5

Author Darren Banks
Editor David Tremayne
Designer Clare Godden
Front Cover Stuart Dent archive and Motorsport Images
Rear Cover Chris Walker/Kartpix
Printed by The Manson Group

Publisher

Performance Publishing Ltd
Unit 3 Site 4 Alma Park Road,
Grantham, Lincolnshire, NG31 9SE
Great Britain

Contents

Rounding Shaw's hairpin at Mallory Park in 1971, one of Gerry's most impressive F2 performances. *(David Marshall)*

Acknowledgements

Gerry on the limit in his highly-modified, Climax-powered Chamois at Ingliston in August '68. ***(Eric Bryce)***

As always with books of this type, numerous people gave up their valuable time to reminiscence about their connection to Gerry in whichever capacity they encountered him. Whether their memories are substantial or brief, all are equally important, and add considerably to the story. I am deeply indebted to the following for their help, honesty, patience, support and candidness, in all matters pertaining to Gerry.

Firstly, the stand-outs, who went the extra mile and, in some cases, many extra miles to do their utmost to help make the story the best it could be.

Top of the list by some margin is Gerry's widow Margaret, who from our first meeting back in 2017, when she granted me the all-important permission to begin work, has been a joy to work with. Her contribution is unrivalled, both in its quality and quantity. She's the only person to have read the whole manuscript before publication and has offered constructive advice throughout. Her pragmatism and honesty are much admired. I sincerely hope I have captured the Gerry you knew and loved. Thank you, Margaret. It's been a pleasure.

Another permission sought and granted without hesitation was that of Gerry's brother Graham. Without his and Margaret's permission, the book you hold would never have happened, so equal thanks to him. On our first meeting he was candid, honest and recalled with clarity memories of the early days back in the early '60s and of the subsequent years, up to Gerry's move south towards the end of the decade. Subsequently, he answered many queries promptly and courteously. I look forward to meeting up again to present him with a copy of the book.

It is no exaggeration to say that without the assistance of Andy Morrison, whose immense knowledge of the Scottish motor racing scene proved invaluable and whose contact book saved me considerable time and effort. The combination of those two things greatly enhanced the quality of the finished product. In my limited writing experience things just click with one person in particular where you feel that you will keep in touch way beyond the completion of the book. Andy is one such person. Thank you for your patience and friendship.

John Catt, Gerry's loyal and trusted mechanic, took some tracking down but was well worth the effort. A morning spent in his company reminiscing about days long ago, but not forgotten, was a joy.

John Stanton, Gerry's backer and friend. His enthusiasm, patience and help at all times was always appreciated. It's a shame we never got to meet face to face, something which is my fault entirely.

Kenny Baird and Raymond Goodman played vital roles in supplying a vast amount of material on Bo'ness, Rest and Be Thankful, Ingliston and other lesser-known Scottish events by allowing me access to their archive of programmes and *Top Gear* magazines. The information contained within was invaluable, so it added a great deal, not just to Gerry's story, but also a unique insight into the Scottish racing scene.

Last, but by no means least, a huge thank you and appreciation to Stuart Turner, a man who should need no introduction to hardened enthusiasts, for his heartfelt Foreword.

In alphabetical order, thanks are due to: Han Akersloot; Thomas Ammerschlaeger; Roger Barr; Andy Barton; Arnie Black, for his generosity; Denise Bloor; Barry Boor; Claude Bourgoignie; Dave Brodie; Brian Churcher; Peter Connew; Adam Cooper; Michael Cotton; the late Andrew Cowan; Bob Curl; Peter Danaher; Ian Dawson; Sandy Denham; Stuart Dent; Mike Doodson; the late Tony Dron; Eric Dymock; Bill Dryden; Neil Edwards; Steve Entwistle, for the loan of his treasured early '60s copies of *Motoring News* and all things rallying related; Robin Emslie; David Finlay; John Fitzpatrick; Yvette Fontaine; Gillian Fortescue-Thomas; Graham Gauld; Peter Gaydon; Dieter Glemser; George and Ronnie Grant; Mike Haysey; Hans Heyer; the late John Hogan; Steve Holter; Gordon Horn; Michael How; Terry Hoyle; Ray Hutton; Mike Jiggle, of *Auto Tradition/Racing Spirit* magazines; Hans Knotte; Gerd Knozinger; Mike Kranefuss; Eddie Labinjoh; Frans Lubin; John Mackenzie; Andrew Marriott; Jochen Mass; Dave Matthews; Sandy McCracken; Brendan McInerney; Jimmy McInnes; Bruce and John McTavish; Greg Mills; Mike Mitchell; Mike Moreton; Logan Morrison; Alan Muir; John Murray; Andrew Mylius; Jean-Pierre Antoine Navarro, of Firestone France; Jochen Neerpasch; Iain Nicolson, for friendship, the loan of his treasured copies of *Top Gear* magazine and all things Ingliston; Paul Owens; Stuart Parker of Veterans of Scottish Motorsport Association; Ian Phillips; Julian Pratt; Phil Read; Andreas Riehl, for interviewing Dieter Glemser in Munich and much more; Johnny Rives; Stuart Rolt; David Ross, for knowledge and friendship; Tim Schenken; Lutz Schilling; Douglas Shannon, for memories of his father Hugh; Sarah Sizer of P&A Wood; Tom Sleigh; Quentin Spurring, for supplying all of Gerry's *Competition Car* columns; Sir Jackie Stewart and his staff; Madeleine Stewart; Simon Taylor; Gunther Trauss; Tony Trimmer; Neil Trundle; Alan 'Plum' Tyndall, for permission to quote from his excellent book on Crosslé and all matters relating to the renowned Irish race car manufacturers; Colin Vandervell; Ian Wagstaff; Jeremy Walton; Gunter Warthofer, for help with all former Cologne personnel; John Watson; Grahame White; Vernon Williamson; Jeff Wilson; Chris Witty; Derrick Worthington; Terry Wright; Robert Young.

I am deeply indebted to all the above and if I have omitted anyone, my sincere apologies.

For permission to use extracts/quotes from *Autosport*, my thanks to editor Kevin Turner and assistant editor Marcus Simmons. The same applies to Joe Dunn, the editor of *Motor Sport* and Matt James of *Motoring News*.

You can almost hear the tyres protesting. On the limit at the Parabolica at Monza ***(Motorsport Images)***

Stepping into the Editor's chair again is esteemed award-winning author David Tremayne. To have such a consummate wordsmith offering help and advice is a privilege I never take for granted. You could not wish for a more generous friend. To find the time to help/guide me, considering his immense workload, is something that continually impresses me. Thank you, DT.

Once again, Adam Wilkins of Performance Publishing has shown great patience and understanding in waiting for what is now the third book we have produced together. His loyalty – a character trait that tops my list – is highly appreciated. No matter what happens in the future, I won't forget that it was Adam who had the faith and confidence in my first effort that enables me to continue to undertake projects such as this.

We are like-minded individuals who are keen to tell the stories of the lesser-known personalities who have graced the world of motorsport. I hope to continue to work on many projects in the future with Adam and his small team who have managed to achieve the deserved recognition of their efforts in the small time they have been producing motor racing titles.

Clare Godden, who has stepped in as graphic designer for the first time on a Performance Publishing title. Her patience and attention to detail while proofs were going back and forth was unwavering.

Thanks, too, to my family and friends who have helped me through what have been some difficult times the past couple of years. You should never underestimate the support of people who understand you and are always there for you, no matter what. Take it from me, don't bottle things up. Never be afraid to open up. It's not a weakness to admit you have a problem.

Finally, to my lovely wife Ann, who allows me all the time I need to work on my writing, which is something she knows means so much to me. Without her support and understanding, none of what you are about to read would have happened. Love you.

Photo Acknowledgements

Gerry with his brother Graham at Ingliston in the late '60s. Graham, as always, looked immaculate. ***(Eric Bryce)***

I am deeply indebted to the numerous photographers, both professional and amateur, who have supplied images to be considered for inclusion. Also, family, friends and rivals, who have been willing to share their private collections. Inevitably, not all have made the final cut but are still worthy of acknowledgement.

Pete Austin; Graham Birrell; Jeff Bloxham; Alan Bowles; Eric Bryce; Peter Carey; Robert Clayson; the late Esler Crawford; Crosslé Car Company (Paul McMorran); Jack Davidson; Mike Dixon; Robin Emslie; Jutta Fausel; John Fitzpatrick; Graham Gauld; Kate Haston; Mike Hayward; Henk Hazelaar; William Henderson of the Bill Henderson Collection; Thomas Horat; Michael How (SMRC); Udo Klinkel; Alfred Koch; John Leck; Robin Liddell; Colin Lourie; Michael Malcolm; David Marshall, Tim Marshall; H Matheson Collection; Josef Mayrhofer; Peter McFadyen; Bruce McTavish; Greg Mills; Andy Morrison; Motorsport Images (Zoe Schafer); John Murray; Niall Murray-Lyon; Paris Normandie (Isabelle Desarmagnac); David Pearson; Rob Petersen; David Ross; Christian Sandler; Alex Shore; Margaret Shore; John Stanton; Madeleine Stewart; Dick Vergers; Chris Walker of Kartpix; Robert Young; and Charlotte Ward, Warren Crone and Jamie Myler of the Ford Motor Company.

Iain Nicolson deserves a special mention for not only supplying two photos but also for his patience and tireless help on all matters photographic.

The mere mention of Gerry's name, even after all these years, conjures up many feelings. Gerry was everything you would want in a racing driver. Quick, intelligent, diligent and easy on the car – his engineering background helping there – all of which were combined with a dry wit, a cheerful disposition and an engaging personality that made you want to spend time in his company.

I consider myself fortunate to have witnessed him at work, whether it was representing Ford in competition, testing and developing new products or promotional work, he was a complete professional. He followed the example set by those two great Scottish champions before him, Jim Clark and Sir Jackie Stewart – who was a close friend. I've often thought that there must be something in the water up there to produce such talents.

The author, Darren Banks, has tracked down a vast number of people, including family members, to offer their recollections of Gerry, who all have nothing but fond memories of either racing against him, working for him, or becoming friends. Many friendships forged in the early days when he was preparing cars for his brother Graham endured even though he moved down south, then subsequently began to travel worldwide. On his rare visits back to the Auld Country, he would look up old friends and be the same Gerry they all remembered. Success and fame in motorsport circles didn't change him, one iota.

I'm delighted that Darren has chosen to tell Gerry's story, something that was well overdue, in my opinion. I've learnt many new things about him or been reminded of things long forgotten. It is a fitting tribute to a fine racing driver and an equally fine human being. Enjoy!

Stuart Turner
Chipping Norton
November 2022

Le Mans '72, waiting for the off with Stuart Turner. ***(Alfred Koch)***

Gerry drove a variety of Capris for numerous teams. This one is the Frami Racing example at Crystal Palace in '72. ***(Peter Carey)***

Arguably, the period from the mid-'60s to the mid-'70s was one of the most dangerous to be a racing driver. The number of fatalities, not just in Formula One, which garnered the most headlines, both in the specialist journals and in the broadsheets and tabloids was, frankly, appalling.

The advent of wings and slick tyres, both of which increased cornering speeds to unprecedented levels, meant that in simple terms, the cars had outgrown the circuits. The latter had often failed scandalously to improve or, in some cases, even maintain, the required safety standards necessary to allow races to take place in an environment that gave the drivers the best chance of survival should they suffer any kind of mechanical/tyre failure or personal error.

Despite the efforts of the Grand Prix Drivers' Association (GPDA) led by Jackie Stewart, who spearheaded the campaign and was on the receiving end of some unwarranted, unfair criticism for his stance to improve standards, the powers-that-be just weren't taking any notice of the evidence at their disposal. Every time a driver left home or his hotel room, whether it was for a test session or a race meeting, there was a one in three chance of him not returning. What a damning statistic.

The governing body seemed weak and powerless to effect any influence on the relevant motor clubs/sporting organisations who were responsible for the safety of the circuits under their control. Invariably, they baulked at the costs involved at the suggested changes put forward by Stewart and the GPDA. While you can have a modicum of sympathy for their plight if insufficient funds weren't available for improvements, what you can't excuse or forgive is their complete disregard of getting the basics right. Surely, there wasn't too much cost involved in setting the support posts for the Armco barriers in concrete, rather than just pushing them into soft earth, and once installed fastening them together properly. That wasn't too much to ask, was it? In the case of Rouen-les-Essarts in Northern France, apparently it was.

The failure to even do those simple, basic tasks resulted in the tragic loss of Gerald Hussey Buchanan Birrell, better known to all as Gerry, an up-and-coming Scottish driver of immense promise, who many felt was destined to follow in the footsteps of his illustrious countrymen, Jim Clark and Jackie Stewart, in not only reaching the pinnacle of his chosen sport, Formula One, but going on to claim the sport's greatest prize.

His loss was felt keenly throughout the worldwide motorsport community, not just because of his popularity but, also, because it was preventable. Even today, nearly 50 years

A fine study of an artist at work. Gerry in the March 722 at the Rothmans 50,000 at Brands Hatch in '72. ***(Ford Motor Company)***

on, the events of 23 June 1973, still foster feelings of anger and despair, in both people directly involved and followers of his career, particularly, in the Auld Country.

While he was a known name among keen enthusiasts, what first comes to mind if you had to be pressed into pinpointing a precise memory or achievement? Quick in the Cologne Capris? More suited to saloons, than single-seaters? A good-all-rounder? Those would be my immediate thoughts.

While the first and third statements are true, there was much more to Gerry Birrell than I thought. Highly-respected test driver. Engineer. Mechanic. Ambassador. Family man. On and on it goes.

Personally, I under-estimated his speed, consistency and achievements in single-seaters. You don't win back-to-back championships in your first two full seasons on circuits you have never seen before, and progress up to, firstly, Formula Three, then to Formula Two, just one rung from the top, without a high level of all-round ability.

The rise up the single-seater ranks – once he moved south after six years of racing on home soil – was quite meteoric, only a slight stagnation in Formula Two halting his rapid progress to the top.

His successes led to a contract with the Ford Motor Company, not just to race and develop a variety of competition machinery, but also to undertake road car development duties. This was how he earned his living and where many saw his future.

Personally, I feel the association with Ford is the primary reason Gerry's career in single-seaters is often overlooked. When you think of Ford of that period and most since, you think of tin-top racing and rallying.

Opinions are divided on where he would have ultimately ended up. Would he have replaced the retiring Stewart at Tyrrell for the 1974 season? Or longer term, would he have continued his relationship with Ford and run their motorsport affairs? The thought of Gerry running a Ford Formula One team isn't too far-fetched.

Draw your own conclusions from the following pages. Personally, my eyes have been opened to what a talent Gerry Birrell was. He should be forever remembered by those with a passion for motorsport – of which I am one – as one of the most professional, complete drivers of, not just his era, but of all time. And a bloody good guy to match!

Darren Banks
East Neuk of Fife
December 2022

A momentous day. On 24 September 1961, at Charterhall, Gerry had his first ever race in Graham's A40, only a few weeks after his 17th birthday.
(Graham Birrell/Darren Banks archive)

CHAPTER ONE

EARLY DAYS

Gerry was the youngest of the three Birrell boys, arriving on the scene in July 1944. Graham, the eldest was born in October 1940, with Iain coming along in March 1942.

They lived on the outskirts of Glasgow in the affluent town of Milngavie (pronounced mul-guy). The ability to live in such a place was down to the hard work of their father, Jack, who was a successful businessman. Typical of the times, the boys' mother, Florence, worked equally hard at bringing them up and fulfilled the role of a housewife, admirably.

A benefit of their acquired status and moderate wealth was the ability to send all the boys to Kelvinside Academy, a highly-respected, fee-paying seat of learning in the West End of Glasgow, just off the Great Western Road. "The old man worked bloody hard to fund the fees to send the three of us to such a school," remembers Graham. "We went there from the age of four or five to 15 or 16. In the main, we all went on the bus (a blue Alexander) from the Strathblane Road terminus, Milngavie to central Glasgow, a journey of about six miles. On some occasions mothers' aunt, who had stayed with us during the war, and after, took us when we were young."

Unfortunately, it appears the calibre of school was wasted on Gerry and his elder sibling. "Gerry was about as good at school as I was," recalls Graham. "He was known as 'excuse

A rare photo of the three Birrell brothers together, with their mother Florence. Graham left, Iain right with Gerry next to Florence. ***(Margaret Shore)***

Graham (left) sampling an early go-kart, alongside an unidentified driver at the Meadowbank Stadium in Edinburgh. ***(Graham Birrell/Darren Banks archive)***

boots Birrell' on the occasions he would duck out of anything which required boots. Sport, cadet training, or whatever. He couldn't wait to leave and get into the garage."

The garage in question was Wylie and Lochhead's, a Renault main dealer on Berkeley Street in Glasgow. "It was the perfect place for Gerry to serve his time as an apprentice mechanic and get a good all-round education on all manner of vehicles," offers Graham. "As well as the Renault agency they had a commercial workshop due to the other line of business they were involved in being furniture removals."

Gerry's interest – nay, obsession – in cars or rather more accurately, cars to be modified/raced, seems, like most boys who have elder siblings, to have been influenced by their hobbies and interests.

"I had an enormous desire since about the age of 10," recalls Graham. "I was always, always interested, not in cars, but always racing cars. There wasn't any motoring/racing background in the family. Father wasn't interested at all.

"I was allowed to drive his Ford Zephyr, which was his business car. Then when I went to work with him he bought me a new Austin A35. I was told, very wisely, by him, that if I was seen or reported doing over 60mph anywhere, the car came away, which was sound advice. The only thing was that I did 60 mph everywhere! I mean *everywhere*!

"I competed in my first event in September 1959, a sprint at Heathfield in Ayrshire, in the A35, with Gerry along as mechanic. He would get behind the wheel and warm the car up. He had just turned 15, so obviously didn't have a licence. That was my only competition outing in the car. I've no idea where I finished.

"I replaced that with an A40, which Gerry ripped to bits and made into a racer for the 1960 season. I raced at Charterhall and competed in other events that the car was eligible for, such as rallies, sprints and hillclimbs. For my first

Before he passed his driving test, Gerry would take every opportunity to get behind the wheel of Graham's car when on mechanic duties. Here he is fooling around in the Austin A40 at Heathfield, a sprint venue in Ayrshire, in early '61. ***(Graham Birrell/Darren Banks archive)***

ever rally, the Highland, which started in Glasgow, I had an engine built by Merchiston Motors, home of Ecurie Ecosse. Unfortunately, I couldn't afford a rev counter. The result was engine failure – it ran its bearings.

"I was always popping into Ecurie Ecosse on my travels. Their patron, David Murray, would sell me a set of tyres on their Dunlop contract for £20. It wasn't just them I would buy tyres from. In the years ahead, I would buy 'scrap' tyres from various people, keeping the best ones and selling the less good to other competitors like John Nicholson. I even ran the A40 on the road with racing tyres. Not a good idea!"

The programme of events undertaken was typical of the Scottish motor racing scene at that time, with Charterhall

As well as looking after Graham's car, Gerry was much in demand helping out friends and rivals. Here he runs to assist Tom Sleigh in his Lola-Climax. ***(David Ross)***

Airfield in the Borders being the only available race circuit. It was necessary to take in Sprints at places like Heathfield, hillclimbs at the Rest and be Thankful in Argyll and Bute, Bo'ness, near Edinburgh and rallies in the Glasgow area, just so that you competed regularly.

Throughout the season, Graham would do so in all the aforementioned disciplines with the modified A40, the registration of which was GB 201. A modicum of success was attained, a first in class at the Rest and be Thankful hillclimb being the highlight of the eight events undertaken.

Gerry was there throughout keeping the car in fine fettle and taking every opportunity he could to get behind the wheel, testing brakes, steering, etc. He would run up and down the paddock, so he would be sufficiently skilled and confident to pass his driving test at the first time of asking the following year.

It wasn't just in the paddocks of the various venues that Gerry gained driving experience. Doubtless unbeknown to his parents, he had come a cropper in Graham's Mini van while travelling on the back roads around Milngavie. This only came to light after an incident a few months later involving a fellow racer and friend of Graham's, Bill Dryden. "I did the Scottish Sporting Car Club anniversary run in 1960 in my father's Vauxhall Victor," remembers Bill. "No racing, it was more map reading, which Gerry was good at, so he came with me. Gerry would have been 16, so couldn't drive. No helmets or any of that nonsense with it only being a 'run'. I do remember he was wearing a pork pie hat.

"We set off from Milngavie at one-minute intervals and were not much out of Milngavie going into a long left-hander about 50 yards behind another car. I came around the corner and suddenly there's a tractor with a flat-bed wooden trailer reversing out of a field on the left. The car in front went around its outside and I went to follow him, but a motorbike and sidecar were coming the other way. It was either hit them or try to go between them and the trailer. I tried to go between them but the left-hand windscreen pillar went down the side of the trailer splitting the wood, resulting in it coming through the windscreen. I went through the windscreen and the wood went through the back seat and out of the back window with Gerry's hat swinging on the end.

"Jimmy Stewart, Jackie's brother, was next round in an E-Type, not racing or anything. He got out of the car and was sick because he thought Gerry's head had been taken off. So did I. I picked myself up off the road, having hit my shoulder, and ran back. We were both scared to lift his hat up but then, to our relief, we heard a cry from the car, 'Get me out. Get me out of this effing car.'

"It turned out that he'd been looking at the map, saw the wood coming towards him, and instinctively dipped his head and it just went over it. Then he said, "Look I can breathe without opening my mouth." He had a small hole through his cheek from a splinter from the piece of wood.

"We got the wood out of the car and the car itself was hardly damaged. It had just opened up like a tin opener but it was still driveable, just no windscreen and no back window.

"What are we going to do?" I asked.

"Let's finish the rally," says Gerry.

"We finished it and we lost some points due to the delay, and that was it.

"A day later, Gerry's face came up like a football. You couldn't see his eyes and nose. It was ginormous and he was taken into hospital. I was working at the Glasgow Motor Show on the SMT stand (my father's company) and used to nip out at lunchtime and visit him. He would be in bed with this great big swollen head.

"It turns out all the nurses knew him because he'd been in the same hospital about six months earlier when he'd crashed Graham's Mini van. Apparently, he'd hit the brakes which were snatching and the thing turned left and hit the wall. No seatbelts, so he fell out but his feet were trapped behind the pedals, which meant he went bouncing along the road on his backside. He had to go to the hospital and get his backside looked at. The nurses were all saying you've been in here before, what have you been doing this time?"

Due to the nature of his work helping Graham, Gerry was making a name for himself as someone who was at his happiest getting his hands dirty, and when not attending to his brother's needs he could often be found with his head under a bonnet or his legs sticking out from under a fellow competitor's car. This led to the nickname of 'Grubby', not a very flattering moniker to have bestowed on you. Gerry, by all accounts, took it in good spirits.

Established names such as Tom Sleigh and Eric Liddell, who came from moneyed backgrounds, were just two who benefited from Gerry's ability to make things work. No disrespect intended, but they would have stood around bewildered at how their car actually worked. They had the financial wherewithal, but not a clue on how to maintain the car. That was for the poor people who got their hands dirty. Even at such a young age, Gerry would have been thinking ahead, to forging long-term relationships with these people. If I do the donkey work – no payment involved – then I might just get a go in the car in the future.

Due to the variety and the limited number of events in Scotland, the entry lists tended to contain the same drivers, no matter what the event. This led to a close-knit bunch of diverse characters who took things very seriously in competition but knew how to let their hair down afterwards. Many friendships were born in that period, and endure today.

One such friendship involved David Ross, who at the time was just beginning to compete. He would continue spasmodically in a wide range of vehicles in the years ahead and would remain friends throughout both Graham's and Gerry's careers. He went on to become a motoring journalist.

"The first time I set eyes on them was when they came to Aberdeen – which was where I lived – to compete in the Highland Rally in an A40," recalls David. "It was a weekend rally and involved autotests, which were taking place on the Aberdeen Promenade. They were doing handbrake turns, which was something I'd never seen before.

"Believe it or not, the A40, which was all stripped out – it did have a rollcage – had only the one seat and was used by Graham when travelling around seeing clients during the day.

"We just hit it off immediately. I would make frequent trips to Glasgow and would often stay over at Atholl Cottage, their home in Milngavie. Their father had a huge train set. It went out into the back garden and back in again. Graham used to say to me, 'If father asks if I've seen the train set, just say yes.' Their mother was a wonderful Irish woman, particularly in bringing up three boys. Something I did find strange was that when she brought the food through into the dining room, she would put it on the table, then go and sit down by the fireplace on her own.

"Gerry navigated for me on the Cats' Eye Rally – which came out of Glasgow – and we won our class in a VW Beetle. I've still got the trophy, which is in the shape of a mug. There's no date on it but it was before Gerry had passed his test, so it must have been '59 or '60.

"We would compete in university club rallies in Glasgow, and on one occasion they fixed me up with a co-driver when they found out I didn't have one. Gerry was navigating for Graham on that event.

"Gerry would navigate/help out anyone, just to be involved. He loved messing with cars. On the Scottish rally one year he was either navigating or was part of the service crew for Tom Paton. Tom was the ultimate Scottish car dealer. Upon arrival at one of the overnight control stops the brake linings were worn out and it was metal on metal. They were told they couldn't work on the car until the morning and they only had one hour to fix them or they would incur time penalties.

"Somehow Gerry got back to Glasgow and picked up some brake linings, then proceeded to crawl under the fence of *parc fermé*, remove the front wheels and re-line the brakes.

"I remember being told a story of when they were coming back from competing in a Sprint at Heathfield in the A40. They had stopped for petrol and, while Graham was away paying, Gerry had opened the bonnet and was checking the oil when he was approached by a little guy who had got out of an A35 estate. The guy's asking Gerry all sorts of questions. 'Is it tuned up? Is that a Weber carburettor? What chokes and jets are you running in that? Who fitted it for you?' The guy is really giving him the third degree. Gerry had a habit of looking down on people until he got to know them. He's just answering yes to the questions, but when he answered that Wilkie Wilkinson – the legendary mechanic – had fitted the carburettor, the guy seemed to know who Wilkie was. I can imagine Gerry thinking, 'who is this guy?' By now, he's had enough and asks, who am I speaking to?

When the guy replied, Joe Potts, it completely floored Gerry. One minute, Gerry's looking down his nose at him, then suddenly he realises he's just been talking to one of the legendary figures of Scottish motorsport."

Potts hailed from Belshill in Glasgow and was a legendary figure in motorcycle racing, and a renowned tuner of Norton engines. That led him into car racing, firstly racing a 500cc Norton-engined F3 Cooper. Then, believing he could do better, he built his own car, the Joe Potts Special.

The A40 was retained for the 1961 season, with much the same fare on offer. But come Charterhall on 24 September, less than two months after his 17th birthday, Gerry made his competition debut having wasted no time in passing his driving test. "I was at Atholl Cottage with Graham when he was filling out Gerry's entry form," recalls David Ross. "I'm pretty sure at the time Gerry hadn't passed his test but Graham still sent it off. I think Gerry passed his test on the Friday before the meeting on Sunday."

Unsurprisingly, his mount would be Graham's trusty A40, a car he was somewhat familiar with. As was the 'norm' back then, the brothers would share it due to the number of races it was eligible for. This would be the first of many such occasions.

Gerry was entered in Event Three, a 10-lapper, for sports cars. (An A40, a sports car? That was stretching the imagination just a tad.) An entry of over 30 cars – some initiation – featured the usual array of seasoned, experienced campaigners, plus in car number 27 (Gerry was number 28) was a certain AN Other in a Marcos. This was, of course, the pseudonym used by a certain John Young Stewart – known to the entire universe these days as Sir Jackie – to prevent his mother from finding out about his racing exploits. Needless to say, like most mothers she soon did!

Back in those heady days of a new decade, Jackie was just a 21-year-old indulging himself in his love of cars and motor racing, having made his debut earlier in the season at Charterhall. He was already making a name for himself in cars belonging to Barry Filer, a customer at the garage owned by Jackie's father, Bob, and where Jackie was earning his keep in the lubrication bay. Dumbuck Garage was a long-established Austin and Jaguar dealership on the Glasgow Road in Dumbarton, a mere 10 or so miles from the Birrells in Milngavie. Jackie and the garage were very much part of not just the Glasgow motoring scene, but the whole Scottish motoring and racing environment.

"The Birrell family were great people," recalls Sir Jackie, all these years later. "I knew the whole family. Gerry was the 'wee' boy of the three brothers, and so enthusiastic. Graham was the same, while Iain was always around but never really got into it the way Graham and Gerry did.

"You have to remember at that time Scotland had some top drivers. Ron Flockhart, Innes Ireland, Ninian Sanderson – and Jim Clark was just beginning to emerge. Ecurie Ecosse was a patriotic and internationally renowned racing team, having won the Le Mans 24-hour on two occasions in the '50s. Scotland had some pedigree and we were all hoping to follow in their footsteps. For a nation the size of Scotland to have had that level of success at that time, and in the years ahead, is unbelievable.

"I started out in motor racing in a modest way and the Birrells were part of that. The three of them would come down to the garage and help me prepare my 'wee' Marcos. Motorsport at that time was in its infancy in Scotland, so the Birrell brothers were well-known. We would see each other at places like Charterhall, Bo'ness, Rest and be Thankful. All the sporting car clubs had dinners and functions which we would attend. They did some rallying, as well. I only ever did the one rally. I got tired at three in the morning and left.

"Gerry didn't work as a mechanic for me at race meetings at that time. He would have been busy with Graham. But we did spend a lot of time together.

"Gerry was a great enthusiast and came down to the garage when he heard we had one of the new E-Type Jags, registration FSN 1, in as a demonstrator. At that time, it was the first E-Type in Scotland, so I took him for a ride in it. No speed limits in those days!

"I must say they were some of the happiest times, not of my professional life, but the amateur side of my life."

The part Dumbuck Garage and Jackie Stewart played in those early days should not be under-estimated. Both would feature prominently in the years ahead.

After his first appearance – which turned out to be his only outing of the season – had failed to get Gerry a mention in the specialist Scottish magazines of the time, such as *Scottish Clubman*, you have to presume he was somewhat out-classed in both car and ability department. Hardly surprising when he was up against what was reportedly described by one eye-witness as the 'hordes' of cars battling it out at the first corner.

While Gerry's exploits failed to attract attention, those of his brother, or rather their car, did lead to the report for the under 1300cc GT cars race stating that 'the car of Graham Birrell was noisy, brash and indecently fast.' You can sense the influence of Gerry's handiwork in the garage at home in those comments.

After a couple of seasons of hard labour, the A40 was replaced by something far sportier, a Lotus Eleven, powered by a 998cc BMC engine. What you might call at that time 'a proper racing car'. It was eligible for use on the road, however, a fact that Graham would make use of in the year ahead.

For the 1962 season the usual varied events – circuit races, hillclimbs, sprints – would be undertaken with added trips further afield. The brothers would venture south for the first time, taking in races at well-known venues such as Oulton Park and Mallory Park, but also lesser-known venues as Elvington Aerodrome, which held its first-ever meeting that year.

As before, Gerry's main role would be that of a mechanic to Graham, but when the opportunity – and money – became available, he would don a cleaner pair of overalls for his stint behind the wheel.

In previous years the A35 and A40 had been driven to the venues to compete. For the Lotus, Graham decided to buy a Mini van to tow it the length and breadth of the British Isles. Typical of the Birrell thinking, that wasn't the only reason for that choice of tow vehicle.

"The Scottish Sporting Car Club re-wrote the regulations which meant I could compete with the Mini van in sprints

Gerry's second competition outing was aboard his father's road car, a Vauxhall VX/490 at the Bo'ness hillclimb in June '62. ***(Eric Bryce)***

and driving tests," recalls Graham. "I may even have competed in both, the Mini van and the Eleven, on the same day at places like the Rest and be Thankful.

"When we went south with the Eleven we towed it with the Mini van, which also doubled up as our accommodation for the night. Luxury!

"When heading south we always made sure Penrith was on the route, no matter where we were going. Father had an account with SMT for petrol and they had a depot there, so we could fill up and charge to his account. The old man was never pro-motor racing but he didn't stop us. Plus, he would contribute the odd pound or two."

The first outing for the pair in the Eleven would be on the familiar surroundings of Charterhall in April. Gerry was entered in the event for racing cars up to 1100cc and would be up against other Lotuses of varying types, Coopers of assorted vintage and a couple of Elvas. One was piloted by boisterous Yorkshireman Tony Lanfranchi. Gerry came up against some decent opposition in his early outings.

He seemed set for his usual busy day with his race being event seven and Graham's outing in the GT cars race, event five. The effort put in to prepare and race the car didn't reap any reward in the form of any worthwhile result.

Next time out, a couple of months later, at the Bo'ness hill-climb on the outskirts of Edinburgh, Gerry would have a car of his own to use for the first time. Well, it wasn't strictly his own. He was entered in a Vauxhall VX4/90, which was his father's road car. Before you jump to the obvious assumption, he was using it with parental approval. Graham would be sticking with the Eleven.

They would be joined on this occasion – another first – by the other Birrell brother, Iain, who would be out in a Mason Special, which was a 750MC machine. Previously, Iain had played very much a background role and hadn't competed before. Quite a historic occasion for the Birrell household.

Yet again, Gerry would be in the class for Sports/GT cars – in a VX4/90? An odd idea of a Sports/GT car, this time for over 1500cc and up to 2000cc cars. His opposition comprised vehicles that were more like sports cars. MGAs, TR3s, a Sunbeam Alpine, an AC Ace, even a Cooper-Monaco.

It would be no surprise to learn that Gerry's best time of his two runs, a 45.78s climb, was some way – over 10s – off the pace of the class-winning run of the aforementioned Cooper-Monaco of Josh Randles and was also outclassed by the other more experienced, better-equipped rivals.

No doubt a few days later when the latest issue of *Motoring News* arrived at the Birrell household, Gerry, along with Graham, would have been a bit irked to read that in the report from Bo'ness, Iain had got a mention, albeit not a very flattering one. 'Iain Birrell (Mason Special) only just managed to get over the top of the hill'. You can read into that what you will. But you can bet that Gerry and Graham would have 'ribbed' Iain mercilessly on the possible reasons for that sentence.

According to all friends/acquaintances/rivals who knew the Birrell brothers well – particularly, Gerry and Graham – the rivalry and the competitiveness between the three of them was something else. "To say they were competitive would be a complete understatement," offers Andy Morrison. "They made Olympians look like Boy Scouts. It wasn't just in motorsport but in everything. I mean everything!"

The name Andy Morrison is probably not one that is instantly recognisable when you get around to discussing the racing Birrells and the Scottish motorsport scene of not just the '60s and '70s but of any era. Always passionate about cars from an early age, he would cycle the many miles from his home to the Dumbuck Garage, just to gaze in the window at what the latest offerings were. His first job would be – somewhat inevitably – at Dumbuck Garage, as an apprentice. It was the first step on what would become a long and successful career in motorsport.

He was a regular attendee at Ingliston upon its opening in various capacities. A subsequent involvement with Broadspeed in the late '60s would lead eventually to a return to his roots when offered a position at Wylie's of Glasgow, running their newly created racing department. This led to his first direct involvement with the Birrells, Graham in particular.

He is an authority on all things concerning the Birrell racing history and his name would feature prominently in the years ahead as Graham and Gerry progressed further and further up the racing ladder.

The outing at Bo'ness was just the start of a busy week for the brothers. The following day, they would make their first foray south to RAF Ouston – along with most of the Bo'ness paddock – where a temporary circuit had been laid out. On this occasion, they would be back to sharing the Eleven, the VX4/90 relegated to the role of tow car. It appears nothing noteworthy was achieved for their efforts.

To complete their travels on the following Saturday, it was a 40-mile trip from Milngavie up the side of Loch Lomond to the famous Rest and be Thankful hillclimb in Argyll and Bute.

This time it was Gerry's turn to earn himself a mention in *Motoring News*: 'A notable performance was that of Gerald Birrell in his father's VX4/90 who finished fifth in the 1500-2000cc class.'

Gerald... It makes Gerry sound more like a bank manager than the aspiring racing driver, more so when behind the wheel of a Vauxhall saloon car. Throughout the majority of his Scottish career, he was entered under an assortment of names. The aforementioned, Gerald. GHB Birrell (Gerald Hussey Buchanan). GH Birrell. And, of course, the more well-known he became, Gerry. With Graham often entered in the same meeting with the same car and number (when sharing), and latterly, in the same race and type of car, entered under GB (Buchanan) Birrell, it makes for some confusion for historians and researchers.

When Gerry and Graham weren't either racing, chasing money or dreaming up their next modification, a trip to the British Grand Prix was regularly on the agenda.

"We started going from the mid-'50s or so," remembers Graham. "Silverstone, Aintree, even Brands Hatch. We went as a family to Cornwall most years and under pressure, our parents would include a trip to the grand prix."

Once they had their own transport, Gerry and Graham would make their own way there, usually as part of a gang of fellow Scottish racing enthusiasts which usually led to some adventures, near-misses and, presumably, much hilarity, once the dust had settled. One such occasion is remembered by a member of the travelling gang, David Ross.

"I think it would have been the grand prix in 1963 when Graham asked me if I'd pick Gerry up in Glasgow because he was setting off in the Mini van with his then-girlfriend, Fiona, and Gerry was still at work. I was going down with my girlfriend Doreen in our Mini Cooper, which, from memory, used to do about 50 miles per pint of oil.

"We were driving through the night and stopped at a cafe near Brough. Inside were the McCrackens and a few others who were doing the same as us. When we were leaving Tom Sleigh pulled up in his Jensen CV-8 and we had a quick chat. Gerry had recently been working on the car for some reason.

"Tom soon caught us up and passed us but when we got near to Silverstone early in the morning he had broken down. You could see Tom thinking, here's Gerry, he'll fix it. Gerry is working on the engine and says he thinks there's a fuel lock. He pulls the fuel pipe off and forgot the pressure was already there and fuel pours out all over the Chrysler V8 engine and whoof, the whole thing went up. On the C-V8 the whole front came up. We all looked up and saw this huge Jensen on fire. Of course, we're all panicking, what are we going to do? I think it was a guy called Gideon Scott who grabbed a tiny fire extinguisher out of the car, and put the fire out pretty quickly. Amazingly, all it did was burn the HT leads. They went away to get some more and got it going.

"We eventually met up with Graham and Fiona who had gone down the day before and made our way to Silverstone. As usual, we were stuck in a traffic jam up the narrow road leading to the main entrance. Occasionally, a car would come past us and try to nip in front of us to jump the queue. Gerry got fed up with this, so he gets out, still in his grubby overalls – which he always seemed to wear – after working on Tom's Jensen and stops the traffic. The next guy who tried it ended up blocking the road. Suddenly, from one of the other cars, Innes Ireland gets out walks over to the car blocking the road, grabs the guy by the scruff of the neck and throws him down the bank."

When their racing activities resumed, Gerry was only required on the spanners on a couple of trips across the border. Firstly, to the first-ever meeting at Elvington Airfield, near York and the prestigious Gold Cup meeting at Oulton Park.

He was back behind the wheel on three occasions in September. In between a trip up the road to the 'Rest-and-be' and a trip to Charterhall in the Scottish Borders was another venture down south, this time to Mallory Park – a mere 700-mile round trip in those pre-motorway days.

The race at Mallory in the Eleven was significant in that Gerry led a race for the first time but his glory was short-lived after three laps when reportedly his visor came adrift forcing him to slow, which allowed his two closest rivals to move ahead by the finish.

Better fortunes were had at the Rest and be Thankful, with a second in class in the VX4/90. The result was matched by Iain who was out in the Mason Special, but

An exodus down south to the British Grand Prix was an annual event. Graham in the dark shirt and Gerry in pork pie hat (partially obscured) with a gang of friends atop Bill Borrowman's bus attempting to see the action. ***(David Ross)***

An outing at the Rest and Be Thankful hillclimb in a newer model than he had competed with a year earlier.
(Graham Birrell/Darren Banks archive)

both were eclipsed by Graham who took class honours in the Eleven and his trusty Mini van. The performance of the Mini van in particular drew praise from Graham Gauld in his *Motoring News* report: 'Graham Birrell in his Mini van, took 77.2sec and proved that there was more to that van than meets the eye.' In reference to the presence of the three brothers in four classes went on to add: 'This Birrell family is everywhere.' With a car to drive and three to tend to, Gerry must have been one extremely busy Scotsman that day. Ultimately, the efforts of the entire Birrell equipe were rewarded with quite a trophy haul.

The reason for the performance of the Mini van was that it had been worked on by the legendary BMC tuning wizard, Don Moore. While that was great for competing, it did lead to problems when used for more mundane matters as David Ross recalls: "Graham was heading up the road at one helluva speed when he was stopped by the police. They clocked him at 90mph when the top speed of a Mini van was no more than 70. They were convinced it had more than one carburettor, so when Graham opened the bonnet to reveal just the one they couldn't believe their eyes. I'm sure they let him off with a warning.

"On another occasion I came across the Mini van in a lay-by near Lockerbie when I was heading home from down south. I stopped to see if I could help and found the car deserted, so I went to Milngavie to see what was wrong. Upon arrival, Gerry and Graham were just getting their coats on – having got a lift back – to go and fix it.

"Nothing seemed to faze them. They were both terrific company. For some reason, they very rarely called me David. It was usually 'D Ross.' That was probably Gerry's idea, he had a name for everything. There was a cinema on Union Street in Aberdeen called The Majestic. Gerry always called it 'The Magic Stick' and Eric Dymock once turned up in a Ford Classic and immediately he called it 'Ford Drastic'."

The last outing of the year at Charterhall saw Gerry and Graham sharing the Eleven. Disappointingly, after recent improvements in performances, neither warranted a mention in the specialist press.

High hopes of building on their experiences and limited success the following year were dashed by that perennial old problem. "No money!" states Graham, emphatically. "Wrapping the Eleven around a tree when a backmarker moved over on me at Oulton Park in May didn't help."

With Gerry fully ensconced in his apprenticeship, he was unable to help out in the financial department on his meagre wages.

Of the four events he took part in – two in the Eleven and two in the VX4/90 – the highlight by far was the Bo'ness hillclimb in his father's newer VX/490. Was his father was worried about the excessive wear in the brake and tyre department, hence the need for the acquisition of a newer model?

After the two runs and a fierce battle with the Dryden brothers, Bill and Dennis, Gerry lost out to the pair to end up in third position. The margin to the victor, Bill, was just over a second and a half. "I believe I had the latest Pirelli Cinturato tyres before Gerry did, which gave me an advantage," remembers Bill, modestly.

He was a close friend of all the Birrells, Iain in particular. "Iain was probably the wildest, but Graham wasn't far behind. Gerry just hung on," reflects Bill. "I lived in Bearsden, a couple of miles from them in Milngavie. We spent all of our time buzzing about in cars.

"There was quite an age gap between Graham and Gerry. Maybe, four or five years. In those days when you were growing up, that was quite large. But they always seemed pretty close. Obviously, the racing helped. I don't think Iain was close to either of them.

"Graham was involved with girls and Gerry wasn't. Iain, Graham and I were all after the girls at the Whitecraig Tennis

Club. We'd go across there on a Saturday night and have a 'jig' and see what was on offer. Gerry wasn't into that at all.

"We had great times, we really did. I'm in my late '70s now and wonder how I got here. We did some crazy things."

All in all it was a bit of a nothing season that failed to build on the momentum of the previous couple. The main reason seemed to lay with the Lotus Eleven.

"We had all sorts of problems with the Eleven which kept Gerry busy," recalls Graham. "The first car I bought from Robin Galloway, a Butcher in Glasgow who also sold a few cars. When we got the car home we threw a bucket of water down the driveway and ran the car through it. The car was running off terribly. I took the car the car back and threatened him with all sorts of things. Eventually, he agreed to pay for the cost of getting the chassis repaired.

"We took it down to the Progress Chassis Company in London and they put a new front on it for £110. Lotus quoted us £500 and would have taken it to the same place. Progress made all the Lotus chassis in the first place!

"Another thing Lotus did was to sell the BMC engine we had arranged to buy from them. The bastards! We ended up buying a good one from Don Moore instead, which was John Whitmore's spare F3 motor.

"I ended up buying Series 1 and 2 Elevens in various states of disrepair from insurance companies because you were allowed to use them on the road. Gerry would cannibalise all the best parts. In the end, I ended up with a car with all the 'trick' bits on and some better bodywork.

"Unfortunately, it wasn't until the end of the season, which had been ruined by the car constantly breaking gears, that Gerry discovered a hairline crack in the gearbox case. All in all a fairly terrible year."

The early end to their season – they hadn't raced since the end of June – due to the aforementioned problems, meant that the ambitious brothers had time on their hands to re-evaluate their plans for the 1964 season.

They decided on a Cortina GT with the intention being for it to remain in standard specification so it could be used for both Graham's business use and competition purposes. But we are talking the Birrell brothers here.

"In our previous, slightly more ambitious efforts, we tended to spend so much on the preparation that there was no cash left to race with," offers Graham. "The general idea was to make the car semi-competitive without spending too much money on it. We left all the trim, seats, carpet in the car. The only thing we removed was the bumpers.

"But while visiting the 1964 Racing Car Show in London, we arranged with the Willment organisation to convert the suspension to their 'sprint' specification, which consisted of new front struts, rear dampers, heavier anti-roll bar etc. The engine, which arrived two days before the car's first outing at Charterhall, caused a monumental panic to fit it in time.

"The whole cost of the above was around £130 excluding the labour which, of course, was supplied by Gerry."

The car had a rather inauspicious debut after Graham sought some advice – from Jackie Stewart – on how to get it off the line. "Take it to 5000rpm and let the clutch out, advised Jackie," recalls Graham. "The result was an almighty noise and a broken engine mounting." Thanks, Jackie!

Further insight into how the Birrells went racing at that time is offered in an in-depth article in the Scottish weekly magazine, *The Motor World* dated 4 September 1964, by Graham Gauld. Graham was the doyen of the Scottish motor racing scene, of not just that era, but from any you care to mention. He was an ever-present part of the scene and knew, pretty much, anybody worth knowing. In the years ahead, he would get to know Gerry extremely well.

The article is reproduced in full on the following pages and makes for interesting reading on just how much money was involved and just how hard Gerry and Graham worked it.

Sporting the latest in headgear, Gerry in the Cortina GT at Evanton in '64 before the controversial incident with Andrew McCracken. ***(Eric Bryce)***

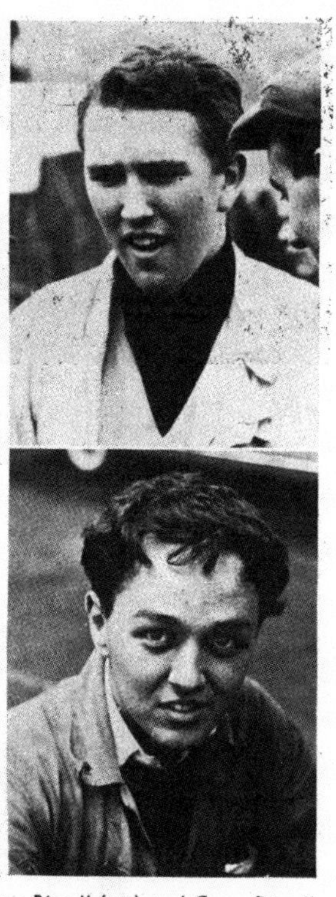

Graham Birrell (top) and Gerry Birrell.

EXPENSIVE RACING ON A SHOESTRING

by GRAHAM GAULD

THESE are the palmy days of motor racing when a top class driver can earn a five figure bank balance fairly easily, earning himself a few trips to far off places around the world into the bargain. To them motor racing is highly profitable. Next down the ladder comes the first-class national driver, the man who occasionally is named as a reserve driver in a formula I team or who possibly uses a good car and races in good company. He probably makes a profit at the end of the year but to do so he has little choice and has to work hard at it. Further down the scale comes the successful club driver who has marginal sponsorship but who pays a lot of his racing himself. If he is lucky he will scrape through a season covering his expenses knowing that he is possibly on the threshold of getting a break. Finally, there is the out and out amateur, the man who races because he wants to enjoy himself. At the same time he hopes that he will have enough success to allow someone to come along and offer him a car to drive. However, as he stands, he is learning on his own and paying for it. He will 99.9 times out of 100 never come even close to covering his expenses and he is probably representative of 65 per cent. of British racing drivers.

Here in Scotland we have many amateurs, indeed the club driver represents possibly 85 per cent. of all racing drivers in Scotland, so what does it cost if you aspire to race in Scotland in 1964? Well most drivers are inclined to shroud their racing activities and the cost of racing rather well so as to blanket the true cost of their exploits. However, recently Graham and Gerry Birrell, who shared a Ford Cortina G.T., decided to retire from racing after half a season because it cost too much. When we approached them to give us a breakdown of their expenses they agreed and so for the first time we are able to give you an idea of all the costs involved.

Before beginning there are a number of things to be remembered. Firstly, Graham Birrell is not directly involved in the motor trade though recently he has set up business in a very limited way selling motor accessories. His brother Gerry has one year to go in his apprenticeship as a motor mechanic and at 20 years of age is normally seen working on Renaults with the distributors in Glasgow, Wyllie & Lochhead.

Both have been involved in motor racing for a couple of years, Graham having driven an Austin A40 and then a Lotus Eleven Austin.

In September of last year they bought between them a Ford Cortina G.T. and around Christmas decided to race this car during 1964. They had a rough idea what it would need to make the car race-worthy and started to read up on the various modifications offered by companies down south. They made up their mind to tackle the John Willment company because "they were the only people last year who had been very successful with Cortinas."

From the very start the idea was to keep the car in Group II trim and first of all the suspension had to be modified. Graham Birrell had to be in London in January in his line of business and he arranged with Willment that the suspension bits should be supplied and fitted by them. This saved carriage charges to Scotland at least.

This alone cost £36 7s. 3d. and consisted of fitting and modifying the front and rear springs, modifying the rear shock absorbers, adding a heavy duty anti-roll bar, and fitting the new Macpherson front suspension struts.

In detail what was done was this. Take these front struts, they are shorter and have a different bounce and rebound setting so stiffening up the front. In fact the stub axles are bent into a different shape. At the rear, flat springs are fitted with the rubber eyes removed and metal bushes in their place, and Willment believe in Armstrong non-adjustable shock absorbers, so these too were fitted.

This then was the first expense. Next came the engine modifications which cost in total £81 14s. 9d. These were sent to

Chapter One

Glasgow where Graham and Gerry got down to fitting them themselves. The changes were what one might imagine, lighter valves, heavier valve springs and an increase in compression to 10.5 to 1. The head is beautifully done being gas flowed for the best possible efficiency. Deeper down in the works they fitted a G.T.5 camshaft (£11) which is the hottest cam made for use on the road.

Cost, of course, was very much at a premium and they decided to stick to one Weber carburettor for a twin Weber set up would have cost them another £38 10s., but for £1 10s. Willment fitted different jets and chokes to their standard carburettor. Actually at this time the Birrells were under the impression that with a twin Weber set up they would only gain around 6 b.h.p. but they were subsequently to find out that the figure was nearer 11 b.h.p. and in a later race they actually borrowed a twin Weber set. The Willment inlet manifold is dowelled to the head, fitting tightly and with the re-jetting of the carb. they found that they had to retain the air cleaner and element otherwise the car wouldn't go properly. The normal progressive double choke Weber was used even though a different one which ran on two chokes all the time could have been used. Firstly it was too expensive and the car would have been hopeless on the road because of an enormous flat spot in the range. (As it was, racing fuel consumption was 8-10 m.p.g.!)

It is very critical with the Cortina when racing to have competition main and big end bearing shells and when you fit these shells you have to modify your oil pressure relief valve. This is due to the additional clearance allowed by the competition shells. Lotus Cortina con-rods were also essential but it was not until May that they managed to get them and through Perdal Developments in Newcastle which is run by George Percival. These alone cost £13 10s. for four plus 18s. for two sets of White Dot big end bolts. It is also necessary when fitting the head to use the Formula Junior steel/copper and asbestos cylinder head gasket and these cost 27s. each. Another interesting thing is that you need a heavy duty dynamo strap (£2) for when racing the dynamo is inclined to drop; indeed even with the heavy duty strap the Birrells broke two back plates during the season.

The final drive has also to be adjusted for the standard 3.9 to 1 differential is no use for racing. You have to fit a 4.1 or a 4.4. and as a 4.1 was available second-hand at £8 10s. they snapped it up. Ideally, of course you would fit a limited slip differential but as they are made by Hewland for the Cortina they are both hard to get and expensive. The Birrells decided to take a short cut and welded up the differential which resulted in a few involuntary spins during the season but certainly helped to get the power evenly on to the road.

So now the car was almost ready

With a welded up differential you lose a bit of control and end up like this. Charterhall July 1964.

mechanically. The cost in total had been almost £150 so far plus, of course, the cost of the Cortina G.T. (£750). But you can't race on ordinary tyres so they approached Dunlop for racing tyres—Goodyear had been considered but they were only developing their tyres at that time and they were not for sale. These tyres were Dunlop D12s which cost between £10 and £11 each plus tubes. The gearbox was left standard because Buckler gears would have cost another £35.

It is all very well having the bits and pieces but you have to put everything together and then tailor the car. You have to have a bucket seat for a start and between them they made their own. Then there are safety belts, etc. The fact that Gerry Birrell was a mechanic in his own right meant that both could get on with the job and work on the car in their own time. Indeed in conversation we found out that by far the most costly item for anyone who did not have some knowledge of what he was doing would be for labour, assuming you could find a garage or a mechanic to put up with the long hours involved in preparing a car. For instance, the quickest time taken by the Birrells for an engine re-built is eight hours but it is done in their time and as enthusiasts, time is not as important as if you were paying for it. They probably drove their car harder for they knew that they could cope if anything did go wrong.

So came the season and the first race meeting at Charterhall. The 4.1 axle hadn't arrived and Graham asked Jackie Stewart for some advice about taking the car off the line. "Take it up to 5,500 r.p.m." was the reply and the result was a torn engine mounting and a stalled engine. So the first lesson they learned was that if you took the Cortina off the line at more than 3,500 r.p.m. it would stall. The idea was to slip the clutch at 3,000 r.p.m. and the interesting thing is that the clutch was a standard unit as a competition clutch would have cost around £30. Mind you they changed the clutch every time they had the engine out, which brings us to the running costs and general post-race service.

After a race and with say another meeting the following weekend they would start on a Wednesday and would change the engine oil (every meeting) and the filter (total cost 30/-). They would strip and clean the carburettor, check the valve springs and tappets, check the brakes, suspension and generally clean the car. When they bought the special racing wheels with the wide rims (£12 12s.) they had been warned that the hubs might fracture—in their case they never did—so they checked the hubs after every meeting.

After every three meetings they changed all the big end bolts, fitted a new head gasket and fitted a complete new set of bearings. Three hundred miles in racing conditions were sufficient for one set of bearings and bolts!

Now, by this sort of attention to detail, the Birrells had a season where nothing really broke in the engine but when you add to all the above the cost of new plugs every meeting at £1 per set, new brake pads after every three meetings and tyres every four meetings plus the other oddments such as an interior roll-over bar (£1 10s.), a laminated windscreen (£13 10s.) and then the travelling expenses, you can find, as the Birrells did that it becomes very costly. As for the returns, well they get some travel expenses and stand to win £10 if they take first place in their race. In total they earned probably £50 in prize money but this was just a drop in the bucket when you now add up the costs. If you include the price of the car you will find that these two brothers competing in what is considered the least expensive form of motor racing—save maybe the 750 Club formula races—spent in one year around £1,000. If you add the depreciation when they sell the car—which could be £150— and the staggering number of man hours which they devoted to racing you can see that motor racing today, even at club driver level, is a very expensive sport,

Gerry flat-out at the Bo'ness hillclimb in Graham's Lotus 11. *(Eric Bryce)*

The wherewithal required to make it all happen was very much Graham's domain, something he never shied away from, working tirelessly, travelling up and down the UK in his line of work as a manufacturer's agent.

"I followed on from my father because it suited me," offers Graham. "I did the same job as a sales representative but I'd do it for around half a dozen companies."

Meanwhile, Gerry was in his element, creating what was for all intents and purposes, the first, fully-modified, ground-up, high-specification racing saloon car of his fledgeling career. To undertake all that work, while still only 20 years old and not yet a fully-trained motor mechanic, shows just how much

Gerry clowning around at Charterhall. *(Eric Liddell/Robin Liddell archive)*

information he absorbed. Being around an elder brother, with his connections and the likes of Jackie Stewart, plus other vastly experienced drivers and mechanics, who were around the Scottish racing scene at that time, clearly influenced him greatly. All the lessons learnt then would be carried forward and used to his advantage at every opportunity.

It wasn't just the on-track department in which the brothers had sought an improvement. The trusty Mini van tow car – and part-time racer – had made way for a larger vehicle. "On our travels throughout Scotland and down south to Rufforth, Croft, Oulton Park etc, we borrowed the ex-British Rail Pullman service truck belonging to Stanley P Morrison," recalls Graham. "He was better known as 'Tim' to us. It served us well. No road tax, insurance or other such necessities."

Keeping the car in tip-top condition for Graham to undertake a more ambitious programme of events clearly restricted Gerry's activities behind the wheel of the Cortina. But in his sole outing at Evanton, in Ross-shire, he would earn a mention not just for the use of his hands when operating a steering wheel, but also, when using his hands – or rather one of them – for an entirely different reason.

The scene had been set in an earlier race involving Graham and Sandy McCracken, who was in a Lotus Cortina, which was on paper superior to a Cortina GT. They had enjoyed a battle royale with Graham finally taking victory on the last lap after a grassy moment had let McCracken through earlier in the race.

In a later race, Gerry was up against Andrew McCracken,

Just moments after the coming-together. Andrew 'Fat' McCracken was in the car business in Glasgow, and his escapades would fill a couple of books. ***(Unknown)***

who was Sandy's team-mate and was also out in a Lotus Cortina. Too many Birrells, McCrackens and Cortinas!

From the start the pair diced for the lead but due to their fierce battle, they let Bill Borrowman seize the initiative and open up a fair lead. *Autosport* takes up the story: 'There were bags of cut and thrust as they jockeyed through the corners together until the seventh lap when Birrell, in a big effort to get past, took a wide, fast line at Paddock and McCracken sliding round tightly on all fours, went smack into his side as he came in. McCracken managed to sort himself out first, but by then Birrell was on the move again the Lotus Cortina had opened up a fair lead on him. Two laps later McCracken was black-flagged and retired with his shattered wing rubbing on his wheel and Birrell was left with a clear run to second place.'

Apparently, after the race, they were some 'afters', which wasn't reported in *Autosport* and *Motoring News* but was witnessed by a spectating Stan Wilson.

"The Lotus Cortina came into the paddock closely followed by the Cortina GT," remembers Stan, all these years later. "When the drivers got out of the cars, Gerry went to throw a punch at McCracken with the words, "McCracken, you want to fucking learn how to drive." They were quickly separated.

"The larger-than-life character, actor James Robertson Justice, who was standing close by, witnessed the whole fracas. He lived part-time in the Highlands in the small village of Spinningdale and used to drive around very fast in a Mercedes 300SL Gullwing, often visiting the local bars."

"I don't recall Gerry throwing a punch, but he was very angry," offers Graham. "Andrew 'Fat' McCracken definitely punted Gerry off. Sandy and Andrew were cousins. 'Fat' Andrew was in the car business. His escapades could fill a couple of books."

"I don't think McCracken was ever forgiven for that," offers Andy Morrison. "Scotland is the biggest village in the world. Once you've hit one, you've hit the lot of 'em. They never forget."

Other than his single outing in the Cortina, Gerry would be seen in yet another VX4/90 belonging to his father at his usual haunts of Bo'ness and Rest and be Thankful. As in previous years, much the same results were achieved, due to the opposition consisting of far more exotic machinery.

The day after the aforementioned Bo'ness outing, Gerry was entered in the Omega Special – a car made famous by John Miles of Team Lotus fame – at Ouston. There is some doubt that he actually turned up due to the lack of a mention in any reports, which is all the more strange when according to the race programme he would start in pole position – the grid positions were drawn by ballot – for the over 1000cc Sports Car race.

"The Omega belonged to 'Tim' Morrison and I don't ever recall Gerry racing it," offers Graham. "Iain was the one involved with that car. He drove it in a sprint and by all accounts, it was a very unpredictable car!"

Gerry (in jacket) helping Graham fix the Cortina at Charterhall, while the race continues. ***(Graham Birrell/Darren Banks archive)***

To round off their year, in late October Gerry and Graham, along with Eric Liddell, Agnes Mickel and her husband Gray, were back at the Rest and be Thankful to form a five-car team to commemorate an event held 36 years previously when a Singer model, the Porlock, derived its name from making 100 climbs of Porlock Hill. The five would make a total of 100 climbs and descents – 20 by each driver – in a Singer Chamois.

The epitome of '60s cool. ***(Eric Liddell/Robin Liddell archive)***

"I remember it being 50 times up and down," offers Graham. "I was the quickest downhill. It was good fun."

As 1964 drew to a close the whole Scottish motorsport scene was about to undergo a major transformation with the opening, in time for the start of the '65 season, of the first permanent race track north of the border. The creation of Ingliston in the grounds of the Royal Highland Showground, on the outskirts of Edinburgh, was the brainchild of Ian Scott-Watson, who was better known for his involvement in starting Jim Clark on his way to becoming one of the all-time greats – if not *the* greatest – of all time.

With the cessation of racing at Charterhall, Ingliston was badly needed and would provide the ideal training ground not just for Gerry and Graham, but for thousands of aspiring Scottish drivers for many years.

These were exciting times to be associated with Scottish motor racing and the Birrells were very much a part of it. For such an ambitious pair, it couldn't have come at a better time. The lessons learned over the past few years would be incorporated in the building of two cars for the coming season. Gerry, now having served his time as an apprentice, was able to play a bigger part financially in what was known as Graham Birrell Racing.

And the new season would see the emergence of Gerry's talent behind the wheel and him coming out from beneath the shadow of Graham, to stand, not quite alone, but to start to forge his own reputation.

CHAPTER TWO

INGLISTON AND MUCH MORE

It would be a two-pronged attack for the coming season with a Singer Chamois, suitably modified by Gerry for racing purposes being the first 'prong'. The car had been supplied by Claud Hamilton (Motors), a well-established Singer dealership in Glasgow. This was the beginning of a very important relationship, not just with Claud Hamilton but also their General Manager MGH 'Mike' Leeke. Both would play a pivotal part in Gerry's future projects and successes.

The second 'prong' of the attack would be a Ford Anglia belonging to Graham, which was built with the help of Hall Marshall, a Glasgow coachbuilder. "They helped us with the body," offered Graham in an article he wrote for the March 1966 issue of the Scottish magazine *Top Gear* (not to be confused with the later BBC publication of the same name). "They combined two wrecked cars. One had hit a lamp post – hard. And another which had been burnt out. David Marshall did a bit of restyling at the front, and because we didn't like the reverse rake rear window he changed that, too. The doors were steel with the insides removed but the bonnet and boot lid were made from fibreglass. All the windows, except the windscreen, were replaced with Perspex – which was expensive. David's business partner, Ian Hall, added a metallic blue paint job to finish it off.

"The total cost of the bodyshell bits was about a tenner. By doing most of the work ourselves – mainly Gerry – we kept the costs down. I hate to think what it would have cost otherwise."

The restyling at the front centred around the adding of a Perspex bubble over the standard, angular looking headlights, giving the whole front-end a more streamlined appearance.

"The modified headlights were like something from an Aston Martin DB4," offers Andy Morrison, who was still at Dumbuck Garage and a frequent visitor to the Birrell household to check on what they were up to. "David Marshall was a lovely guy. Very talented.

"My over-riding memory of that car is when I was at Dumbuck Garage one night and you could hear this noise, it was like a Lancaster bomber going overhead. We – Jackie and his old man – came outside to see what was going on. You could it thing for miles. Then this thundering noise arrives. It was Graham coming from Milngavie.

"About thirty seconds behind was Gerry in their back-up vehicle, which was an Anglia estate car. It was painted blue with orange wheels – just like the race car – and it looked as if it had been painted in the dark. And it carried the GA 3 registration plate, which all of Graham's race cars had. Both the race car and the road car had the same number plate. We were just bewildered by the whole thing," concludes Andy.

"The Anglia was built at a filling station in Auchentoshan belonging to Claud Hamiltons about three or four miles up from Dumbuck Garage," remembers Graham. "We used to test the car at night on the Dumbarton Boulevard which ran up from Dumbuck. The local police kept us briefed on the whereabouts of the traffic cops! We were around Dumbuck Garage regularly.

"The Anglia Estate had a 1500cc engine and towed the racing Anglia."

The one area Gerry wouldn't have been involved with was the engine. That was the responsibility of Perdal Developments, the establishment set up by George Percival (the 'per' in Perdal) and Peter Dalkin (the 'dal') in Newcastle. This was a continuation of the relationship forged when buying parts for the Cortina.

Working as a mechanic for Perdal at that time was Jeff Wilson. "I knew Gerry extremely well," he recalls. "He'd come to stay with us in Newcastle for three or four days and build the engines and take them back with him. He was a good engineer. We had a workshop with space for about seven cars and a room in which to build engines, where we also had an ex-Cosworth dyno. Quite advanced for the time.

"He had a metallic blue Cortina GT, totally stripped out, just a driver's seat. Perdal were main Weber dealers, so he'd take carburettors and manifolds back from us, all for Graham's shop. Gerry was always on the up and up."

Jeff would go on to have a long and successful career in motorsport. Firstly, as a highly respected mechanic and engine builder, which led on to a highly successful career behind the wheel when he was involved in the Special Saloon 'boom' of the '70s and '80s. His most famous mount would be the ex-Doug Niven V8 Chevy-powered VW Beetle, which he campaigned with great aplomb, mainly at Croft, Aintree and Ingliston. He's still involved today both in the workshop and occasionally still on the track.

Looking pleased with his mode of road transport, which incorporated various modifications. ESN 1D was put to good use, both for 'courting' purposes and the collecting of engines. ***(SMRC/Graham Gauld)***

The shop referred to by Jeff was on St Vincent Street in Glasgow and was a new venture for Graham selling everything the motorist and racing fraternity could wish for. He would expand to open another shop in nearby Clarkson, a suburb of Glasgow, and would take a mobile shop filled to the brim with spares to all Ingliston meetings, where it would be situated behind the grandstands. Gerry, now a fully-qualified motor mechanic would run the shop. It soon became *the* place, not only to buy the latest gear but also a real meeting point for the regulars involved in all areas of Scottish motorsport.

It wasn't just in the retail sector of this burgeoning business that Graham saw potential earnings. A separate wholesale operation would supply many outlets, such as garages and petrol stations with whatever they needed, throughout Glasgow and the surrounding areas. The brothers had established themselves as highly-respected individuals, Gerry more for his mechanical skills, while Graham would today be termed an entrepreneur.

Graham now had a lot on his plate, with the shop, his manufacturer's agency and an ever-increasing racing programme. On Gerry's recommendation, Alan Muir was brought in to run the agency.

"I have no idea why Gerry approached me and thought that I was the man for the job," recalls Alan. "At that time, I was far more interested in motorsport, building engines and things like that. I had no sales experience. But after an interview Graham offered me the job. One of the attractions was a company car.

"I was universally known to the Birrells and their friends as Sam for a couple of reasons. My middle name is Samuel, so my initials are ASM and Graham's main agency at that time was for Royale Baby Carriages, which was a direct competitor to the more well-known Silver Cross prams. Sam rhymes with pram, so it all led to the moniker 'Sam the Pram'.

"By the time of the job offer I had known Gerry for a long time, probably since his early Charterhall days, 1960 and '61. I raced primarily with John Nicholson, who had a Lotus Eleven at the same time as Gerry and Graham.

"I was once dispatched from Glasgow to go for the engine for the Perdal Anglia. I drove down to Newcastle and arrived

Graham (on his knees) along with many helping hands attempt the remove the broken exhaust from the Anglia on its debut at Ingliston in May '65. ***(Eric Bryce)***

The offending item removed, Gerry is waved frantically on his way to rejoin the fray. ***(Eric Bryce)***

there at some ungodly hour in the morning and had to wait for them to open up. I introduced myself to the apprentice who opened up – he turned out to be Jeff Wilson – and said, 'I've come to pick up the engine for the Anglia.' To which, Jeff replies, 'We haven't built it yet.' I sat in the Perdal workshop all day while Jeff slaved away putting it together.

"We socialised a great deal, mainly in the Malletshaugh Inn near Newton Mearns where I lived. It was the social hub of many of the people involved in motorsport, not just racing but rallying as well. Gerry lived on the opposite side of Glasgow and yet used to travel across. Girls would come from Aberfoyle and places like that all the way to the Malletshaugh Inn. It was definitely the place to be. Particularly at that stage in our lives.

"Another place was the Whitecraigs Tennis Club which held weekly dances with live music. You would be thrown out of the Malletshaugh at 10pm in those days but the dance at the Tennis Club went on until 11.30, so everyone would decant down there from the Malletshaugh.

"Gerry, being a non-drinker, would stand there with his ginger beer and lime, while we would be getting rat-arsed."

The Malletshaugh Inn would also be the venue for, on this occasion, an important, non-racing related moment in Gerry's life.

"That was where I first saw him," remembers Margaret (the future Mrs Birrell). "It was our local and as Alan (or Sam as I knew him) says, it was quite a way from Milngavie for Gerry. Sam was part of our crowd that would meet there on a Saturday night and we always had a laugh with him. We had parties which were usually held in the houses of friends whose parents were on holiday.

"Thinking back it was a pretty grotty pub."

"I take exception to the term 'grotty pub'. Providing you kept moving your feet you didn't stick to the carpet," says Alan, his tongue firmly in his cheek.

The opening of Ingliston would alter Gerry's goals, allowing him for the first time to chase after some championship honours. More so now that he had a car of his own to campaign.

Typically, he wouldn't be exclusive to the new home of Scottish motorsport. He would still indulge in the odd sprint and for the first time, be seen along with Graham among the forests of the British Isles when they would try their hand at rallying. When he wasn't tending to most things mechanical in connection with the car, he would be in the passenger seat dealing with all things navigational.

The first-ever meeting at Ingliston took place on 11 April and surprisingly Gerry didn't get the chance to sample the delights of the new narrow, twisty course, located in and around the Royal Highland Showground site. The programme for the event lists him as second reserve in two events but no evidence exists of him having competed. Two factors would have played a part. Firstly, due to the narrowness and length of the track (0.76 miles/1.2km), a maximum of 10 starters was permitted. Secondly, unsurprisingly, all races featured either full or over-subscribed entries.

He was, of course, still in attendance in his mechanic role to Graham. He would have benefited from having some shelter from the typical Scottish weather of rain, sleet and a howling gale – welcome to Scotland in April – with the use of the concrete stalls, usually occupied by cattle and such like being used to 'garage' the cars. These shelters were considered a luxury for the time and are still remembered by all those who occupied them, not always for the most flattering of reasons. The smell, a memory that lingers the most.

Before the next Ingliston meeting the following month, Gerry made his way down the A1 towards Newcastle again. But this time he would continue further south to the outskirts of Darlington to race at the recently opened (first meeting August '64) Croft circuit. No doubt he popped in to pick up more spares for the shop on his travels, too.

This would be his first outing in the Anglia and his long trip was rewarded with a sixth-place finish in the GT race.

Once rejoined, Gerry was going flat-out to make up lost ground when...
(Bill Henderson Collection)

...A con-rod decided it needed fresh air and pitched him into a substantial pole. The result was one sorry looking race car. ***(Bill Henderson Collection)***

The car was predominately Graham's and would be shared by Gerry, as per usual, when time and the finances allowed.

"Ingliston always had races for Saloons and Sports/GT cars," offers Graham. "I would do the saloon race, leaving Gerry to do the other, if he wasn't occupied with his Chamois."

To contradict the above and to confuse matters further, the next outing at Ingliston in May would see Gerry out in the Anglia and Graham in the Chamois. As things turned out, Graham was to be thankful that was the case.

After dominating the early stages of the GT race for over 1200cc cars, Gerry had to pit to have a loose exhaust pipe removed. 'This was deftly removed with a lump of concrete, which dropped him to third place.

Thereafter, Birrell turned up the wick, but lost the lot at Vets and stuffed the Perdal Anglia into a solid post,' wrote the Scottish correspondent for *Autosport*, Bill Henderson. Bill, as well as reporting on events, was the doyen of photographers north of the border.

"Vets was the left-hander before the pits," says Graham. "The engine threw a con-rod, broke the crankshaft and seized the engine. It turned square left into a big steel pole, which left us with a destroyed engine and a sorry looking car. Rather a setback."

The brothers were never the type to be daunted by such a major setback, however. They set to and acquired a damaged Anglia van that formerly belonged to a Glasgow butcher. With help from David Marshall, Gerry then proceeded to weld the good half – the front – of the Butcher's van onto the one good surviving half – the rear – of the race car. Just like that!

Fortunately for them, the next Ingliston meeting wasn't until the end of July due to the circuit being situated on the showground. Its main use was for agricultural purposes and the largest event in Scotland for those involved in that area of business was the Royal Highland Show, held annually in June.

Not content with rebuilding the Anglia, Gerry found time to make his rally debut alongside Graham on the Scottish

Much better fortunes came next time out at Ingliston, when Gerry scored his first-ever race win. ***(Bill Henderson Collection)***

Previously, Gerry had shared cars with Graham. Now he had his own machine, a Singer Chamois. Here he's on his way to third-place at Ingliston in August '65 in the race for saloon cars under 1200cc. ***(Eric Bryce)***

The same day, this time aboard Graham's Anglia and an improved finish when he came home in second place. ***(Eric Bryce)***

International event in a Chamois (another one) supplied by Claud Hamiltons. A suspension failure in the forests brought about their retirement.

Better fortunes were hoped for on their return to Ingliston – they couldn't get any worse – in July. And, boy, did Gerry's improve! He scored his first-ever race win in the repaired Mk.2 Anglia in the over 1200cc Saloon race after a fierce battle with the Volvo-engined Marcos of Harry Ballantine and took third place in the Chamois in the up to 1200cc saloon race. To make his day even sweeter – Graham scored in a win with the Anglia in a later race and in view of the intense sibling rivalry – was that Graham trailed home two places behind in fifth place in yet another Claud Hamilton Chamois (how many were there?) in the up to 1200cc race. Bragging rights to Gerry on this occasion.

That performance seemed to take the monkey off his back. From then on in the remaining three Ingliston outings he would take two runner-up and a third-place finish in the Chamois and runners-up spoils in his only other outing in the Anglia.

According to Bill Henderson in *Autosport*, the Anglia outing was pretty eventful: 'The 2-litre Perdal Anglias of Bob Blaylock and Gerry Birrell circulated with nothing between them until the Mini of Ed Labinjoh tried to prise them apart on the penultimate lap at Brewers. Result: Gerry and Ed all but visited the Highland Show stands with a 1275 Mini Cooper engine almost filling the Anglia's boot – both continued at unabated speed.'

In between those Ingliston outings, a trip down the road to Gask Aerodrome on the outskirts of Perth for a sprint event and another trip south to Croft were squeezed in.

The outing at Gask must have been hectic. Of the seven classes being run, Gerry was out in three of them in three different cars. Adding to that, Graham was out in two of the three classes, sharing the car.

Graham took family honours in the Perdal Anglia beating Gerry by over two seconds to claim the class spoils. The next outing in the Singer Chamois saw the pair sharing the car with Mike Leeke and Eric Liddell. It was good there was a large entry, giving them time to take their individual runs and have a change of driver. The Chamois was outclassed by the multitude of Mini Coopers. The fastest of quartet, Graham, ended ninth. Gerry would up 12th, the third fastest of the quartet, being pipped by Liddell by a couple of tenths.

Gerry saved his best for last with a shared outing in Eric Liddell's Lotus Elan and only just missed out on beating the car's owner by half a second to end up class runner-up. Perhaps it wasn't good form to bite the hand that feeds.

The Croft outing resulted in another run in Eric Liddell's Lotus Elan and a third-place finish, after a close, race-long battle in atrocious conditions with another Elan of Bill Dryden and the Ginetta of Chris Meek. The Ginetta man came out on top to finish runner-up, some way behind the victor, Julian Sutton.

To round off his busiest competition year, thus far, Gerry took part in the gruelling International RAC Rally alongside Graham in yet another Claud Hamilton Chamois. To come away with second in class honours in only their second international rally outing is a testament to Gerry's and Graham's versatility, adaptability and skill in mastering all facets of whatever task they undertook.

Not content to be busy with their on-track activities, the brothers were also active on the social scene and would be frequent visitors to any motoring-related event. Especially to all the end of year sporting club dinners/award ceremonies.

One such event towards the end of the year was a talk they gave to a large crowd in the green room of the Royal Scottish Automobile Club (RSAC) in Glasgow. The assembled masses listened to a very detailed and interesting account of their adventures on the RAC Rally.

A slight change of direction was the plan for 1966 with Gerry forging closer links with Claud Hamiltons by starting to modify what had, up until then, been a pretty 'bog standard' Chamois. The whole car would be looked at in detail with upgrades to the suspension, lighter body panels and an increase in engine size from the standard 875cc to 1140. Quite an increase and not easy to accomplish. Enter one Hugh Shannon, who along with the continued presence of Peter Dalkin of Perdal, would work wonders with the powerplant. Gerry, despite being busy with all the other non-engine modifications, would still offer his thoughts.

In an in-depth article in *Cars and Car Conversions* in September 1966, titled A Canny Shammy, Mike Leeke of Claud Hamiltons explained the reasons for getting involved with the Birrells – Gerry in particular – and the amount of work and the development undertaken to get the car to the track. Here are some extracts:

'The whole operation was mounted for publicity purposes initially. It is now interesting to find that everyone involved in the project is dead keen to get the car into the winner's circle.

'As with all ventures of this sort we are picking our way

blindly gathering little bits of information from here and there with our resident spies, Graham and Gerry Birrell, crawling under every competition Imp they could find at the English race meetings. This led to a funny incident. They came back from one meeting filled with hope that they had found a weak link in the strategy of teams like Alan Fraser and Roger Nathan, both renowned Imp specialists. They noticed that both retained the big steel fuel tank up on the bulkhead. They thought that if you removed this and substituted a smaller tank you would save some weight. So Gerry removed the tank and then wondered why the doors kept flying open and the scuttle kept shaking; Gerry forgot that the fuel tank on the Chamois is an integral part of the front end stiffness!

'To get the capacity up to 1140cc the only way was to increase the stroke which meant modifying the crankshaft. Perdal did such a good job that Hugh Shannon didn't believe at first they had done anything. We then had a problem with the piston crown and top ring protruded above the liner. Thinking the whole thing over, Gerry, ever mindful of the Cosworth principles, suggested that the conventional Chamois piston could be trimmed down from three rings to two. This modification thinned the piston crown so Gerry had to get down to hand-filling the piston crowns to match, which took him something like eight hours per piston. He then had to re-cut the valve grooves because of the slightly different positioning of everything.

'During the first assembly of the engine, Gerry decided to use Valvoline oil and now swears by it. He remarked that with the crank, bearings and caps in place he could still spin the crankshaft quite easily.

'The previous year we had raced the car with a full-specification body. The Birrells had worked all winter on a lightened bodyshell made up from two write-offs we bought for spares. They removed the rear window assembly which saved considerable weight. The doors were lightened and even the heavy door hinges were replaced with lighter ones.

'They lowered the engine mountings by four inches to get the centre of gravity down even further and Gerry designed his own rear springs. These were short and fat and the rear wheels are offset by about four inches, which we feel will make it stick to the road better.'

What an illustration of the amount of thought and work Gerry was putting in behind the scenes to modify the car to a higher-specification and his need to gain an advantage in the mechanical engineering of the car. At that time, this was almost unheard of.

"We tended to stumble around in the dark, to a certain extent, in those days," offers Alan Muir. "We just weren't technical, unlike nowadays. But Gerry was different. He always seemed to plough his own furrow in many respects, something he would do in the years ahead on numerous occasions. He was prepared to do something different. That mentality, if you can get an edge on something or somebody, he would be quite happy to try it."

On his way to the first victory in the much-modified Chamois at the May '66 Ingliston meeting. ***(Eric Bryce)***

An area in which Gerry wasn't out of his depth, and competent, was how to build engines. But he must have realised that you can't do everything yourself. We will never know if he sought out the services of Hugh Shannon or if that fell into place. Either way, he was smart enough to spot a good thing when it was presented to him.

This was the beginning of a relatively short working relationship, but a long-lasting friendship with the highly-respected engine man, and all-round skilled engineer. When it came to engines, he was the man to go to in Scottish racing circles. His two most famous associations, previously with Tommy Dickson (father of Norman) and Jimmy Mackay, had brought much success to the pair. They had benefited enormously from having aligned themselves with him, something Gerry would have been well aware of.

All the indications are there of him seeking to branch out on his own. For the first time, there would be no sharing of cars with Graham – excluding their rally outings. The Chamois would be partly his creation and for his sole use at Ingliston. There would be no sprint and hillclimb outings, and a more condensed programme, probably driven by monetary concerns, would be on the agenda. The six meetings at Ingliston were now the priority.

For the first one in April, Gerry gave his new, highly modified car its debut but had to make do with 'a rally cooking engine' after the 'big' engine for the Chamois failed to materialise according to the report in *Motoring News*. A fourth place was the best he could do up against a plethora of more-powerful Minis and Imps. 'Wait till next meeting,' was his parting shot in the *Motoring News* report.

With the new 'big' 1140cc engine now installed – Gerry had been working on it for most of the night before according to Eric Dymock's report in *Autosport* – he certainly delivered on his promise with a resounding victory in atrocious conditions once his main rival, Bill Borrowman, had spun on the opening lap. He wasn't alone apparently, the race being described as 'one of the wildest saloon car races up here.'

A day for the history books. All three Birrell brothers leave the grid, the first time they had competed together in the same race. Graham leads Gerry while Iain in the Mini (66) languishes in the pack. ***(Eric Bryce)***

The Ingliston race programme cover from 24 July 1966. ***(Iain Nicolson)***

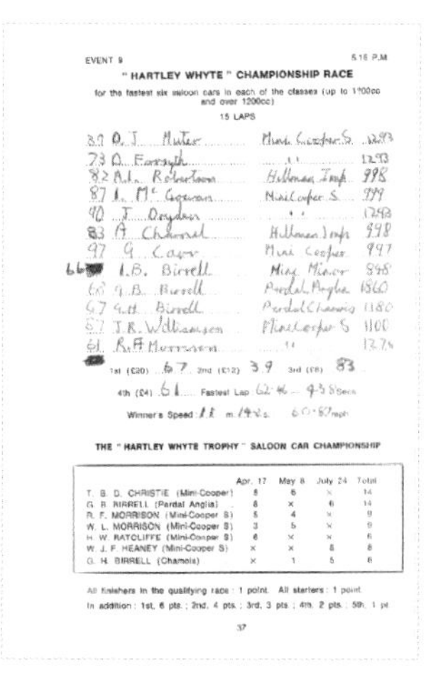

EVENT 9 5.15 P.M

"HARTLEY WHYTE" CHAMPIONSHIP RACE

for the fastest six saloon cars in each of the classes (up to 1200cc and over 1200cc)

15 LAPS

39 D. J. Muter ... Mini Cooper S 1293
73 D. Forsyth ... " 1293
82 A. L. Robertson ... Hillman Imp 998
87 I. McGowan ... Mini Cooper S 999
90 J. Dryden ... " 1293
83 A. Charnell ... Hillman Imp 998
97 G. Carr ... Mini Cooper 997
66 I. B. Birrell ... Mini Minor 848
68 G. B. Birrell ... Pardal Anglia 1860
67 G. H. Birrell ... Pardal Chamois 1180
57 J. R. Williamson ... Mini Cooper S 1100
61 R. A. Morrison ... " 1275

1st (£20) 67 2nd (£12) 39 3rd (£8) 83

4th (£4) 61 Fastest Lap 62·46 – 43·58 secs

Winner's Speed 11 m. 14.2 s. 60·67 mph

THE "HARTLEY WHYTE TROPHY" SALOON CAR CHAMPIONSHIP

	Apr. 17	May 8	July 24	Total
T. B. D. CHRISTIE (Mini-Cooper)	8	6	×	14
G. B. BIRRELL (Pardal Anglia)	8	×	6	14
R. F. MORRISON (Mini-Cooper S)	5	4	×	9
W. L. MORRISON (Mini-Cooper S)	3	5	×	9
H. W. RATCLIFFE (Mini-Cooper S)	6	×	×	6
W. J. F. HEANEY (Mini-Cooper S)	×	×	8	8
G. H. BIRRELL (Chamois)	×	1	5	6

All finishers in the qualifying race: 1 point. All starters: 1 point.
In addition: 1st, 6 pts.; 2nd, 4 pts.; 3rd, 3 pts.; 4th, 2 pts.; 5th, 1 pt.

37

Qualifiers for the Hartley Whyte race, 24 July 1966. A quarter of the field are Birrells! ***(Iain Nicolson)***

Next time out in July, in glorious, much-improved conditions, Borrowman exacted revenge but only after a race-long battle which saw Gerry, reportedly, using a great deal of road to stay in front in the early stages. In the later Hartley Whyte Trophy race – which was for the top six finishers in both the under 1200cc and over 1200cc Saloon car classes – Graham led off the line with Gerry in hot pursuit but they both had to settle for second and third, respectively, behind the Mini of Heaney.

Before the next Ingliston meeting Gerry ventured south to Silverstone to take part in the Birkett 6-hour relay race as part of the 'Scottish Rootes' team of four cars, which consisted of the Imps of Tony Charnell and Alistair Robertson and the pair of Chamois for Gerry and Graham. Despite being up against a huge field, the vast majority of which were far more powerful, the Scottish quartet ran out the winner by two laps. Their cause was aided somewhat by the diabolical conditions at various stages of the race but still, to come away with the spoils was an impressive performance. "That whole event was really good fun," remembers Graham.

Back on home soil the following weekend, Gerry and Graham were joined for the first time by sibling, Iain, who was making his circuit racing debut in a Mini 850. While on many occasions, two brothers have competed at the same meeting or in the same race, there can't have been that many occasions, if any, that three brothers had competed at the same meeting.

Iain got the ball rolling with a third place on his debut in the first event of the day, the up to 1200cc saloon race for the less experienced drivers. Graham and Gerry won their respective races which meant that all three of them qualified for the Hartley Whyte encounter. Twelve cars took the start and 25 percent were driven by Birrells! Graham took the lead at the start but came under severe pressure from Gerry. Such was their pace they lapped Iain and the other slower cars on lap seven. That must have been galling for Iain. Just when it looked like it would go down to the wire, Graham's con-rods came out looking for some fresh air, which meant instant retirement for his Anglia, leaving Gerry to take the family honours. Taking into account the legendary competitive nature of the three brothers, their home back in Milngavie wasn't a place you would have wanted to be that evening. To say there would have been an atmosphere would be a huge understatement.

You would have thought that at the conclusion of the Hartley Whyte race which was the ninth of the 11 planned races – by that stage, they had competed in four of the nine races – the Birrells would have been done for the day. But no, immediately after winning the Hartley Whyte race Gerry jumped into a Lotus Elan entered by Graham to come third in the Marque Cars race. Then, in the final race of the day, Graham debuted the brand-new Ecurie Ecosse-Imp in the race for racing cars under 1200cc. He came home a respectable fifth behind four F3 Brabhams of various vintage. Gerry would get to sample and help develop this machine, along with several Ingliston regulars, in the months ahead.

The remaining two meetings at Ingliston brought mixed fortunes. The first encounter saw the presence of some serious opposition from down south with the appearance of two Alan Fraser Imps for Nick Brittan and Ray Calcutt. According to Bill Henderson in *Autosport*: 'The pair cleaned up the saloon car races, trouncing the local fast men.' Gerry had taken an early lead in his only outing against them but before he could show his mettle he encountered engine problems in the early stages. To have suffered from such an uncharacteristic problem must have been immensely frustrating for him as he would have relished the opportunity to take on the established big boys from down south. He had better fortunes in the Marque Cars race when another outing in the Lotus Elan resulted in a second place finish.

It was back to two brothers at the next meeting but not the usual two. Graham was away in Germany rallying, so Iain

Graham (in the Ford Anglia) and Gerry aboard the Singer Chamois circulated together a month later at the August Ingliston meeting. Gerry came away with two victories. ***(Eric Bryce)***

Another outing in the Lotus Elan at the September meeting saw him go one better with a second place. ***(Eric Bryce)***

was the 'other brother' on this occasion, again driving his Mini 850.

"I'm sure Iain only raced because we did," recalls Graham. "He was never that bothered. That race at the August meeting was the only time we all raced together. He did enter an Austin-Healey Sprite the following season but I don't remember him racing it.

"Gerry used to say that to Iain every nut's a plier size and that you don't need to fit locking washers if you cross-thread the nuts."

Part of the reason for Iain's failure to continue was reportedly due to his importance as a whisky blender and that his employers had made him decide between that and racing. He chose the former and would go on to a successful career.

Disappointingly, Iain, despite numerous approaches, didn't have the courtesy to reply to my request for his involvement. Presumably he has his reasons.

In the season's finale, normal service was resumed for Gerry with first and fourth place finishers in his two outings in the Chamois.

The campaign at Ingliston had been a successful one with four victories from his nine outings and other numerous top three finishes and with just the one retirement the indications were that Gerry and Hugh Shannon had formed quite a formidable pairing, which they would take forward with even more ambitious plans for the following season.

Before such plans were acted upon, an outing on the RAC Rally as part of the service crew proved rather eventful. The Claud Hamilton entered Chamois was to be driven by Graham, with journalist Mike Cotton alongside.

"I got to know Gerry through Mike Leeke, who previously to his time at Claud Hamiltons had been the MD of a Rootes Group dealership in Caterham, Surrey. My sister, Anne, was his secretary," remembers Cotton.

"We had a mutual love of motorsport, especially, rallying, I was the editor of *Motoring News* at that time. I co-drove alongside Mike on the Scottish with Graham and Gerry in another Chamois as part of a two-car team.

"On the RAC with Graham, we had a head-on collision with a non-competing car somewhere in Scotland. The car had slid on to our side of the road on an S-bend over a level crossing. Our right front wheel was pushed right back in the wheelarch, against the bodywork. Gerry was quickly on the scene, and with brilliant improvisation, he got the wheel off the hub and used the scissor jack to force the buckled suspension forwards. He did this so well that the tracking was about right, and the car handled perfectly well from then on.

"Another incident was an encounter with a Ford Cortina GT which overtook us, one foggy night, on a special stage. Graham immediately asked who it was and after consulting my handbook gave him some unwelcome news that it was a female driver by the name of Jenny Nadin. Graham was none too pleased and found some extra speed, and chatted her up at the next control. In time she became Mrs Jenny Birrell."

"My memory differs slightly to Mike's," offers Graham. "Jennifer was in a 1.0-litre Imp (she worked for Rootes) and we did the passing. He is right about me chatting her up. The rest is history."

If all that wasn't enough, something much more serious was to befell the pair, Graham in particular.

"Upon arrival at the last stage at Silverstone, Graham became unwell and collapsed," continues Cotton. "He was taken away in an ambulance to Northampton General Hospital with what turned out to be a perforated stomach ulcer. I remember that Jenny was very concerned about this. Gerry too, of course. I had to drive the final stage on the circuit, and then Gerry joined me to complete the crew on the final leg to the finish at London Airport (now Heathrow). We had to confess to the organisers that the crew had changed and we might have been disqualified, but they took pity and gave us our position, seventy-something."

The 1966 Scottish Rally saw the Birrell brothers finish second in class. Gerry was on navigation duties on this occasion. *(SMRC/Graham Gauld)*

The 1966 International Gulf London Rally, and the brothers look in good spirits before the start. Another second in class maintained the smiles. *(Graham Birrell/Darren Banks archive)*

Thankfully, when Gerry was alongside Graham as co-driver, he had a far less eventful time than Mike. They had undertaken three outings intertwined among their racing outings. The first, on the Circuit of Ireland, resulted in a non-finish after an accident. The Scottish and the Gulf London events brought better fortunes, as on both occasions second in their class was achieved. All outings were in a Chamois entered, as usual, by Claud Hamiltons.

It was towards the end of the year that a significant change occurred in Gerry's working life when he left the employ of Graham and accepted an offer from Claud Hamiltons to run their specialist tuning department based at Broomloan Road, Glasgow. The job would not only give him access to the latest performance parts but also the use of the workshops and equipment after his working day. It was a job made in heaven for Gerry.

The forging of ever-closer links with Hamiltons and Mike Leeke seems to indicate yet another effort to achieve independence from his brother. Almost immediately, Gerry struck up a close friendship with the Wholesale Manager, John Murray.

"We just got on great right from the start," recalls John. "Within a couple of weeks, Gerry mentioned that he was keen to race the Chamois at Brands Hatch on Boxing Day. I was planning to visit my parents in Southam, near Silverstone, over the Christmas period. I said he could come and stay with us to break up his journey and I'd come along to help out.

"He arrived on Christmas Eve in a Singer Vogue with the Chamois on a trailer and we left on Christmas day, which didn't go down well with my father who was a parson, and stayed at a little hotel at the bottom of Wrotham Hill near the circuit.

"The paddock in those days had what looked like bicycle sheds you put your car under. Gerry would always wind the engine over from cold to get the oil circulating before starting it up. The car was still on the trailer, so it was more or less at eye level. I hadn't noticed but there was a group of girls standing behind the car right by the big fat exhaust. Gerry fires it up and a huge cloud of black smoke covers all the girls from head to toe. It was so funny. They were laughing, as well, eventually.

"It just carried on from there. We were close friends. I'd stay behind after work with him, often until the early hours, and help out with some pretty advanced modifications he had planned. Mike Leeke had supplied a car. I don't know how he got away with it. Mike was all big-time and quite charismatic with it."

The modifications were yet another example of Gerry constantly on the look-out for improvement and not being afraid to experiment with some previously untried materials.

"I'm pretty sure he was the first to use honeycomb material to stiffen the car," continues John. "He used it to make a completely new floorpan. We used all the correct materials and it certainly stiffened things up. I used to help with that sort of thing.

"He had an incredible ability to adapt things and make them work. He was much more than just a driver. He analysed things from an engineering point of view. He was very clever."

The work didn't stop there. Revised suspension was designed and fabricated to make the best use of the wider wheels fitted all around. Other detailed, subtle modifications were incorporated, which ultimately made it one of the most highly modified Chamois of its time.

Needless to say, Gerry's loyal and trusted engine wizard, Hugh Shannon, built an engine worthy of inclusion in such a highly-modified, high-specification machine. This time it was a 1140cc Coventry Climax unit.

Hugh was based in the small Scottish village of Methven which is on the outskirts of Perth. A trip to Methven from

The first Ingliston meeting in '67 saw Gerry claim victory the first time out in his further modified Chamois, but he had to settle for second place in the Hartley Whyte race. Here he is harried by the Mini Cooper of Dave Muter while the late Andrew Cowan in another Chamois prepares to join the battle. ***(Eric Bryce)***

Gerry's parents' place in Milngavie would take around an hour in those pre-motorway days. It would be a journey he would make frequently. His regular companion on those many trips would be Margaret; after their first meeting in the Malletshaugh Inn, some 12 months previously, they had gradually become an item.

"A whole crowd of us would go through to Ingliston regularly to watch," recalls Margaret. "I was interested in racing before I went out with Gerry. It was good fun. My best friend Joannie and I both had Minis and we'd do crazy things. Joannie ended up going out with Gerry's mechanic, Mike Barr. I was going out with Gerry by then.

"We would drive up to Hugh's on most Friday nights (it seemed like most!), either to deliver an engine or pick one up. Very romantic courting! A Sgt Pepper LP was the nearest I got to chocolates and flowers! I must say I preferred the LP.

"The drive up in those pre-motorway days was like being on a rally stage. We'd spend most of the journey trying to avoid rabbits, deer, etc... We once hit a rabbit and you could see the shape of it on the front of the Imp. We called the car ESNID due to the registration being ESN 1D. He also called his sheepskin jacket Cedrick! Sad, but true. I'm making him out to be slightly mad! He was of sound mind, honest.

"Hugh had a workshop behind his house. When they had done what they had to do, we would go to the Bell Tree pub which was just up the road. When we travelled up from down south to see family in Glasgow years later, we always took Hugh and his wife out for a meal.

"He was a lovely man with a great sense of humour, which I experienced first-hand a few years later when I worked at the National Heart Hospital in London. He was in for a major heart operation and the Senior Registrar asked to see his legs (for potential vein grafting) and he just says, 'It's under the bed'. He'd not told them he had a wooden leg.

"Another thing was that he and his sons had really broad Scottish accents. Even I struggled to understand them. I had to act as a translator between Hugh and the surgeon and in the pub across the road from the hospital, his boys couldn't even order a drink! I had to step in there as well."

It seems Gerry certainly knew how to show a lady a good time. Trips on a Friday night after work involving engines and workshops. How did he get away with it?

On the odd occasion Margaret was unavailable, John Murray, who remembers the trips fondly, would tag along. "Hugh's workshop was very posh, it had carpet on the floor. He was such a lovely man and very clever. His background was being involved with the Royal Navy and at that time they were changing over to the Phantom jet-fighter and Hugh had a part in the fitting of British engines.

"We would go up after work in a Singer Vogue estate car which got tattier and tattier as time went on. It was always loaded up with an engine and we'd bring a freshly rebuilt one back with us. I don't recall him ever coming to the races. He seemed happy to be in the background."

Sadly, Hugh died in late 1978 from a heart attack. His youngest son Douglas, continued to build engines for many Scottish competitors, mainly in rallying, after his father's death. He was only 11 years old when Gerry used to visit, but remembers not just those visits, but other occasions when he would accompany his father to Glasgow.

"Gerry was quite a hero to me at that time," offers Douglas. "As well as delivering/picking up engines, dad and Gerry lowered the front springs on an Imp on one occasion. There was always something going on. This all went on quite late at night. Gerry had a lot of respect for dad and vice versa.

"I have a nice picture which was presented to Dad by Claud Hamiltons at a dinner dance in 1967. Also, some photos of when I went with dad to Glasgow to install the Climax engine. I was very young, so just sat in the office. I do remember him making some engine mounts from scratch. He was a very good engineer."

With the work completed, the car had been shaken down at the pre-season Ingliston test day – a luxury then – it was time for its first serious outing. The season opener at Ingliston in April offered up the usual fare with a good size entry of the regular faces and a sprinkling of new names to bolster the numbers. Gerry would again be running in the Scottish Saloon Car Championship in the under 1200cc class. As before, this usually involved two outings per meeting with a good finish in the championship round resulting in you going forward to compete in the final race of the day, the Hartley Whyte Trophy race.

It looked like all the hard work had paid off, reported *Top Gear*: 'Gerry Birrell always makes a fast start and, once he is through the Esses in first place, there is little likelihood of anyone overtaking him. Bill Borrowman in his usual Cooper S tried extremely hard to get on terms, but gradually the Chamois opened up a safe lead, eventually winning by 3sec'. Some debut!

Looking straight at the man pressing the shutter. Eric Bryce was a top-class amateur lensman and a regular figure at all Scottish events who knew the Birrell brothers well. ***(Eric Bryce)***

Never one to waste an opportunity to compete, Gerry took the Chamois to the Fintry House hillclimb on 25 June 1967 for the first time and came away with second place in his class. ***(Jack Davidson)***

In the Hartley Whyte encounter, Gerry had to be content with second place, sandwiched between the two Mini-Coopers of the victor, Logan Morrison and Dave Muter. Even though the order didn't change for the entire race the crowd who had remained were treated to a thriller. Andrew Cowan in an ex-Fraser Imp joined in the battle towards the end. At the finish, less than half a second covered the four cars.

The following month at Ingliston saw an even better return with victories in both the Saloon and Hartley Whyte races. The meeting was run in extremely wet conditions, proving the car was just as adept in the wet or the dry.

According to the June issue of *Top Gear*: 'Gerry had made the usual arms-length set of modifications to the Shannon-Chamois. The trouble with Gerry is that he needs two cars to work on, to use up all the ideas he has. Meanwhile, Hugh Shannon stands by with a quiet smile on his face and makes the necessary changes to the engine.'

With Ingliston having its annual break due to the staging of the Royal Highland Show at the venue, Gerry, as in previous years, took in a couple of other motoring disciplines: rallying and hill-climbing. And he would make the annual pilgrimage to the British Grand Prix, which that year was being held at Silverstone.

The Scottish International Rally in June would see his first appearance behind the wheel on such an event and his vehicle, a Singer Vogue, would also be making its first rally appearance. Mike Leeke would assume co-driving responsibilities.

A pretty much trouble-free four days resulted in a very impressive 12th place finish overall and the winner of the Group One class plus an award for the best Scots finisher. What a debut – or it was until, to quote Graham Gauld's report in *Autosport*, 'He was bombed out of Group One for having three spotlights.' This was after a protest by the third-place finisher, Peter Johnston. The rules were unequivocal that only two spotlights were allowed.

Ross Finlay in *Top Gear* explained in more detail other factors behind the exclusion of the car. 'It seems that there had been hints before the rally that the Vogue should have been entered in Group Two due to it having had strengthening parts welded to its front suspension and various other odds and ends. To leave it in Group One was nothing less than chancy.

'Apparently, the scrutineer, in the ridiculously short time available for examining the car assumed it was in Group Two.'

All the above, especially, the modifications to the suspension, you would have to suspect was further proof of Gerry's need to engineer an advantage. To stretch the rules to the maximum. Unfortunately, on this occasion, it resulted in a disqualification.

There was no such controversy on the Red Hackle Rally, which was a regional Scottish championship event starting and finishing in Perth. From a sizeable and strong entry of Lotus Cortinas, Mini Coopers and Imps, Gerry's Singer Vogue claimed an impressive third place overall and even set the fastest time on stage nine at Glenisla. His performance drew praise from AP of *Motoring News*: 'Birrell's immaculately prepared and sportingly driven Claud Hamilton Singer Vogue finished well clear of the fourth-place finisher.'

The hillclimb outing at Fintray in Aberdeenshire – the venue's first national event – was in his usual Shannon-Chamois in the under 1300cc class. He wound up a fine second, splitting the Mini Coopers of Tom Christie and Jim Dryden, only a couple of tenths covering the three of them.

As in previous years, it seems the trip to the grand prix was a memorable one for several reasons. "There was Gerry, myself, John Nicholson and a couple of others all went down in Graham's bloody transporter, the ex-British Rail Pullman truck," reflects Alan Muir. "We had a couple of days to spare, so instead of heading straight there we'd heard that North Wales was supposed to be quite good for women, so we ended up in Prestatyn. Of course, none of the campsites would let us in with the truck.

"We ended up at Silverstone three days before the grand prix. In those days you literally parked across the road in a small industrial estate. We slept in the back of this bloody truck. No facilities, whatsoever. We used to go to London in the evenings and on one memorable evening saw Spike Milligan's latest show.

"When it was time for the meeting, we were short of money and, more importantly, had no tickets. Because we all knew Jackie (Stewart), Gerry managed to blag his way into the paddock – far easier in those pre-Ecclestone days – and got us tickets and paddock passes for the three days. It was brilliant.

"By the time we were on our way home we were all a bit 'wiffy' to say the least. We decided to head for Blackpool and went to the swimming baths to get ourselves cleaned up. We thought we'd treat ourselves and stay the night. We ended up in this god awful boarding house. I vowed that day to never go back to Blackpool, and I haven't."

After the trials and tribulations of the past few weeks, Gerry must have been pleased to be back in his preferred environment with the re-commencement of racing at Ingliston. He would be busier than usual this time out, not only would he be in his regular Chamois but he had been invited by Team Volkswagen GB, along with fellow Ingliston regular Bill Dryden, to compete in the first Formula Vee race on Scottish soil. The formula had been introduced in England at the start of the '67 season and was attracting stronger entries as the season progressed. This would be the first round of a four-race Scottish championship.

The Formula Vee race would be Gerry's first competitive outing in a single-seater. He had been entered in the Ecurie Ecosse-Imp on a couple of occasions as a team-mate to Graham, but these drives had failed to come to fruition.

Compared to his usual performances, a somewhat disappointing sixth place was all he could achieve after a fierce race-long, battle with Peter Danaher, a reportedly, fist-waving, grass-mowing, Bill Dryden and Dutch glamour girl, Liane Engeman. A consolation would have been beating Bill Dryden to be top Scot. Both Gerry and Dryden were up against it from the off when they had been allocated the Dolling chassis which was outclassed by the Beach chassis of the other Team VW runners.

It was back to normal with a roof over his head when he took the honours in both the saloon and Hartley Whyte races after race-long battles with his arch-rival, Logan Morrison, who was also now behind the wheel of a Chamois, albeit with a 1000cc motor compared to Gerry's 1140cc unit. To round off a splendid day, Gerry also set a class lap record.

While his racing career was on the up and up, the same couldn't be said of his personal life. In August, his girlfriend left for America to carry on her career as a medical technician. "I didn't feel the relationship was going anywhere and my career was important," recalls Margaret. "I didn't have the money for a gap year as they do now. I paid my way out there by working for a family looking after their children and working at a hospital in Boston as a technician. I intended to see a bit of the world and stay out there. But that's not the way it turned out."

Having got the jump at the start, Gerry leads the field through the Esses at Ingliston in July '67. This image with the agricultural buildings, the trees and the proximity of the barriers encapsulates everything about the track. ***(Eric Bryce)***

On the same day, he took part in the first Formula Vee race north of the border and finished in sixth position. Here he follows Danaher and Haysey, who are both in the more modern-looking Beach chassis compared to his Dolling. ***(Eric Bryce)***

The next two outings in August and September at Ingliston in the saloon championship yielded victories on both occasions, making him unbeaten thus far in that particular series.

Unfortunately, his first mechanical gremlin of the year struck at the September meeting in the Hartley Whyte race when the coil lead came adrift out on the circuit. A quick stop to re-attach it resulted in a fourth-place finish.

At the final meeting of the year, Gerry's hopes of maintaining his 100 percent unbeaten record in the saloon championship were spoilt when veteran northerner, Tony Lanfranchi, albeit by then southern-based, appeared in an Alan Fraser Imp and pulled away to win in the atrocious conditions. But Gerry had done enough by that stage to be crowned the Scottish Saloon Car Champion. Despite a couple of troubled outings in the Hartley Whyte Championship, he still managed to come out champion by just a solitary point from Logan Morrison.

He wasn't finished there, adding the Scottish National Speed Championship Trophy to his already considerable haul of silverware. Again, Logan Morrison was the bridesmaid.

The only thing he didn't win was the Scottish Formula Vee Championship, ending up as runner-up to Nick Brittan. After his initial disappointing outing, the further three outings yielded runner-up finishes in each. In the first two Gerry was behind Brittan but in the last round at the wet October meeting, he was beaten by fellow Ingliston regular and friend Bill Dryden.

"I was asked by Wooler Engineering to race their new Austro chassis," remembers Bill. "They were agents for the car and it was, I believe, its first appearance in the UK. Even though I'd not driven it before practice, I could tell immediately it was far superior to the Dolling chassis I had raced previously on two occasions.

"All the regulars were entered, Brittan, Muir, Hayselden, Danaher, and, of course, Gerry, who was now driving the Beach chassis which was the car to have.

"By the time of the race it had started to rain and the car felt good. I always felt that in wet conditions if I did two good laps, I was away. I ended up beating Gerry by 11 seconds in the 15-lap race.

"I got out of the car afterwards and Wooler's team manager Mike Moore came running up, embraced me and kissed me on the lips! It was the first time in my life that a bloke had kissed me on the lips. Mike said, 'You must drive for me next week!' I said, 'I can't I'm getting married.' 'What am I going to do?' was his reply.

"I recommended he give Gerry a try, saying he was single and could move about. And was desperately keen to get on in racing. Gerry went to race for them and, in a way, that was the start of his professional career."

The acceptance of the offer from Mike Moore to contest the 1968 National Formula Vee championship in one of their Austro chassis didn't require Gerry to turn professional. He still had plans to race his Chamois on home soil, so he would commute between his parents' place in Milngavie and England. Most people would have been daunted by such a thing, but not Gerry. He would have seen the travelling as part and parcel, a necessary evil, of his continued climb up the racing ladder. But that was all for next year. He hadn't finished with 1967 yet.

The following month, now Beach-mounted, he leads Brittan and the future Mrs Graham Birrell, Jenny Nadin. Brittan eventually got past to claim victory by just over a second. ***(Colin Lourie)***

A rare trip down south to Mallory Park in October would round off his circuit racing activities for the season when he was invited to join brother Graham to drive one of the Ecurie Ecosse-Imps for the well-known Scottish stable, and what a trip it was. Gerry scored his first-ever single-seater victory in a Formula Libre encounter with Graham repeating the feat in the other car in the second Libre race, making the long trip all the more worthwhile. With one trophy each, the bragging rights were shared for once.

That shouldn't have been the culmination of Gerry's season – but it turned out to be. A planned outing on the RAC International Rally in a Rootes Motors-entered Sunbeam Imp, again with his regular co-driver, Mike Leeke, was cancelled at the last minute due to an outbreak of Foot and Mouth disease.

While that may have been the end of his racing exploits, it was by no means an end to Gerry's travels and adventures for the year. The longest trip of the year awaited him. The destination was the United States of America and the small matter of a question he needed to ask a certain lady.

"He came out around Christmas time," remembers Margaret. "It was my 21st birthday on 1 January and we spent it in New York and he asked me to marry him. He wanted me to come home straight away, but I said, no, I'll wait until my year is up which meant I came back in the August of '68."

Typical Gerry, the marriage proposal wasn't the only reason for the trip. Claud Hamiltons had arranged for him to pay a visit to Chrysler Motors in Detroit to have a peek at their competition department.

In a lengthy feature in *Top Gear* titled Gerry and the Road Runners by Graham Gauld, it seems that as Gerry told it, he had problems immediately upon his arrival on American soil.

'I wandered up to the TWA desk at Kennedy Airport, flung my ticket down for Boston, only to be told that the flight I booked had been cancelled months ago and the alternatives were cancelled due to snow.

Waiting in the assembly area at the season-ending October meeting on a typical Scottish autumnal day. ***(Micheal Malcolm)***

All suited and booted on the Claud Hamilton stand at the Glasgow Motor Show 1967. On the far right is John Murray, Gerry's future best man. To John's left is Mike Leeke, a director and the general manager at Hamiltons, who was of great assistance to Gerry. ***(John Murray)***

Posing with his impressive sticker collection, garnered on his Stateside travels. ***(SMRC/Graham Gauld)***

'We were all taken back to New York. I got off the airport coach clutching all my bags tightly as I had been told that all Americans are out to steal your luggage. I was asked if I needed a hand by a young man. I asked him for directions to Grand Central Station. This guy picks up all my luggage, sprints around the back of the bus, twenty yards across the street and into Grand Central. Then he complained I didn't tip him enough. Welcome to America!

'After fighting my way aboard the train to Boston, surviving the kicking, pushing and shouting, I thought that maybe British Rail travellers weren't so bad after all.

'My only time behind the wheel didn't go much better. It was in a 1964 Rambler Classic estate car with a column change that didn't change and an almost automatic clutch. I guarantee I didn't drive at over 45mph. I wasn't helped by the traffic lights either. I came to one set near Arlington Heights which showed red and yellow. After asking Margaret what that meant, she said, 'cross now'. So I started to bomb across only to be greeted with Margaret screaming STOP! It appears that she meant the pedestrians can cross now, not me.

'A few days later I flew down to Chrysler's Highland Park plant near Detroit for a pre-arranged meeting with the guy in charge of the competition department. I had phoned ahead and it sounded like he was trying hard to forget I was coming. He was helpful in the end but obviously had a million other things to do rather than show me around.

'The next day it was on to the Plymouth Special Vehicles Division which covers everything from Hemi-Chargers to taxis. I could not have had a more friendly welcome. I would have loved to have taken some photos but cameras weren't allowed in the place. It was fascinating to see the production line and the thoroughness of the component testing.

'I was determined to come back with car stickers as mementoes which were all the rage in America. I was led over to meet the head storekeeper, who apparently had a reputation for irascibility. We had ended up getting on like a house on fire and I staggered out with a huge pile of stickers. It turned out his grandfather came from Armadale!'

Gerry came back with a head full of ideas that would be put to good use, not just on his own car but on those of others. By this time he was acquiring quite a reputation for both his skills in developing a car and his mechanical knowledge. Both facets would undoubtedly lead to other offers. It looked as if 1968 was set to be his busiest year of his life.

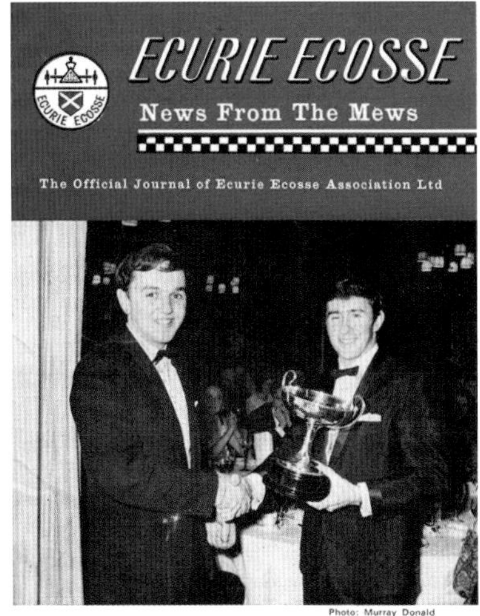
ECURIE ECOSSE

News From The Mews

The Official Journal of Ecurie Ecosse Association Ltd

Photo: Murray Donald

Gerry Birrell (left) winner of the Ron Flockhart Trophy, receives the cup from previous winner Jackie Stewart.

2/- Vol. II No. 4 March 1968

Old friends reunited. ***(Author)***

Gerry on his way to one of his many victories. ***(unknown)***

CHAPTER THREE

THIS IS GETTING SERIOUS

Before the commencement of on-track activities, Gerry's presence was required at the various engagements involving the presentation of the awards from the previous season. He was in for quite a haul. The Scottish Motor Racing Club (SMRC), the organisers at Ingliston, were first up, Gerry coming away with three trophies. The Scottish Saloon Car Champion, the Hartley Whyte and the Scottish National Speed Championship. That perennial bridesmaid, Logan Morrison, was runner-up in all three.

The Ecurie Ecosse Dinner Dance was next up. A black-tie affair attended by the great and the good of Scottish motor racing. Gerry added to his already mounting collection by coming away with the Ron Flockhart Trophy which was awarded annually to the most promising up-and-coming Scottish driver of the season

The trophy was a mounted and inscribed hub cap from Flockhart's 1956 Le Mans-winning Ecurie Ecosse Jaguar D-Type which Flockhart had presented to the Esso Oil company at a dinner in Edinburgh to celebrate the victory. Following his death in 1962 the trophy had been given to the SMRC who had since presented it to whom they felt was the most deserving recipient.

Gerry's name would join other illustrious drivers on the roll call and it was one of those previous recipients, Jackie Stewart, who presented him with the award. Jackie, by then, was already a grand prix winner. A far cry from when a young Gerry, along with his brothers, would visit him at the Dumbuck Garage.

It was down to the serious business now with a trip (some trip!) to Thruxton in early March to sample his new mount for the season ahead, the Wooler Performance Equipment entered, Porsche-built Austro Formula Vee. A general test day had been arranged for those wishing to sample the venue for the first time before the inaugural meeting on Easter Monday featuring a round of the European Formula Two Championship. Gerry would be on the supporting programme when the European Formula Vee contingent visited the UK.

He emerged from the day a fraction slower than the previous year's champion, Nick Brittan, who with the continued support of Volkswagen (GB), would be concentrating on the European series. Gerry, reportedly, expressed satisfaction with his day's work.

All the ingredients looked in place for Gerry, despite his lack of experience of many of the English circuits, to emerge

They weren't the prettiest of race cars, but who cares if you are winning? *(Bruce McTavish)*

Gerry became quite used to being interviewed after such a dominant season. *(Unknown)*

as the favourite for championship honours in both the National Formula Vee series and the Lydden Hill-based series sponsored by Financings.

To enable Gerry to complete his many commutes from Milngavie to most points of the UK, he would spend many hours in the air. It would have been impossible to attempt such a schedule by road. It was certainly the flying option that was required for his first Formula Vee outing of the season at Lydden Hill in deepest Kent; a thousand-mile round trip by road. A decent size entry and the tight confines of the track meant that two qualifying heats were required to sort out the starting order for the final, which counted towards both championships.

Gerry took an easy victory in the first heat of two. According to Paul Harrington in *Autosport*: 'His only spot of excitement came on the last lap when he came up to lap Peter Ross's Abridge Engineering Beach: Ross appeared so amazed at the speed of Birrell's Austro that he spun on the straight.'

The final was a little more closely fought with the heat two victor, Mike Hayselden's Monaco, making a superb start to lead for three laps before Gerry took over for the remaining twelve tours. The significance of leading those laps was that the championship organisers, as an added incentive, was awarding £1 for each lap led. 12 laps led = £12 + £25 for the win. Not a bad payday, which I'm sure wasn't lost on Gerry. More so, if it's true what they say about the Scots and their money!

From that first round at the end of March until the first weekend of August at Thruxton, Gerry would remain unbeaten in both British championships, taking an unprecedented twelve wins, which consisted of three heat wins and nine overall victories.

His only defeat during that time came at the inaugural meeting at Thruxton on Easter Monday when a large European contingent arrived on these shores to contest a round of the European Vee Championship. A loose coil wire stopped him out on the circuit. He managed to get it going but a pit stop to have it fixed properly put him well out of contention. Before the problem, he had been the leading British championship regular in sixth place.

Every outing in the national championship just seemed to confirm his superiority. A couple of visits to Silverstone, in April and June, brought flag-to-flag victories and lap records. Another £20 in the pot for the laps led – to go with the £50 prize money – with them both being ten-lappers. Brands Hatch, in April and May, brought the same outcome. Two wins and new lap records. Another payday! Solitary visits to Castle Combe and Mallory in May and June, respectively, resulted in the same outcome. Kerching! A couple of visits to Lydden Hill in July saw him for once put under some pressure from Mike Hayselden, who managed to get in front on both occasions but had to yield to Gerry come the chequered flag.

The first defeat came at Thruxton – seemingly, not his best hunting ground – at the hands of Mike Haysey. "As a driver for Team VW GB, I remember well the arrival on the grid of Gerry and the Wooler Performance Equipment team," recalls Haysey. "I knew that the combination would be a difficult act to beat. The Austro chassis combined with a Porsche-developed engine was fantastic. I drove Nick Brittan's Austro once at Brands Hatch and although stuck in third gear, broke the lap record, which stood for three seasons.

"At Thruxton, Gerry and I both made good starts and by the first bend, Allard, we were joined by Mike Hayselden and one other. As we entered the tight Campbell bend we were all bunched up. I knew Gerry would be aggressive and not give way so I did the same. We touched a couple of times but I managed to get clear leaving Gerry and Mike to fight it out."

The battle for second place didn't last long due to the engine in Gerry's car unable to pull maximum revs, which dropped him to a disappointing fifth place at the finish.

He made the cover of Safer Motoring, the in-house VW magazine. ***(Author)***

After two defeats it was back to winning ways at Silverstone in late August. Here he leads away from pole position. ***(John Murray)***

He did have the consolation of sharing the fastest lap with Haysey, which leads you to believe it was an intermittent fault.

Having suffered his first defeat, Gerry would have been determined to get back to his winning ways at Cadwell Park a couple of weeks later but was thwarted, not by mechanical woes this time, but by the return of Nick Brittan, who was having a break from his European activities.

According to the report in *Motoring News* by HWJ: 'At the front the in-fighting between Brittan and Birrell was a joy to behold, the championship leader trying every trick in the book to out-fox, out-brake and out-drive the Londoner. He met his match for Brittan matched his every ploy and ran out the victor by 0.2sec, after a most interesting and entertaining battle of wits.'

Someone who can testify to how intense their battle was their closest rival Haysey: "Following qualifying Nick (Brittan) gave me a few tips on where I could make up time. This resulted in a great start for me to lead into the first corner. Gerry passed me after a couple of corners, then Nick passed me on the second lap. From then on I sat back and watched the two ex-saloon racers up to their usual and somewhat dangerous tactics. From memory, they touched so many times I thought, I hope they both go off and hand me the race, but Nick just held on from Gerry."

During their heated battle, Gerry set a new class lap record but that would have been scant consolation. To have been beaten by Brittan in what was his first outing of the season in the championship would have been a difficult pill to swallow.

The presence of Graham, who had made a rare foray south with his Escort Twin Cam, added to his woes. Especially, when he claimed victory in the saloon car race.

Another reason for Graham's presence was a rare appearance of the Ecosse-Imps south of the border. The brothers would compete in the Formula Libre encounter amongst a plethora of Chevron GTs, which must have dwarfed the tiny single-seater. They did enjoy a close battle, swapping places on a couple of occasions – neither was in contention for the race victory – but after only a few laps both would retire. Graham car's broke a front wishbone. Gerry was brought in and retired as a precautionary measure.

The return of Nick Brittan to the series must have been a way of trying to drum up some good press for the series, which due to Gerry's domination, wasn't attracting the sort of coverage and calibre of drivers Volkswagen (GB) was hoping for. As well as is abilities behind the wheel, Brittan was a renowned PR specialist and was in charge of the promotion of this new formula at the behest of Volkswagen. At that time, he was also actively involved with the promotion of Formula Ford 1600, both in the UK and Europe. It was this category that was clearly winning the popularity contest.

The press coverage in the motorsport weeklies seemed to focus more on Gerry – for obvious reasons – than the quality of the racing in the category. Ian Titchmarsh reporting in *Autosport* on one of Gerry's Mallory Park victories stated: 'Gerry Birrell in his Wooler Performance Equipment Austro Vee can swing an axle better than most.'

Andrew Marriott (ARM) was rather more succinct in *Motoring News*: 'When will someone give the lad an F3 drive?' Marriott, at that time, was a junior reporter. He would continue to follow Gerry's career and would achieve fame of his own in being recognised as one of the leading writers/commentators of the past 50 years.

The next race at Silverstone saw Gerry exact revenge on Brittan and on this occasion both Gerry and the formula got good press from that man Marriott in his *Motoring News* report: 'Every man who ever criticised Formula Vee racing should have been present to watch this race with its mind-bending battle for the lead. It was simply terrific. It was Birrell and Brittan in front with their swing axles swinging in unison. The battle continued with the lead continually changing.

'By half-distance (six laps) Brittan seemed to have the edge and hung on to the lead for five laps, but then Birrell swept by again. On the penultimate lap, Brittan successfully reversed the manoeuvre and led across the line to start the final lap.

Looking delighted with his day's work after finally beating arch-rival Nick Brittan at Silverstone in August. *(John Murray)*

All the action was at Becketts where Birrell decided to stop tracking Brittan and went ahead again and just scraped out of the corner in first place. He held the lead down the club straight, around Woodcote, to take the flag with Brittan only inches behind. With Brittan returning to British Vee racing the class has really livened up. Not surprisingly, Birrell bettered his own class lap record.'

With Brittan absent at the next round at Crystal Palace, Gerry romped away in the atrocious conditions to win by over 20sec, mastering the conditions with ease. Again, his performance drew praise, this time from Michael Cotton (MLC) in *Motoring News*: 'Being an accomplished rally driver was something of an asset in those conditions.' That's something Michael is well qualified to comment on, having accompanied Gerry on the 1966 RAC Rally.

That win – his fourteenth in total – took place in mid-September and was enough to clinch the British Championship. Having already taken the less prestigious Lydden Hill-based Financing-sponsored Championship a month earlier, Gerry was quite justifiably crowned 'the king' of Formula Vee.

Unsurprisingly, in the three remaining races, Gerry didn't let up in his determination to dominate. No doubt he was still seeing pound signs in his eyes for all the laps led.

Another dominant win by more than 7sec at Brands Hatch, further increased his considerable bank balance. Yet again more praise was offered up in *Motoring News*, this time from Mike Doodson (MGD): 'Nothing short of a bombing raid will stop him from taking another maximum points haul in the National Championship.' Mike is another one, like his colleague, Andrew Marriott, who would follow Gerry's climb up the racing ladder, along with that of his own.

The final two outings at Thruxton – his 'bogey' circuit – and Silverstone yielded third and second-place finishes, respectively. On both occasions, Brittan took the honours, an on-form Fred Saunders sneaking between the dominant pair at Thruxton.

At the aforementioned final round at Silverstone, Gerry was invited by Saunders to try out his twin-cam engined Crosslé 12F in the event closing Formula Libre race. Typical of Gerry's thoroughness and attention to detail he arranged for the Wooler team to look after the car. In what was quite a step-up in power from his usual mount, he performed highly-respectably against a typical Formula Libre field of a V8 engined ex-F1 Cooper, F3 Brabhams, and even a GT40. It was the ex-F1 Cooper of Martin Brain that handed Gerry a fortuitous but deserved win by blowing its engine on the last lap after a race-long battle.

In his next outing in the car at Brands Hatch a couple of weeks later he had to settle for second place – for once – when he was soundly beaten by the 'King of Brands' Tony Lanfranchi.

It just seemed no matter what Gerry got his Nomex-clad backside in at that time, he was going to come out on top on most occasions. The combination of confidence and momentum are such vitally important factors when you are trying to climb up the racing ladder.

That outing was the culmination of his circuit racing activities in the UK. What a first season it had been. Two Formula Vee titles to his name and a full bank account from all his laps led. The presence and success of Nick Brittan in the latter stages took the gloss off an otherwise, memorable season.

Enabling him to achieve that extraordinary level of success was a team of equally skilled people at Woolers which was a division of CT Wooler Engineering based in Ealing, London. The mechanic responsible for Gerry's car was Kiwi Bruce McTavish, though with a name like that, you'd think he was a fellow Scot.

"I'd arrived from New Zealand in the middle of '67 and joined Woolers towards the end of that year," remembers McTavish. "My main job was to assemble the 5-speed gearboxes which Ford supplied for use in the 105Es, Cortinas and Escorts which were modified by Woolers and had Hewland gears. These were fine for the twin-cam but became obsolete when the BDA came along. Woolers used to make all sorts of accessories, oil coolers, wheel spacers and lowering kits. The work on the race cars was fitted in around all that.

"I must have met Gerry for the first time at Woolers in '68 and with the success we were having the race car maintenance gradually took over from the gearboxes. Because we were beating the works Team GB VW cars it was decided that Woolers took over the race preparation of their cars. So now, with help from the Team VW guys, I was looking after four cars: Gerry's, Mike Haysey's, Jenny Nadin's and Nick Brittan's, who was doing more races on the continent.

"Gerry's car was a '67 Porsche-Austro chassis, Brittan's was the latest '68 Austro. The cars of Mike and Jenny were US-built Beaches. Mr Peacock, who ran Woolers, and I, were trying to reconfigure the two Beaches with the Austro tweaks, as well as doing work on the engines. We did a little work on

Never content with just the one or two outings, Gerry was also out in the second round of the Scottish FF Championship in a converted Lotus 20. A disappointing first-lap retirement was the outcome. ***(SMRC/Graham Gauld)***

Back on familiar territory at the season opener at Ingliston in April '68. Arch-rival and eternal bridesmaid Logan Morrison is on two wheels trying to stave off Gerry's challenge. ***(Eric Bryce)***

modifying some VW engine parts for customers but didn't assemble any customer engines.

"We didn't see much of Gerry between races. I think he was still working at a Rootes dealership in Glasgow and living with his parents. I do know he was still racing other cars in Scotland."

All the while Gerry had been dovetailing a full campaign back on home soil with his hectic schedule down south. You wonder if Gerry's days had more than 24 hours in them.

To defend his numerous Ingliston titles, Gerry had retained his Climax-engined Chamois. Never content to leave the car in the same specification, the engine had been enlarged by his much-trusted engine man, Hugh Shannon, from 1140cc to 1298 and, to cope with the extra power and torque, a 5-speed gearbox had been fitted. In recognition of his efforts, the car would be entered on most occasions as a Shannon Chamois.

Most racing drivers would have been content with just a fraction of Gerry's planned schedule but, typical of Gerry, he would continue his association with the once-great, Ecurie Ecosse behind the wheel of the Ecosse-Imp in Formula Libre races and would compete in the inaugural Scottish Formula Ford Championship in a Lotus 20, which was originally a 1961 Formula Junior, he converted to Formula Ford specification.

The car was owned by a group of Scottish motorsport enthusiasts, Tony Evangelisti, Robin Trail, George Stewart, Ian Callender and Bob Callander (different spelling, no relation). They ran under the name of Equipe Centro-Scot, you sense the influence of Tony Evangelisti there.

"They also ran under another name," recalls Graham Birrell. "Falkirk Automobile Racing Team or FART, for short." A dose of Scottish humour there. I prefer the latter!

Sadly, no members of Centro-Scot survive but Madeleine Stewart (George's widow) offers her memories. "The team was based at our home Dunipace Mill House, Larbert, near Falkirk, where they worked on a variety of racing cars including at different times, a Crosslé, a Lola and a Chevron.

"George and a couple of the others drove the cars in races and hillclimbs. I know that Gerry drove for the team but I am not aware of where or how often, but I do remember him coming to our home to discuss progress on the cars with his friend and mechanic, Mike Barr. Margaret – we knew her more by her nickname Tingh – occasionally came too before going to the States. I recall one New Year, Gerry, Tingh and some friends driving from a party in Glasgow to our home to celebrate again with us."

"I was *very* drunk that Hogmanay," remembers Margaret (surprisingly). "Madeleine took me upstairs to sleep it off, offered me some broth and I felt even more sick! Her memory is a real blast from the past."

The season-opener at Ingliston in April which was the first outing for the re-worked Chamois got off to a sombre start with a short commemoration to Jim Clark, who had tragically lost his life the previous Sunday.

Unsurprisingly, the car suffered from the usual new car gremlins. Graham Birrell in his regular column in *Top Gear* stated: 'Gerry had problems with the handling. The engine wasn't performing as well as expected. Plus, the new 5-speed gearbox was apparently very tricky to make a quick change from first to second gear when leaving the start-line.'

Despite all the problems, it wasn't all doom and gloom. A second-place finish behind the Mini of Jim Dryden in the over 1000cc saloon race saw Gerry qualify for the Hartley Whyte encounter. As was the norm, the top six finishes from both saloon races went forward to fight it out for honours. According to *Top Gear*, that's just what happened: 'This was probably as exciting a race as has been seen at Ingliston. With Gerry Birrell not quite hitting it off with his mount, he was involved in a battle royal with the lesser-powered cars of the in-form duo of Jim Dryden and Logan Morrison. The trio enjoyed a fierce, close battle until at two-thirds distance, Birrell retired with a fuel-line failure.'

In yet another outing, only his fourth at the May meeting, Gerry drove the Ecosse-Imp in the Adam Wylie Formula Libre race. Here he follows Graham, who is driving the newer version. Another first-lap retirement was the result on one of his least rewarding days. ***(Colin Lourie)***

Gerry leads Mitchell, Danaher and Nadin on the first lap into Gerard's at Mallory Park in round six of the F Vee championship. Victories in his heat and the final brought his series tally to eight wins from eight outings. ***(Mike Mitchell)***

Despite the urgent need to be on a plane bound for Thruxton to compete in the European Formula Vee encounter the following day, Gerry discovered, to his horror, that, having moved the brake pedal, he had screwed up the master cylinder arrangement and the brakes were building pressure in the system. As the race progressed, the brakes were steadily being applied without him touching the pedal. By the time the single-seater was back in the paddock, the problem was so severe it had to be carried on to the trailer.

His busy itinerary led to the inevitable clash of dates due to the Ingliston meeting in May being the same day as a round of the Financing Formula Vee Championship at Lydden Hill. Ingliston won the day due, you suspect, to the number of possible outings that would total four. The usual two (hopefully) in the Chamois plus, a first outing in the Centro-Scot FF after its no-show at the April meeting and a rare appearance in the Ecosse-Imp. By the meeting's conclusion, he would have wished he had gone to Lydden instead.

All seemed rosy to begin: a victory in the over 1000cc saloon race, despite a broken exhaust manifold resulting in a slight loss of power. The victory was made sweeter due to Graham following him home. Admittedly, he had a cam follower break, resulting in a bent valve and a loss of power.

From then on, things went pear-shaped. The outing in the Ecosse-Imp in the Libre race lasted a few yards when the clutch cried enough off the start-line. Although he had been entered on numerous occasions to handle the tiny single-seater, it was mainly Graham, Bill Dryden, Willie Forbes and Eddie Labinjoh, who got the nod. Graham had the pick of the two cars. A fuel-injected and more spacious example had been built for him but he found the carburettor car, very uncomfortable – you tended to sit on it, not in it – but the faster of the two.

The Formula Ford appearance lasted a little longer but would end in retirement. It was the same story for the Chamois in the Hartley Whyte race. The serious matter of a broken crankshaft meant an instant retirement. Reportedly, the crankshaft was supplied by Racing Preparations for experimental purposes. The conclusion of this experiment: Make it stronger next time.

You would have thought that after such a busy and ultimately disappointing day, Gerry would have welcomed some time away from the driving seat but, when the opportunity arose the following weekend to sample yet another, different machine, how could he resist.

Among the cars in the Centro-Scot stable was a 1964 Lola T55 F2, now powered by a 2.0-litre SCA engine. Tony Evangelisti was entered in the Formula Libre and Allcomers handicap races at Croft, and with Gerry wielding spanners. He wouldn't have needed asking twice if he wanted a go.

Unfortunately, neither *Autosport* nor *Motoring News* mention his presence in their reports but take part he certainly did. We have photos to prove it! Irrespective of who drove in which race, nothing noteworthy was achieved.

During the break in activities at Ingliston, and when not racing the length and breadth of England, there was talk of a big modification to the Chamois, which was a talking point in Graham Birrell's column in *Top Gear*: 'Gerry was muttering about fitting a supercharger. This should be very interesting, provided it doesn't blow up. However, with his schedule, it may be a few months before he sorts out his ideas.'

The next meeting at Ingliston was the most controversial thus far in the racing career of the Birrell brothers when the inevitable clash between the fiercely competitive pair finally happened. Unsurprisingly, accounts differ on where the blame lies. Bill Henderson in *Autosport* offered: 'Gerry had unaccustomedly qualified on the second row and reportedly, wasn't a happy man. In front of him on the grid were his brother, Graham, in his Escort Twin Cam and John Handley's Mini. The race would start in damp conditions and these caused the Escort and Mini to struggle for decent traction off the line. In contrast, Gerry made a blinder and went to go between the pair. It was at this time that his brother's car found traction and made contact with Gerry's car and slewed into the barriers. End of the elder brother's race.'

Euan Taylor in *Top Gear* offered: 'The start was one of those calculated to strain the best family relations. Through no fault of his own Gerry nudged Graham's Escort which clouted the barrier and ended its race there and then.'

Richard Thomas in his Wheelspin column in the same magazine made no excuses for sitting securely on the fence when stating that: 'Graham will have his say in the GB column. All I can offer is that Graham wasn't very happy about the incident. I could tell by the smoke coming out of his nostrils! Third brother, Iain, acted the mediator when he stopped the pair coming to blows after the race.'

Graham in his GB column seemed to have calmed down – it was a month later – when he offered his views and a sensible way to prevent such a thing happening again: 'In light of my experience at the start when I was subjected to 'stock car' tactics. I suggest it might be safer at wet meetings to think about making up the grid in a two-by-two formation rather than in the conventional 3-by-2-by-3 arrangement.'

Gerry's problems didn't end there. Handley put him under enormous pressure until in the dying stages when he decided to make a bid for the lead. By that time, the rain had eased and a dry line was emerging. Unfortunately for Handley, he got off the dry line and clipped the back bumper of Gerry's car and slammed into the barriers causing damage to his front end. The collision sent Gerry into a spin. By the time he had got going again, Dave Muter had swept past into the lead but a quick bit of thinking by Gerry at Vets Corner saw him re-take the lead and claim a surprising victory. Phew!

Seemingly, there were no hard feelings between the pair, Handley accepting a lift back to the paddock from Gerry on the slowing-down lap and commenting that he would certainly be coming back for more; if only to lead young Birrell across the line!

Thankfully, the outing in the Formula Ford race was a more timid affair, not something you normally associate with Formula Ford. Australian Dave Walker, who was one of the leading runners in England, had ventured north in his works Russell-Alexis to take on all the locals and would have been expecting to have things his own way. Seemingly, Gerry didn't read the script. Euan Taylor in *Top Gear* stated: 'Gerry Birrell was stoking the boiler furiously, gradually closing up on the leader Walker.' Gerry finally lost out by a couple of seconds to come home in second place. To have been so competitive in only the car's second appearance against one of the leading car/driver combinations is further proof – if any were needed – of Gerry's prodigious talent in not only the building of the car but also, his ability to hone and develop the machine.'

At previous Ingliston meetings, Gerry had been averaging two or three outings, but at the August meeting he would take

A much-improved FF outing at Ingliston in July brought a second-place finish. *(Eric Bryce)*

part in five of the nine races. Graham was only marginally behind with four outings. With the pair in the winner's circle regularly – and Graham with his ever-present mobile shop – you have to wonder if the SMRC, ever considered changing the name from Ingliston to Birrellston. Just a thought!

Despite being seen in five of the races, none brought any results of note, only the two outings in the Chamois bringing any results to speak of but these were only third- and sixth-place finishes. The other races brought retirements in the Formula Ford event with a damaged sump and a broken wishbone on the Ecosse-Imp ended his second outing in the Formula Libre King Hussein Trophy race. Part one of the race had seen Gerry come home a disappointing seventh.

He did have better fortunes away from the track with the return of Margaret from America. "I came back in August, as promised, and got a job at the Glasgow Royal Infirmary" she recalls. "I'd try to go and watch him race as often as possible. If he was racing down south, I would try and get away on Friday then come back late on Sunday night or Monday morning. You could get the Vanguard mail flight for £9 and if you got the midnight one, you could sit in first class because the mail was in the back. My father didn't particularly like it because he had to come and pick me up from the airport.

"Mind you, you could go up and down to London in about four or five hours by car even though there weren't as many motorways, there just wasn't the traffic there is nowadays."

The next two meetings, which concluded activities at Ingliston for another year, were both run on the newly extended circuit. The lap distance increasing from approximately 1 mile to 1.3.

Neither of the meetings brought much in the way of success, the highlights being third and fifth-place finishes in the two Formula Ford outings. The lowlight was being involved in a start-line shunt in the Hartley Whyte race with Morrison, Borrowman and Muter. The quartet all ended up hitting something hard. That was the last intended outing in his trusty Chamois. With the car up for sale, it wasn't exactly the glorious end he would have envisaged for a car that had served him so well.

You would have thought that, by the culmination of activities at Ingliston in early October, he would have been ready for a break. Not Gerry. It would be early November at Brands Hatch in one of the aforementioned Formula Libre outings that would bring his hectic season to a close. Well, that's what he thought.

A nice sit down to reflect on his achievements. Make plans for next year. Spend time with the lady in his life. They all went out of the window with an offer to compete in the gruelling 23-day London-Sydney Marathon Rally. Just the sort of offer you need in November after a gruelling season of close-on forty races. Most people would never even have considered the offer for more than a millisecond. But Gerry wasn't like most people. We are talking about a guy who just loved to get behind the wheel of any car and compete.

The opportunity had come about due to his connections with the Rootes Group. He was still working at Claud Hamiltons – although I can't imagine how he fitted that in – and had been recommended to be part of the crew of a factory-entered Hillman Hunter, joining Andrew Cowan and Brian Coyle on the epic trip.

At least that was the intention until leading up to the start of the event he was hospitalised requiring a hernia operation. Reportedly, it was a problem he'd had a while following an accident in his mis-spent youth. Unsurprisingly, he had a steady stream of visitors, one of whom was Richard Thomas of *Top Gear* magazine who wrote in his Wheelspin column: 'If anyone had told Gerry about the operation beforehand he would never have allowed himself to have it done. The sight of Gerry hobbling about his room was like a lion with a bellyache and was not a pleasant sight.'

While lying in the hospital recovering Gerry must have suffered from mixed emotions when following the event's progress. On the one hand, relief at not having to endure such a tortuous journey, but on the other, the missing out on being part of the winning crew and the accolades that came with it. Colin Malkin was the lucky, or unlucky man, depending on your point of view, who took Gerry's place.

At least his enforced absence gave him time to focus on what the future held for him. Some important decisions needed to be made. Firstly, there was the small matter of one ring, for one finger, which belonged to Margaret.

"With all the success and his winnings he was able to buy me an engagement ring in December which was almost a year since he had asked me to marry him" she recalls. "Then he announced he was giving up his job at Claud Hamiltons to turn professional, move to London and work for Woolers."

The continuation of his relationship with Woolers was an obvious one. Especially with their plans to be the south of England agents for the new Crosslé Formula Ford 1600 car. The Irish company's first attempt at entering this expanding, increasingly popular category. The arrangement was for the car to be manufactured in Ireland, then shipped over for them to build and sell. All supported with a full spares back-up.

Gerry entertaining fellow members of Centro-Scot. From left to right: George Stewart, Bob Callander, Tony Evangelisti (partially obscured) and an unknown with his back to the camera. ***(Bill Henderson Collection)***

Waiting for the start at Croft in the Centro-Scot Lola T55. ***(Madeleine Stewart)***

So, not only would Gerry race the Crosslé the following season but a position of racing manager had been created specifically for him so that he could oversee the preparation of the cars – which were mainly for export to America – and undertake a development programme. Once built, they would undergo a thorough track-test and would be supplied with a full set-up/maintenance sheet, all courtesy of Gerry.

This must have been an opportunity made in heaven as far as he was concerned. Working with an established, highly-respected manufacturer to develop a new car in his usual, methodical way. He had free rein to try out new ideas which would hone the package to his tastes. All the ingredients were in place for him to display his wide range of skills to a wider audience and to achieve further success.

It had been quite a year. A relatively unknown driver outside of Scotland at the beginning of the year to a full-time professional racing driver at the end of it. Quite a transformation.

What next for the man who was frequently referred to in the specialist periodicals of the time as the 'haggis basher'?

Brands Hatch was wet for the opening round of the European FF Championship. Waiting for a quote is a young Jeff Hutchinson, who from such humble beginnings would become one of F1's leading photo-journalists of the '70s and '80s. ***(Unknown)***

CHAPTER FOUR

MOVING SOUTH AND TURNING PROFESSIONAL

London in the swinging '60s: what a contrast to the industrial backdrop of his home city, Glasgow! Gerry was by now 25 years old and had a wise head on his young shoulders. The experiences of the past couple of years had given him the confidence to deal with the pressure of living in London – which would have daunted many – and to be able to earn a living as a professional racing driver. Plus, it would the beginning of another chapter of his life with fiancée Margaret.

"I didn't join him in London until the January of '69," she remembers. "We rented a flat in Richmond Hill, South West London, and I immediately found work as a medical technician at the National Heart Hospital.

"That was how we started our life together. More or less straight away, Gerry began his preparations for the year ahead."

While waiting for Crosslé to finish his car, which would be chassis number one, Gerry put on his best suit and fulfilled his role as Woolers Racing Manager by manning their stand at the Racing Car Show at Olympia to try to spread the word and, hopefully, take some orders. According to brother Graham in his report of the show in his regular column in *Top Gear*: 'A car was on display in kit form and it features one of the strongest spaceframes which I have yet seen on a Formula Ford but it is still down at the minimum weight, it also promises to be one of the lowest cars seen in the formula as they have concentrated on reducing the drag resistance to a minimum. The car has been selling well and I will be handling the distribution of the car in Scotland.'

Gerry would finally get to sample the car for the first time at Kirkistown in Northern Ireland which Crosslé used for testing and shakedown purposes as it was just a 30-minute drive away from the factory. Reportedly, Gerry set times over a second below the FF lap record and that was with a 'hack' engine. He had been experimenting with different tyres and discovered that when running in the dry his quickest times were set using Avon crossplies of a very soft mix, as opposed to the radial tyres used by all the other runners. When running in the wet, it was a very different matter – the crossplies were agricultural, to say the least.

Certainly, Gerry would have relished the challenge of making the Avons work, as opposed to following the conventional choice of Firestones or Michelins. That was yet another example of his willingness to plough his own furrow. Another factor influencing his choice may have been the memory of a conversation that had occurred a couple of years previously, as Graham recalls: "During the RAC rally a couple of years earlier we were having breakfast at the Devils Bridge Hotel in Wales and got talking to a guy called Les Cowan, a lovely man from Manchester, who was competing in a Cortina. He was being serviced by his brother-in-law Roly who had a Ford Zephyr estate fitted with Avon tyres.

"In the course of the conversation, Roly mentioned how fantastic the handling was and that the performance of the tyres was fantastic. The only downside was a set of tyres only lasted a rally.

"I had always remembered that conversation, as I'm sure Gerry did. When he told me of his Formula Ford plans, I suggested to him that he contact Avon. At that time they had no involvement in car racing at all. Previously, they had supplied tyres to the works Astons in the '50s/early '60s, but, in the late '60s, they were just supplying motor-cycle racing tyres. Alan Blake was the motorcycle tyre competition manager and he would end up being the Formula Ford tyre man as well.

"They were just far, far better tyres than any of the others. That's how the Avon thing came about."

You can imagine Gerry rubbing his hands in excited anticipation in trying to get one over on the established drivers and manufacturers, with both the choice of the Crosslé chassis and the Avons, in what had already become a fiercely contested formula.

He didn't stop there, either. He introduced a new name to the growing list of Formula Ford engine builders when he

Gerry with Brian Hart. They made a formidable combination. ***(Chris Walker/Kartpix)***

Three abreast. Gerry, on the inside, flanked by Ian Ashley with Tony Trimmer on the outside during their frantic lead battle. ***(Chris Walker/Kartpix)***

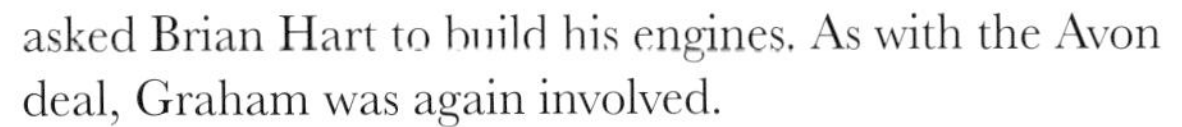

asked Brian Hart to build his engines. As with the Avon deal, Graham was again involved.

"At the time, Brian was building my engines for my twin-cam Escort. Plus, there was a Scottish connection," offers Graham. "The money in Brian Hart Ltd was originally, and quite possibly all the time, from John Romanes. John was a successful businessman and part of Scotcircuits, the owners of Ingliston. He was a very influential man in Scottish motorsport.

"Gerry's was the first and only FF engine Brian ever built. I did notice recently that Brian Nelson used one in his Crosslé later in that season. My thinking is that it would have been Gerry's spare."

Hart, who sadly passed away in 2014, is rightly acknowledged as one of the leading enginemen of the '70s, '80s and '90s. After setting up Brian Hart Ltd in 1969, he was asked by Ford to develop the BDA for rallying. He found success in racing with Ronnie Peterson and Mike Hailwood both winning the European Formula Two Championship with Hart-tuned engines. It was the building of his own Formula Two engine to take on the might of the then-dominant BMW that is the stuff of legend.

His progression to Formula One with Toleman was a real David versus Goliath act. He would perform miracles on a fraction of the budget of the likes of Ferrari, Renault and the other manufacturers.

Gerry and Brian would become firm friends, both having the utmost respect for each other's abilities. If Brian built engines for the formula that Gerry was racing in, Gerry would insist on being powered by one of them.

Having completed a thorough test and evaluation of the car, engine and tyres, all of which were new to Formula Ford, it was time to see the fruits of his labours – and those of his loyal allies – and go racing. Gerry, being Gerry, with a plethora of major UK Formula Ford championships to choose from, didn't follow the norm. Instead, he cast his eye much further afield and focused his efforts on contesting the inaugural European Cortina Formula Ford Championship. The 'Cortina' part of the title was the prize of a new Ford Cortina to the championship winner, generously donated by the Ford Motor Company.

His thinking would have been that having cleaned up in Formula Vee, he had nothing left to prove on home soil and – already with an eye on the future – by racing in Europe he would learn the circuits which would stand him in good stead for any future campaigns. Or was it the lure of a brand spanking new car – if he was successful – that proved the clincher?

Gerry was a canny Scot and always had an eye for a good deal. What's the old saying? 'You can take the boy out of Scotland but you cannae take Scotland out of the boy.'

The championship would be run over seven rounds, one of which would be a hillclimb in Switzerland – circuit racing was still banned in Switzerland following the 1955 Le Mans tragedy. No doubt with his previous hillclimb experience, he would have been pleased with its inclusion.

The championship commenced on the familiar territory of Brands Hatch in March as a support to the Race of Champions. The traditional early-season fixture gave the British race fans their first glimpse of the latest Formula One machinery. You can be certain that Gerry would have sought-out his old friend, Jackie Stewart, who was now a well-established member of the F1 fraternity. Both had come a long way – much further in Jackie's case – from the bygone days of Charterhall and the like.

Gerry certainly gave notice of his intent, causing quite a stir by qualifying an impressive second to line up between the Merlyn of the polesitter Roger Keele and the works Alexis of Ian Ashley. With practice being run in misty, damp conditions, some of Gerry's main opposition had suffered and would surely be more of a threat come the race on the following day if conditions improved.

That was how things turned out in the dry conditions with Gerry embroiled in a close battle with the aforementioned

A second place at Brands Hatch was a great start to Gerry's campaign. ***(Unknown)***

Gerry, looking very dapper, with Margaret at Schiphol Airport in the Netherlands. ***(Bruce McTavish)***

pair and the Michelin-shod Titan of Tony Trimmer, who had qualified, uncharacteristically, on only the third row. Keele got the jump at the start but Gerry was soon through into the lead after making a decisive move into South Bank on the opening lap. Michael Cotton in his *Motoring News* report takes up the story: 'Birrell's blue Crosslé looked to have a comfortable lead, if 20 yards is comfortable in that company. It was a fine debut for a new car and the reigning Formula Vee champion in this class.

'After four laps Birrell's lead had extended to 50 yards and he looked the winner, but then his car jumped out of gear at Clearways, allowing his pursuers to close right up.'

One member of the battling quartet, Ashley, all these years later offers a detailed account of how the race unfolded. "I believe it was as we all entered three abreast into Paddock Bend at high speed that by being in the middle I was best placed, Gerry was too tight and Tony too wide. I shot ahead much like a piece of soap being squeezed between them. Tony soon followed me through and I lost sight of Gerry but assumed he was third.

"I'll always remember the race because of its 'showcase importance' and because after pulling away from Tony by 200 yards, I then half spun, broadsiding the car on the last lap at South Bank leading onto the long back straight. I recovered, but not enough to stop Tony slipstreaming past me into Hawthorns Bend.

"I then tried so hard to retake the lead that I spun at the last corner, Clearways trying to go around the outside! Gerry nipped past to claim second place while I recovered to finish third.

"I spun away the lead due to 'nervous mirror watching'. I remember talking to my parents about it the next morning. I never suffered from that affliction again!"

To accompany his gear selection issue, the report in *Autosport* stated that Gerry had other issues to contend with: 'The rear section of his exhaust had come adrift and the unsorted Avon crossply tyres were causing severe front-wheel judder under braking.' Taking all that into account, second place was richly deserved and a solid start to the season.

The result highlighted just what a tough, competitive season Gerry was in for. Three different makes of car in the first three, none of which was a Merlyn, which had been the dominant car the previous season in the hands of Tim Schenken. Much more surprising was to have three different tyre manufacturers in the first three; Michelin, Avon and Firestone. The Firestones had always been regarded as the tyre to have. Both the Firestone and Michelin radials had been perceived to be the better tyre construction, until Gerry came along. Firestone still held a near-monopoly with only Trimmer on Michelins and two others, apart from Gerry, on Avons. The most notable was a certain James Hunt, who was out in a Merlyn.

A foray overseas to Zandvoort was next on the agenda for the second round of the championship. To travel to this and many more overseas events, Gerry chose – like the majority of his fellow competitors – the VW Combi Transporter which allowed the car to be carried on the flat-back with all the spares and tools in the side lockers and three – sometimes more – people up front in the cab.

As in the previous year, looking after the car-preparation side of things for Gerry was Bruce McTavish. "Another job was to drive the VW Transporter," he remembers. "Gerry and I had set off for Zandvoort, but en-route we had to pick up Margaret at Schiphol airport in Amsterdam. We had some time to spare so we did a bit of sightseeing on the way to Zandvoort. That was made more enjoyable because Margaret could speak Dutch."

"I'm surprised to have made such a good impression on Bruce regarding my speaking of the language," says Margaret. "I only have kids' Dutch vocabulary and what to order food-wise! But I did know where to take them sightseeing as I had spent most of my childhood school holidays in Holland.

"I was born in Amsterdam. My late father was Dutch. My

maiden name was Eltingh and the teachers called you by your surname in those days. I was nicknamed Tingh at school and it stuck. Gerry referred to me as Tingh to his mates but called me 'doll' to my face (very Glaswegian!)

"I also have a Dutch passport. I never changed my nationality when I married Gerry. In those days you could only take £50 out of the UK on a British passport so I was useful for taking money out to Europe when he was racing. I am still a Dutch citizen (I have lived here since I was two years old). It now costs silly money to become British plus I'd have to learn some history and sit a test. I'll stick with being Dutch even though I don't really speak the language!"

While the journey out may have enjoyable, the serious business of the trip was less so. Gerry wouldn't even qualify for the points-scoring final after his engine blew out all its oil during qualifying, causing his retirement. This was all the more disappointing because up until then he had been right on the pace of the other championship regulars, who had been joined by an unknown Brazilian called Emerson Fittipaldi making his first appearance in Europe. As with the previously mentioned James Hunt, you would have had to live on the moon not to have heard of his future achievements.

With the next race being at the Aspern circuit in Austria the following weekend, Gerry and Bruce drove down there from Zandvoort. Margaret had to go to work in England, so needed dropping off back at Schiphol. The journey to the airport is still etched very clearly in her memory, and Bruce's.

"There was one horrifying moment," recalls Bruce. "It was very early on a Tuesday morning, dawn was just breaking. Margaret, Gerry and I were travelling in the VW with the car on the back on a three-lane or possibly a four-lane motorway, on the way to the airport.

"There was very little traffic and I had the accelerator flat to the floor, as usual. Gerry was dozing, as usual, but Margaret and I were horrified to see another VW Combi van coming around a big sweeping bend and heading towards us. He was on the wrong side of the motorway. Fortunately, because of the lack of traffic, I had plenty of room to change lanes, but he never bothered, he just kept going regardless. As he went passed there were at least four or five other people in the van. I dread to think what could have happened. I don't think Margaret has ever got over the shock."

"Bruce is so right. I've never forgotten the shock," Margaret confirms. "But the story of the van being on the wrong side of the motorway is different in my memory.

"I seem to remember we were racing another pick-up truck while we were in the outside lane. We gave up and drove into the inside lane then an American limo (or large car to us in those days) came down the wrong side. It would have been a head-on collision had we still been racing.

"So take from those two stories what you like, but a near miss is the bottom line. Memory is a strange thing. We had some laughs along the way when the three of us went to race meetings."

Gerry leading Emerson Fittipaldi at Zandvoort in the second round of the Euro FF series. This was the Brazilian's first appearance in Europe. ***(Rob Petersen)***

Gerry taking an opportunity to catch up on some sleep after one of his many long journeys around Europe. ***(Bruce McTavish)***

The trip to Aspern yielded a third-place finish, which was followed by two second-place finishes in the two heats to end up as runner-up on aggregate to the Lotus 61 of Belgian Claude Bourgoignie at Zolder, the following weekend. Both of those races were non-championship events. The primary aim of them was to try and raise the profile of Formula Ford in both countries. That was something that Nick Brittan, the supremo of Formula Ford International, and organiser of the European Cortina Championship, was trying to do with the blessing of the Ford Motor Company.

The trip to Zolder is also memorable for Bruce McTavish for an altogether different reason. "Margaret had rejoined us so the three of us took the race car on the VW transporter and this time accompanying us in their Mini Traveller were Mr and Mrs Peacock, who ran Woolers with Mike Moore.

"We had two rooms at the bed and breakfast, both with double beds. One of the rooms had an extra single bed. Margaret had the single bed in with Mr and Mrs Peacock, and Gerry and I had to share the other bedroom. It was the first time I'd slept with a bloke, and thankfully the last.

"And another thing I remember is that if there was ever a football table around I would usually beat Gerry at a game."

"Wow! I don't remember sleeping in the same room as the Peacocks. My memory is definitely shot!" offers Margaret.

Having spent nearly a month on the continent and with the next round of the Championship not for another six weeks, it was back home but, not for a rest. Gerry competed in a

With Graham away racing the Ecurie Ecosse Brabham at Jarama, Gerry filled in for him in the Wylie's Escort at the Ingliston meeting in May. His first time behind the wheel resulted in two wins from his two outings. ***(Colin Lourie)***

couple of races at his regular haunts, Croft and Ingliston.

At Croft he scored his first win of the year driving the Centro-Scot entered Crosslé 16F. The Centro-Scot band of enthusiasts had forsaken their cobbled together Lotus for the newer Crosslé which he supplied.

The following weekend at Ingliston he was out again in the Centro-Scot Crosslé and also back with a roof over his head when he drove the Wylie's of Glasgow Escort Twin Cam usually pedalled very quickly by Graham, who was away racing the Ecurie Ecosse Brabham BT23C in the European F2 encounter at Jarama.

The first of Gerry's planned four outings was in the combined Formula Libre/FF race which was run in wet conditions. His performance drew gushing praise from Richard Thomas in *Top Gear*: 'Man of the race was clearly Gerry Birrell. He held third position overall throughout the race, holding off the F3 Brabham BT21B of the able John Millar with ease.

'Birrell's driving on the streaming wet track was enough to provoke hysterics. Those little, skinny tyres never seemed to touch the ground going through the Esses, so maybe the wet surface didn't matter.'

He was equally impressive behind the wheel of the Escort, which he was driving for the first time, when he managed to equal Graham's lap record during the dry practice. Despite the weather turning wet for the race, it didn't stop him from romping home to an easy victory. Two out of two!

On the same day, it was another two wins in the Centro-Scot Crosslé 16F. ***(Niall Murray-Lyon)***

To complete a memorable day, Gerry won his two further outings to remain unbeaten all day. What makes this all the more remarkable is that after winning the FF race he jumped straight into the Escort to race in the final event of the day. At least earlier in the day, he'd had a race in between in which to gather his thoughts. It was just like the old days.

In complete contrast to the tight twists of the 1.3 miles of Ingliston, Gerry headed off to the 6.5 miles of Chimay in Belgium. This was a superb, extremely fast and dangerous circuit that used the country roads outside of the town.

The race was a classic slipstreaming FF thriller involving Gerry, Bourgoignie and Fittipaldi. For 10 laps they swapped places constantly and at the finish, all three were covered by 0.2sec. Bourgoignie scored a popular home victory with Gerry beating Fittipaldi into third place.

Bruce McTavish offers some clear memories of that trip and why Gerry just failed to cross the line first. "The circuit was roughly triangular in shape. The start line was on a downhill slope which led into a hairpin in the village of La Bouchere.

"Emerson was the only driver Gerry was worried about. Margaret was with us on this trip and was doing the timing. Gerry wanted the gap between whoever was leading the race and himself. This was quite difficult to do because the cars crested a rise just before the start line, so they weren't really seen until they had crossed it.

"With it being such a slipstreaming circuit you could have covered the whole field with a handkerchief so we were unable to give Gerry the information he'd asked for.

"We would have won that race if only the start and finish lines had been in the same place – the finish line was at the back of the grid markings, approximately a 100 yards before the startline. Gerry came over the rise in front of Fittipaldi but behind the leader, Bourgoignie. As he crossed the finish line, he came out from behind Bourgoignie to slipstream past him and win the race before they passed what Gerry thought was the finish line, if you know what I mean."

The next stop on the championship trail, Vallelunga near Rome, would be the first time that Formula Ford had appeared on Italian soil and for Bruce it was a trip to forget for a couple of reasons. "I had driven down from Chimay – just a small matter of 1500km (just over 900 miles in old money) away – while Gerry and Margaret had flown back to England. We'd arranged for me to pick him up at Rome airport on his return.

"Nobody had told me about the time differences and I had got there in plenty of time, so I thought. I was waiting in the carpark for a couple of hours when Gerry and two of his friends came looking for me. It turned out they'd be waiting in the terminal for two hours. A right mix-up.

"Now there wasn't enough room for all of us in the VW cab, so Gerry elected to ride in the racecar on the back of the transporter. Not knowing the area that well, I had apparently taken the scenic route from the motel to the airport, so it was the only way I knew back to the motel. I also knew the VW was very low on petrol but thought I had enough to get to the motel and to a petrol station in the morning.

"It was very late at night by this time, and we then found out that we weren't going to even make the motel as, of course, we ran out of petrol, in the middle of the night somewhere in the boondocks outside Rome. Fortunately, Gerry had the bright idea to siphon the fuel from the racecar.

"I got a bit of a hard time the next morning when upon looking at a map we discovered how close the airport actually was to the motel."

It turned out to be a very long trip for nothing when, after qualifying in fourth place and running with the leading group, Gerry pitted on the fifth lap with suspected serious tyre troubles and didn't rejoin.

"That was down to me," confesses Bruce. "It was extremely hot, especially the track temperature. Not anticipating that, I put the incorrect pressure in the tyres which caused them to blister badly and resulted in the non-finish."

With a four-week break before the next outing in Sweden at the Anderstorp Raceway, it was time to make an honest woman out of Margaret and tie the knot on 5 June.

"I was down in London and flew up on the Friday night to Glasgow," she remembers of her happy day. "Before leaving London it occurred to me that with Gerry travelling back from Vallelunga, he probably hadn't bought a wedding ring. With no means of getting in contact, I decided to play safe and went out to Marylebone High Street in my lunch hour to the first jeweller I came across and bought one. If we ended up with two, so be it, but I had to guarantee to have one. I ended up with the one I'd bought. He had forgotten!

"Another thing he had forgotten after being given the job was to organise the wedding car. He had other things on his mind, like racing, so forgot until the last minute. All the available cars were booked so he turned to his friend Tom Sleigh whose family owned Rossleigh Motors in Edinburgh. The only car he could lend us was one of the royal cars

While on a stop for fuel in Sweden, Gerry clowns around behind the late Tony Broster, while other members of the travelling party look on. Tony Trimmer is on the far right. ***(Tony Trimmer)***

carrying the registration SF 1. My mother was tickled pink when the chauffeur, on arriving at our house, asked for a glass of water which she thought was for his consumption but it was to clean the car.

"You can tell racing came first! The laugh is we only got married that weekend because it was his only one free of racing.

"We were married at Busby Parish Church near Clarkson. The reception was at the Macdonald Hotel at Eastwood Toll, which my parents paid for... mainly for their friends and the Birrells, I might add. I think I had one table for my friends.

"John Murray was his best man. I remember him reading out one of the telegrams which said 'hot rubber slows you down', a reference to his tyre problems at Vallelunga.

"We caught the last plane back to London on Saturday night and flew out to Yugoslavia for our honeymoon on Sunday. After a week of hanging around and sightseeing, Gerry got bored and decided to hire a car. In those days the tyres on the cars you hired were skinny, awful things. They were just like those he had on his Formula Ford!

"He decided we would rally around Yugoslavia. I was hanging on for grim death for most of the time and remember thinking, 'at this rate, I may never get home'. From what I saw, as it sped past the side window of the car, Yugoslavia was a beautiful, fabulous country.

"When we returned, I went back to work and Gerry went off to his next race."

"I think he only asked me to be his best man so he wouldn't offend Graham or Iain," offers John Murray modestly, somewhat playing down the closeness of their friendship.

Becoming a married man seemed to agree with Gerry as he drove a magnificent race at Anderstorp. He passed early leaders Bourgoignie and Dave Walker, both in Lotuses, to claim his first Euro FF victory and put himself right in contention for the championship with three rounds remaining.

With a six-week gap to the next Euro round, Gerry as usual

Gerry and Margaret's wedding day even had a racing car present. The happy couple poses with Graham. ***(Margaret Shore)***

kept his hand in with a busy and varied schedule.

To complement his success on-track, things were going equally well off-track in trying to keep up with the demand for cars. Sadly, Crosslé founder, John Crosslé passed away in 2014 but when collaborating with Alan Tyndall for his excellent *Hidden Glory – The Story of the Crosslé Car Company*, he offered his memories of the partnership with Woolers and Gerry. 'Gerry was a very busy man. As well as racing he was running the production side of the 16F. It was a hell of a change for us, which was the reason for going with Wooler. There was no way that we had the staff, organisation, or experience to build that many cars within the time frame. We were snowed under with orders for thirty 16Fs.

'We made the chassis and all the things that were sensible for us to make, and Gerry arranged the wheels, shock absorbers and some of the castings, which would go direct to Woolers, where the whole package was assembled. By the standards of the day, orders were good. Roger Barr's Formula B success in America helped him sell the 16F.'

Gerry had met Barr at Kirkistown when he first tested the 16F. Roger was over from the States to test the range of cars and they had struck up a firm friendship. Roger was the North American agent for Crosslé, so Gerry would have been in regular contact. The relationship built up in that short time would be beneficial to him later in the season.

It wasn't just on track that Gerry was looking for an advantage at every turn. He was just as adept in ways of not just promoting his own career but Crosslé's too. A good example would be when the Isle of Man Government was looking to publicise the return of car racing to the island and invited two former grand prix drivers, Maurice Trintignant and Tony Brooks to try out the secret circuit. What did they drive? Two Crosslé 16Fs supplied by Gerry. At that time there was a whole host of racing car manufactures who would have been vying to be linked to such an occasion. Unsurprisingly, the evidence points to Gerry being first out of the blocks.

When he returned to matters behind the wheel he was just as busy with a double-header planned in mid-July. Croft on Saturday followed by Ingliston on Sunday. Usually, when racing up north he would use the Centro-Scot Crosslé but on this occasion he was using his regular Wooler entered car. It had been planned for Graham to race the Centro-Scot car at Ingliston to go up against Gerry for the first time in Formula Ford.

Things didn't work out as planned when Gerry suffered a front wishbone rosejoint failure with two laps to go while leading comfortably at Croft. Luckily for him, it was the outer joint, which meant that the wishbone rested inside the wheel rim. Such was his lead, he managed to ease his pace and still take victory by a couple of seconds.

A rare UK outing for the Wooler Crosslé at Croft in July resulted in a victory in a non-championship encounter. ***(Unknown)***

The following day at Ingliston saw the same result. Gerry leads the Hawke DL2 of Tom Walkinshaw and Dave Manners' Lotus 51. ***(Eric Bryce)***

Upon arrival at Ingliston there was reportedly much changing of parts between the Wooler and Centro-Scot cars rendering the Centro-Scot version *hors de combat*, so the planned head-to-head between the fiercely competitive brothers didn't happen.

The hasty repairs didn't seem to have any effect on the car's performance, Gerry taking a straightforward win. But he didn't fare so well in the two-part SMT Trophy race for Formula Libre cars. He was having a one-off outing in Robs Lamplough's F3 Lotus 41. Quite how that came about is anyone's guess. All these years later, Robs himself, has no recollection of the occasion.

In part one, Gerry was going well in among the top six until he was black-flagged for leaking oil onto the track – and his overalls – due to a rocker cover leak. With repairs effected for part two, it was a broken water header tank that caused his demise but not before giving him an involuntary shower. He lived up to his old nickname of 'Grubby' with overalls covered in oil and water. To rub salt into his wounds he suffered the ignominy of having Graham – who had won the race in his F2 Brabham – stop on his slowing down lap to give him a lift back to the paddock.

Gerry's non-stop schedule now took him to Ireland for another double-header – it was getting to be a habit – with Kirkistown on Saturday followed by Mondello Park on Sunday.

Sales of the 16F had been surprisingly slow on Irish soil, so the outings would raise brand awareness. Plus, the final round of the Euro series was being held at Mondello Park in October so Gerry, typically, was thinking ahead.

Victories in both races certainly helped in raising the car's profile. The victory at Kirkistown had only come about after a protest of Patsy McGarrity's engine in his Merlyn. John Crosslé was alarmed that Gerry had been beaten and had his suspicions. So, most uncharacteristically, he put in a protest, and at the same time presented Gerry's Hart engine for inspection. The resulting examination found that McGarrity's cylinder head did not comply with the regulations, hence his loss of first place. The Hart engine was found to have no more than the permitted modifications.

Before recommencing his European adventures it was back to Ingliston in August to take victory in the FF race, this time back in the Centro-Scot car, to keep him in contention for the Scottish Championship. The following weekend Gerry found himself in Switzerland for the fifth round of the Euro series, the Luzzone hillclimb on a two-mile course which ran up a narrow valley from the tiny village of Campo Blenio.

As he'd hoped, Gerry put his previous hillclimbing experience to good use by claiming victory over the aggregate of two runs by five seconds. It had been decided by the championship organisers that, due to the nature of the event, only half-points would be awarded to the first six finishers. So instead of the usual nine points, Gerry came away with four and a half. How significant would that turn out to be?

A rare appearance on English soil came at the FordSport meeting at Mallory Park in early September. He would be still be racing a Crosslé but it wasn't either the Wooler or Centro-Scot car on this occasion but one owned by John Stanton.

Another person present that day in his role as a mechanic to one of Gerry's rivals was John Catt. Both Johns would play highly significant roles in Gerry's future plans.

Stanton recalls when he first met Gerry and how he came to drive for him. "My involvement all came about after a relative of mine passed away and left me quite a lot of money. I was already quite heavily involved in saloon car racing, especially with the Mini 7 Club.

"I had always wanted to open a shop selling car accessories and racing equipment, and with the money I'd been left, I was able to open my first one at the end of '68.

"I would get quite a few drivers visiting the shop who were all asking if I would like to invest in them. They would come up with all sorts of grand plans. I did come up with the idea of offering them a small discount if they carried a sticker on their car promoting my business.

It wasn't the same outcome in the two Formula Libre races at the wheel of a Lotus 41. Here he is climbing out of the car after an oil leak. ***(Eric Bryce)***

Covered in the aforementioned lubricant, he gets a lift on the back of Graham's Brabham BT23C. ***(The Bill Henderson Collection)***

"One driver who came into the shop had a Crosslé FF and he persuaded me to help him on his way to fame and fortune. He would ring me up on most Monday mornings after a race meeting and I would come off the phone feeling gloomier and gloomier. Basically, he was useless. At the time I saw an advert in *Autosport* offering mid-week test sessions at Silverstone. I suggested to him that he should book one of those sessions to get some laps in and that I would pay.

"I go up there to watch and, after a couple of hours, I'm wandering through the paddock when I spot another Crosslé FF, the same as ours. Of course, this was Gerry's car. Obviously, I knew he had been very successful in it. We got chatting and I said that I had this useless driver in my car and was getting fed up with being at the back.

"Gerry very generously and unexpectedly offered to take the car out, so long as both my driver and I were happy for him to do so. I was somewhat surprised and offered that I couldn't guarantee its race-worthiness. Gerry just said 'I'll trust you'. So that was how I first met Gerry Birrell.

"Not long after the test, I entered him in 'our' Crosslé in a race at Mallory and he proved the car was competitive with two top-five finishes, which didn't surprise me at all."

John Catt tells of when he first met Gerry and how the seeds were sown for their future relationship: "Obviously, I'd heard of Gerry from when he was doing all the winning in Formula Vee. He was bloody quick.

"At that time, I was working at Motor Racing Stables at Brands Hatch, on Formula Fords. We sort of looked down on Formula Vee.

"In 1969 I was looking after the Merlyn FF of Ed Patrick, whose real name was Ed Marriage. His family owned Marriage's Flour and didn't want him racing so he changed his name to Patrick. We did a couple of the European FF races so I saw Gerry at those and we were sort of nodding acquaintances.

"The meeting at Mallory stands out because in the qualifying heat, Ed finished fourth just ahead of Gerry and then in the final Ricardo Ashcar in a Merlyn won the race from Tom Walkinshaw with Gerry third and Ashcar's team-mate, Luiz Bueno, in another Merlyn, in fourth place.

"The significance is that the week before the meeting, Ashcar and Bueno had come down to the Merlyn factory where I was now working and asked us to set the cars up. I set both up, the ride heights, the cambers etc... changed a few bits and pieces.

"Anyway, after the final I got talking to Gerry and mentioned that the cars that I had some involvement with had beaten him in his heat and the final, and the other one had been close behind him. That must have stuck in his memory because, when he was making plans for the 1970 season, he contacted me through a couple of other parties and I went to work for him."

The meeting at Mallory Park must have been a busy one for Gerry, not just driving-wise but also socially. Jackie Stewart did some quick demonstration laps in his F1 Matra MS80 before heading off to Monza to clinch the World Championship. Brain Hart was out in an F2 Brabham and Graham was also present in his Twin-Cam Escort and was having a one-off FF outing in an Alexis.

It was back to his usual Crosslé for the next round of the Euro series at Zolder. A dominant win in his heat gave him a front-row starting position for the final. He didn't have things so easy in that when he was involved in a race-long dice with a trio of Lotus 61s driven by Walker, Bourgoignie and Mo Harness. Gerry used all his tactical nous to outsmart them all by letting them fight among themselves, whereupon he made his move and slipped into the lead.

Bourgoignie made a last-lap lunge to keep his championship hopes alive and to take the win on home soil, but had a huge moment and ended up in only sixth position. Gerry took the chequered flag to score an important victory and with it take the championship lead for the first time from the erstwhile leader, Trimmer.

Tony had endured a troubled weekend with an electrical problem in his heat. He did manage to fix it quickly and resumed, but could only finish 12th and thus did not qualify for the final and the chance of championship points.

With Tony's title aspirations seemingly compromised, Gerry was one of the first drivers to petition the organisers to let him start at the back of the grid, and with all the other finalists agreeing the organisers were persuaded to let Tony start.

In a stirring drive, he would finish fourth to add three points to his championship tally and keep his title hopes alive.

That was a fine sporting gesture from Gerry. He could easily have kept quiet and benefited from Trimmer's misfortune, but saw no satisfaction in becoming champion in any other way than beating him in a straight fight on the track. But would this most generous action backfire on him come the final round on Irish soil?

In typical Gerry fashion with a three-week gap between Zolder and the Mondello Park finale, he ventured to Phoenix Park in Dublin to take part in the annual road races. It wasn't a place for the faint-hearted and you wouldn't have thought Gerry would have risked his regular car at such a high-speed, dangerous venue. But according to Brian Foley's report in *Autosport*: 'He was out in his Wooler Crosslé'. It must surely have been another car, as it was hard to imagine someone as meticulous in his preparations as Gerry risking his well-sorted car so close to his most important race of the year. Whichever car he was driving, it all came to an unhappy ending with retirement in Saturday's race with a blown rocker cover gasket.

The showdown for the title – and not forgetting the prize of a new Ford Cortina – would be decided between not just Gerry and Tony Trimmer, who had been the pace-setters all year, but also the Lotuses of Bourgoignie and Walker, who both had outside chances, once the dropped scores ruling had come into effect. The simple maths for Gerry was that if he finished in front of Trimmer, the title was his. The worst-case scenario was that, if Trimmer won the race, Gerry had to finish second to take the title. It was going to be a tense climax.

To help Gerry's cause he would have a team-mate of sorts when Crosslé themselves entered a car for a local ace, Brian Nelson, who would be there to play a supporting role and to hopefully deprive Trimmer of points. The plan seemed to have worked a treat in practice when Gerry qualified quickest with Nelson right behind him. Trimmer was third fastest and equalled the lap record set by Nelson a month ago, which obviously meant the Crosslé pair were under the record.

The first heat was a sign of things to come when Gerry and Trimmer raced nose-to-tail for the entire 10 laps, with Trimmer leading throughout. Their pace was such that they both lowered the lap record further still.

Nelson had an easier time in the second heat winning comfortably, but was alleged to have jumped the start and was relegated to last position and would have to start the final from the back of the grid.

For the final, Gerry would have to fight a lone battle with his title adversary, and battle they did. For the first 20 of the 25-lap final, they really went at it, Trimmer always managing to stay in front despite Gerry's best efforts.

In the closing stages, Gerry eased off ever so slightly, knowing that second place was sufficient for him to win the title and that Trimmer was never going to make a mistake. After just short of 30 minutes of some of the closest, fairest racing, and in front of a reported 12,000 spectators, he duly crossed the line to finish second and be crowned European Cortina FF Champion by the narrowest margins, just one and a half points.

Surprisingly, in *Hidden Glory – The Story of the Crosslé Car Company*, Alan Tyndall recalls that John Crosslé was not pleased with the race result as he felt that Gerry should have beaten Tony. You would have thought that by that stage he would have understood Gerry's approach to his racing. The displeasure couldn't have lasted that long, however, with the running of a full-page advert in the following week's *Autosport* offering congratulations from the Crosslé Car Company.

It had been a long campaign with many miles travelled in pursuit of the title and with it the keys to a new Ford Cortina GT, which Gerry would pick up at the first FF International (FFI) dinner dance and awards presentation at the Royal Lancaster Hotel in late November.

Joining a whole host of Formula Ford drivers and helping the master of ceremonies and FFI supremo Nick Brittan with proceedings was Walter Hayes of Ford. The father of the legendary Cosworth DFV V8 F1 engine, he was the man in control of the racing purse strings of the global giant, and he would certainly have been well aware of Gerry long before that evening due to his close ties with Jackie Stewart.

While Margaret would have been just as delighted as Gerry with their new car, her main memory of the evening is of something completely different. "Money was tight so I used to make my own dresses. At the dinner dance, I wore the same home-made dress which I had worn recently to another racing 'do'. Respected journalist Mike Doodson, who was a great guy, happened to be at both events and commented that he would see me at Brands Hatch in the dress one day. This is the sort of comment that sticks with us women. I'm sure Mike will not remember but it did give me leverage to get a new dress for the following year's functions. So thank you, Mike."

The three main people involved in the season's activities offer their memories of a very enjoyable time.

Tony Trimmer, who had been such a close rival all season and done all he could do by winning the final race, has nothing but good memories of those times, both on- and off-track. "Gerry was a formidable competitor that season. I especially remember our many battles, racing wheel to wheel on many occasions. His racing was precise and clean, but hard, and we would share wins throughout the year. He was certainly one of my main rivals.

Congratulations to

GERRY BIRRELL – CROSSLÉ 16F

ON WINNING THE

EUROPEAN CORTINA FORMULA FORD CHAMPIONSHIP

CROSSLÉ AMERICA RACING
574 New London Turnpike,
Glastonbury.
Conn. 06033 USA.

All plating by
NICHROME (ELECTRO PLATING) LTD.,
308 Albertbridge Road,
Belfast, 5.

GLASS FIBRE BODIES
manufactured by
BRIAN FALOON & CO.,
Brooklands, Hillsborough,
County Down.

Steel Tubing by
LE BAS TUBE CO. LTD.,
472 Shore Road,
Belfast, 15.

Cooling by RADIATOR SERVICES (NI) LTD.,

THE CROSSLÉ CAR COMPANY LIMITED

RORY'S WOOD, KNOCKNAGONEY,
HOLYWOOD, COUNTY DOWN
Tel: BELFAST 63332

AUTOSPORT, OCTOBER 9, 1969 43

"We were friends and would help each other when help was needed and that is how racing should be, something which, unfortunately, is lost in modern times."

Bruce McTavish believes that Gerry's different approach reaped its rewards.

"During this season I got to know Gerry much better, as he was more hands-on at Woolers now. As well as looking after his own car, we were also assembling customer cars with the major parts sent to Woolers from Crosslé. Sometimes Gerry would take these cars to a track and set them up for the customers. Other times he was chasing the myriad parts needed to build one. Some cars were stripped after assembly and packed to be sent to the United States, so we had to be sure that everything necessary went into the crates.

"The Crosslé was a real racecar compared to the Formula Vee of the previous year. There was much more to adjust and Gerry certainly thought a great deal about the set-up. I was very impressed with his skills as to what he required, to the point that even before he drove the car, virtually just looking at it, he seemed to know what was needed. Therefore practice usually went without too much drama. I learnt a lot about setting up a racecar that year, thanks to him, all of which stood me in good stead when I joined fellow Kiwi Bruce McLaren's F1 team towards the end of the year."

It had been quite a year for Margaret, too. She had become Mrs Birrell and had tried to juggle a full-time job with supporting Gerry, not just at home, but travelling whenever possible to watch him race. She was young, full of life and excited about what the future held.

"In those days it was a travelling circus," she reflects. "We travelled together, ate together, we did everything together.

"That was when we first met Emerson Fittipaldi, who'd just come over. Something I used to do was to take money out for them. Tony Trimmer and the rest of them. We did some crazy things. You all helped each other out. It was like one big family really. A big support group. It was good fun!"

With his last race being at Mondello in early October and the claiming of his spoils of victory in late November, you would have thought, like most racing drivers, that it was time for a break. To recharge your batteries and make plans for next season. But Gerry was not like most people as far as racing was concerned.

With an invitation – in recognition of his success – to take part in the Champion of Champions FF race across the pond at the Sebring International Raceway on 28 December he would finish off his year the way he had started it, behind the wheel of a racing car.

Adding yet another skill to his ever-increasing repertoire was a chance to become a journalist of sorts when he was asked by *Motoring News* to write a comprehensive piece of his American adventure. The article – which appeared in the issue dated 5 February 1970 – tells quite a tale and is reproduced in full. To conclude, Margaret offers her thoughts after reading the article more than 50 years later.

Formula Ford at Sebring

All the drivers who had been involved in the European Formula Ford Championship announced early on that they would be going to Sebring for what the Americans promised would be the World Championship Formula Ford race, so I thought that the least I could do as Champion would be to go too.

John Crosslé had some ambitious ideas about sending across lots of cars, but these depended on getting a huge sum of sponsorship money. Unfortunately, it didn't materialise, so I had to find the money myself.

My problem was that, although I had won the European Championship and the very nice Cortina which went with it, there was no ready money for the Champion. Happily, my brother Iain happens to work for the whisky company which makes Red Hackle Scotch and he managed to get them interested because they were doing a promotion campaign in the States. There was also some support from Ford of America, thanks to Nick Brittan, with £150 for each of the FF drivers when they got there or when they raced.

The next problem was what car to use because the Crosslé I had used during the year had already been sold and anyway I couldn't afford to freight my own car all the way to Florida. We had one rather tired spare engine available and could put our hands on an untuned spare. I approached John Crosslé about the possibility of supplying a car, and although he wasn't able to supply one himself, he arranged with US Crosslé importer Roger Barr to lend me a car. It turned out to be a very original car, chassis 02 (mine had been 01).

Roger had been at Crosslé's a fortnight or so before I flew to America, so we joined up at Shannon with both the engines, the gear ratios and various other bits. We flew to Boston with my wife Margaret, who was paying her own way – strictly her own way – I wasn't paying any of it! She had even arranged her own accommodation in the USA with friends in Boston, where she had worked for a year.

Arriving at Boston, Roger and I set out for his own workshop in Glastonbury, about 100 miles south of Boston itself. He's a great guy and was more than helpful to me during the whole of my stay. Travelling across the Atlantic, he had made American Formula Ford sound very technical. The Yanks have a great reputation for demon balancing, head work and gas-flow, which I was inclined to pooh-pooh as being normal American exaggeration. How wrong I was!

Roger himself is not just a race car dealer. He makes his money out of working on normal European type cars (VWs, etc), in a foreign car shop at Glastonbury. He loses his money by working on Crosslé's! He was wonderfully helpful and hospitable, even to the extent of insisting on driving all the way south and wouldn't let me take the wheel for an inch of the 1250 miles.

But first, there was a car to prepare. It had had a new frame, having been pretty extensively shunted and, although I was warned that it was in a dreadfully tatty state, luckily this was a bit of an exaggeration and the car was in quite good nick. Nevertheless, I stripped it down to the last nut and bolt, washed the chassis, re-pop-rivetted everything back on to it and built it right back up again with an old Brian Hart engine and Roger's own gearbox with all the ratios sorted out. The work took me from the Wednesday I arrived right through the weekend (working from eight in the morning until 10 at night), to Tuesday morning, when we got into Roger's transporter to set off. Roger meanwhile had been rebuilding the engine of his transporter, one of the latest new-type VW pick-ups, which is a very nice machine.

It was 11 o'clock on Christmas Eve when we got going, with a light snow-storm falling around us and very Christmassy. We drove all through that day till about 11 at night, stopped at a Holiday Inn and climbed out of bed at 4.30am Christmas day for the last stage of the journey. We drove solidly all through Christmas day until 6.30 that evening, when we got to Sebring. Margaret came down separately with Roger's team manager and regular buddy Dave Logan, who is a really switched-on bloke. If ever I have the money to do a Can-Am season, Dave's the man I would get to team manage. Normally he's a director of a computer firm, but he used to race a bit and then helped Roger finance his Vee programme. Since then Roger has been twice Vee Champion on the East Coast and in 1968 he won SCCA Formula B in a Crosslé.

The first thing we did on arriving was to enjoy our Christmas dinner at the Lake Blue Motel. I also had a swim on Christmas Day, which made quite a change. Florida was a bit disappointing from the point of view that it was obviously mid-winter, and although the sun was there the grass wasn't really green. It was a sort of mid-green, almost as though you weren't quite seeing things right.

We assembled the next day and went up for signing-in at race HQ in Sebring itself. Then we went to 'do the tech' as they call scrutineering, something we'd heard quite a bit about. All the Formula B cars went through first because they'd been promised some unofficial practice, and when we put the FF in the queue to get it weighed and checked the FB's were holding everything up. Fred Opert (who seemed to have entered half of them, including Schenken's), was about three feet off the ground and flapping about as usual because of minor technical troubles. Eventually, things got moving and the organisers sent out assistant scrutineers, assistants' assistants, boys, and anyone who could check the cars. We got a really funny little fellow, about 60, who was only really concerned with being nice to us. He pulled a few wheels, said what a nice car it was and barely glanced at the helmet. So much for the fantastic American 'tech'.

Then we had to stick the car on the weighbridge, according to which (and they took four separate readings), the chassis must have been at least 30 degrees twisted because they got totally different readings at each corner!

At last, we got out for some practice ourselves, and I was interested to find that the special version of the circuit which we were using was very like Kirkistown, believe it or not. Down past the start-finish line and pits you go round a flat-out left-hander (the same as Debtor's), about the same length of straight and into a braking area where instead of a hairpin as at Kirkistown there is a funny chicane made of huge aircraft tyres. You then run at right angles to the straight you have just come from, through an ess, round at right angles and back on to the ordinary 12-hour circuit, bypassing the twiddly bits. Then there's a slightly downhill section through a right-hander which is a bit off-camber. You've got to get this one right because it makes a difference of about 300 revs on the following straight and unfortunately those of us who were using the ordinary Dunlop 970 tyres were losing time through here. Then there's another straight to a hairpin which takes you back past the pits again.

I realised that my top gear was wrong, but so also was my engine, which was not so easily rectified. The trouble was that it wouldn't rev properly over about 5600/5800rpm: It was screaming and rattling, getting me nowhere. We decided first that either the rev-counter was wrong or the engine was and after a few checks, the finger pointed at the engine. Rather than start pulling it to bits, we left it in for the next session of official practice because we didn't have enough time to change it.

On the other hand, the car really was handling well, apart from the understeer on to the start of the straight.

It wasn't very funny for the chap involved, but I got caught up in one amusing incident at the chicane thing. This poor fellow had really stuffed two of the massive tyres, which were bolted or tied together: the whole of his car was bent right up in the air and the car was resting on the chassis tubes. I zig-zagged past him and was about to turn right to go round him when I saw these two huge tyres (which our friend had dislodged) rolling alongside me! If I turned I knew that I would have been run down by them, so I jammed on the anchors and slid through the pylons, listening to the errant markers thudding past me like a big elephant.

So far as British entries were concerned, all the odd bods who said they were going to be there didn't make it. Dave Walker had been out for a couple of weeks, had a beautiful tan and looked very smooth driving about in a Mustang with tinted windows. He had also done a full day's testing the previous Sunday when Firestone had hired the circuit. Tim Schenken and Tony Trimmer were out in new Titans for Fred Opert, reeling around in a big Oldsmobile with their Fred Opert jackets and about 20 minions working on each car. In fact, it almost looked like a Fred Opert-sponsored meeting: there were five of his cars in the FB race and three or four

Fords, all yellow with a blue bit down one side and red on the other, very smart.

Trimmer, like me, was having a few practice problems, but Tim was going as quick as anyone. Then there was American Vee ace Bill Scott, who has done some European racing. He went out in his own car (a Royale) and took the nose off it, then he went out in a customer's car and wiped the rear suspension off that before leaving it for the day. I believe this is a fairly regular occurrence with Bill, who is a bit inconsistent, to say the least.

Before last practice, we took the head off the old engine and found that the valve springs were flat dead. The valves, of course, had not been seating properly, which is why they didn't rev. So we stuck in the standard engine, which isn't very bright, but at least it would run and rev to 6000rpm. We changed the gear ratios slightly and I went off to get some Firestones fitted (at a price of $160!) for comparison purposes. I have to admit that they were superior to the Dunlops, being the YB11 compound, but I suspect that they require some pretty radical suspension changes to make the most of them.

The main trouble out on the track was the difficulty we all had with the local Formula Fordsters, who seemed determined at all costs to outbrake the foreigners. They just cut in without a snowball in hell's chance of getting around the corner they were braking for.

When eventually the practice times were posted, my name seemed to go up and down the list like a yo-yo. First I was given an unofficial fourth fastest, ranging down to 11th, then the official times were issued, and I was fourth fastest again. 'OK,' I thought, but then there were the 'amendments' which put me down to sixth fastest. That didn't seem too bad, but when race morning came around I was put back to ninth on the grid!

There is no doubt in my mind that some gentle fiddling had taken place among the organising officials, which wouldn't have been too bad had there not been a prize of $500 for the fastest man in practice. This was handed to some unassuming youth in a LeGrand: the car is American, so was the driver: need one say more? The poor guy involved was totally dumbstruck and didn't know what to say, except that his pit hadn't got him within five seconds of the time awarded to him by the organisers. Not surprisingly, there was a lot of shouting by the others, and Tim Schenken (who was given a time just behind Bill Scott) did his nut. As it happened, I was the slowest of the Europeans except for Huub Vermeulen, who was also in trouble.

The race itself was supposed to have a rolling start behind a great big Camaro, and this is where Bill Scott's advice came in handy. He told me to watch the starts of the B race on the day before and of the A event which preceded our own, just so that I could see where they were going to drop the flag. This was done when the leading two cars got to within about 50 yards of the line.

I followed Bill's suggestion to the letter, and they worked a treat. I fell back from the others until about 100 yards from the line, then floored the throttle. Because the Camaro was moving so fast, this meant that I was in the right position, but moving much faster, when the flag fell. By the time we came past the pits, I was through with the guys in the second row, coming down the inside for the fast left-hander after the line. Not having a demon engine, though, all those behind were starting to catch me up and by that time they were about six cars abreast. Having forecast that there would be an accident on the first lap, I was already backing off, because at that sort of speed there's really only one line for the corner.

Then it happened. One of the five or so people who had just retaken me spun, taking off one car with his tail and another with his nose. Dave Walker got tied up wheel to wheel with someone trying to share the same bit of road and shot up into the air. I went past the melée with Dave about six feet above me and saw a Merlyn heading straight for the Crosslé, at right angles. Dave nailed him on the way down before he could get me! It's a wide track, about 40ft, but I was running on the verge.

So there I was, heading down to the chicane when I saw something stirring in the long grass on the infield. It was a Lotus wedge, Fred Stevenson's, churning through the undergrowth like an ant-eater with its tail on fire. The front end of the bodywork was ripped off and when he turned back on the track, he nearly rammed me too. Little did Fred know, but the accident which had removed his nose section had also taken away his brake master cylinders. Somehow we avoided contact, and the Lotus slithered to a brakeless halt.

Following that hectic interlude, Dave Logan signalled me that I was fifth. Schenken and Scott were already hard at it, swapping the lead like mad, clear and on their way to a race-long dice. In third was the lad in the LeGrand, then Skip Barber in a Caldwell and me. We both overtook the LeGrand, which shows that it should never have been where it was. I stayed in Barber's tow down the straight (the only way I could hang on) and did him in the braking. He's a fairly switched-on guy and realised that we would be dicing the whole way, so we started waving each other through and enjoying our own little battle for third place.

Tony Trimmer was delayed by something or other and disappeared into the pits. When he re-emerged, it was right in the middle of our little dice and, although several laps behind, he joined in, which made things rather complicated. The only way I could stay in the others tow down the straights was to hang on right behind, and in the warm sunshine, this meant that the radiator could not cope and the engine started to overheat.

With little more than a half-dozen laps to go, I had to drop out of the dice with the temperature needle off the dial in the hope that I could stay in a safe fourth place. But the engine didn't respond when I needed it and I went into a gentle spin. It wouldn't start straight away and five others went past: I counted $50 for each of them because that was what my

Margaret and a girl friend, Sam, in snowy Boston in late 1969/early 1970 pose in front of the lime green Chevy Nova hired by Gerry. ***(Margaret Shore)***

spin was costing me in prize money. I got it going again and crossed the line with a dead engine in ninth place, which was worth $200.

There was still scrutineering to go through, and this is where a lot of ill-feeling arose. The first six cars were all brought in to have their cylinder heads removed and as for Tim – who had just pipped Scott on the line – they were obviously standing around just waiting for his gearbox to be removed. The Americans knew just what Lucas had done and in spite of the special assurances for the Europeans there was obviously going to be a disqualification. The American competitors even knew what the score was and had taken their own racing clutches off for this one race!

It was also very badly handled on the part of Fred Opert, who danced around when he shouldn't have said a word and then instead of putting in a formal protest allowed himself to be talked into believing that his own engine was illegal! The modification was certainly not anything that would have made Tim's car go any quicker. It did seem that the Americans were fed up that an Englishman had walked off with the A race (David Hobbs) and that Reine Wisell had won the B race by such a convincing margin. For the FF men, it was a sad day.

As for the other races, they were great fun. From my point of view, one of the greatest thrills was being briefed at the same time as the A drivers standing along with Mario Andretti and Mark Donohue, both 'greats' of motor racing about whom I had only read previously, was marvellous. Then there was the Formula B dice, just like their battles in F3, between Tim Schenken and Reine Wisell. If Tim had bothered to top up his oil tank, the finish might have been a little closer!

If there's anything I learned from the trip, it's not to spend money on motor racing. I returned from the States out of pocket despite the help I had received in cash or kind from Red Hackle, from Ford USA and Dunlop. Roger Barr was more than hospitable and although I naturally paid him for the parts I had used, he wouldn't take anything for petrol, board and lodgings. But it was a great experience and I hope that it isn't the last opportunity I have of visiting the USA.

It seems that Gerry had warmed to the USA this time around. He was distinctly unimpressed the first time as we know. Speaking of unimpressed, Margaret can't have been too happy about having to pay her own way.

"I remember the trip well, at least my side of the story," she recalls. "When Gerry announced he was going to America he was determined he couldn't afford to take me. I was determined to go because I had a tax rebate to collect from the USA and the original deal was if I came home from the USA to get married and he ever went back, I went too.

"I saved for my fare. I remember Roger as we flew with him from Shannon to Boston. I stayed with my friends there. Not sure how I got down to Glastonbury, probably by Greyhound bus. I remember meeting up with Dave and Lucille Logan at their house on Christmas Eve. I stayed the night and we all got up very early on Christmas morning (there was a threatened snowstorm) and drove directly to Florida with a couple of comfort breaks. I remember taking my head off the pillow in the back seat – somewhere south of New York and north of Virginia – to see several snowploughs in a staggered line clearing the highway. The tyre of the nearest snowplough was higher than our car, a BMW. I instantly went under the pillow again!

"Gerry on principle was going to make me find my own way back to Boston from Florida, but eventually gave in and I got in the transporter with him and Roger. On getting back to Boston Gerry was more relaxed and hired a lime green '69 Chevy Nova.

"We spent time with Maija (I worked with her in Boston) and her husband Aviars. We hung out with them and another friend of mine, Sam. While I was in Boston I visited one of the heart surgeons, John Wright, who I had worked with at the National Heart Hospital in London. He was on a year's sabbatical doing similar research to that I was involved in at the NHH.

"By now, on principle I wouldn't ask Gerry for any spending money (although I had got my tax rebate, which was now spent). I decided to sell my blood without telling him. You got $25 for a pint in those days. Unfortunately, I duly fainted. I did recover but had to tell Gerry, who gave me a telling off as it could have cost him more if I hadn't recovered. He was a generous person but although we got on very well, we were both stubborn. I haven't changed!"

A stunning photo of Gerry airborne going up the Mountain at Cadwell Park. ***(Mike Dixon)***

CHAPTER FIVE

THE NEXT STEP

Even before the sojourn to America the rumour mill had been in full swing concerning Gerry's Formula Three plans for 1970. The most persistent of them was the continuation of his association with Wooler and Crosslé. There was some foundation to these with Crosslé having already completed their first F3 car, the 17F, which was tested by Roger Barr at Kirkistown in December when he was sampling the latest offerings from the company.

Much to the disappointment of all parties, however, neither relationship would continue. The agreement between Crosslé and Wooler Engineering to assemble cars had come to an end midway through the previous year when Crosslé had taken assembly and production back to their County Down factory. The amicable split between Gerry and Wooler was due to their reluctance to match his F3 ambitions. It had been a fruitful relationship for both sides with two successive championships, so the decision to go their separate ways wouldn't have been taking lightly.

It wasn't the lack of ambition on the part of Crosslé that led to another amicable split. 'Undoubtedly we got a bit carried away,' offered John Crosslé in Alan Tyndall's Crosslé book. 'When you win something at international level against everything that others can throw at you, you get a bit excited! We were young, enthusiastic, and prepared to have a go at anything.

'Naturally, we were sorry to lose Gerry, as we had built the 17F especially for him, but there were no hard feelings. I think his idea was to get known on the continent and to learn the European circuits in preparation for Formula Two the following year.'

When the offer came for Gerry to drive a Brabham with support from Sports Motors it was far too tempting to turn down. The Brabham was a known quantity and Sports Motors was a successful, proven outfit with a burgeoning reputation. Reportedly, Tim Schenken, who after a highly successful F3 campaign for them in '69, had got to work on Rodney Bloor, the proprietor, to get Gerry on board. The whole deal had the blessing of Motor Racing Developments, the manufacturers of the car and its designer, Ron Tauranac, who as well as looking after the Formula One car of Jack Brabham, ran the production side of the company which built cars for the lower formulae.

The plan was for a full programme of UK and European events. No particular championship would be chased, the idea being to experience as many of the European circuits as possible to further broaden Gerry's experience.

It wouldn't be the typical Sports Motors-run operation but one put together by Gerry on his own terms. Enabling him to put together such a programme were two men who had been impressed when meeting him for the first time at Mallory Park a few months earlier: John Stanton and John Catt.

"I had a couple of conversations with Gerry about moving up to F3," remembers Stanton. "He said he would call me once he had finished his FF campaign. I never expected to hear from him, but call he did. He came around with Margaret a couple of times for Sunday lunch. My wife said after they'd left one time that Gerry seemed a very nice guy. He had an excellent presence and would be extremely trustworthy. He would do a lot of good promoting the business. How right she was!

"Having tested the water, so to speak, with one shop, I was now looking to expand and open another shop in Harrow, North London, which would also sell racing spares, helmets, fireproof overalls, etc. I saw a gap in the market there with only Gordon Spice retailing that sort of thing at the time.

"The season would end up costing a lot of money, some of which we got back in publicity. There is no doubt that it did the business a lot of good.

"I never regretted getting involved with Gerry for one second. It wasn't all sweetness and light but when I think back to those days, I'm extremely proud to have been involved with him."

That was the money sorted. There was still one piece of the jigsaw to complete: a suitable mechanic to help run and prepare the car.

"Towards the end of 1969/the start of 1970, I was out in Brazil looking after the Royale FF of Ray Allen, who was racing in the Temporada series," recalls Catt. "I'm pretty sure it was Eric Dymock, who at the time was the motoring correspondent for *The Guardian* newspaper, and a good friend of Gerry's, that put in a good word. Gerry had mentioned to him that he was on the lookout for a good mechanic and evidently he said I was the man to have.

"When I got back from Brazil my father said that the phone hadn't stopped ringing with various people offering me work. We hadn't had the phone in that long, it was quite a luxury back then. I could have gone into F5000 with Ed Patrick but wasn't interested and Bob King of Royale had offered me a job on my return from Brazil. In the end, it was Harvey Lee, who was Tony Trimmer's mechanic in FF, who had been talking to Eric, who then had been talking to Gerry.

"By that time Harvey was involved with Gerry looking after the Avon tyre supply business which had come out of Gerry winning the Euro FF championship. Eventually, Gerry rang with a good offer. I was to be employed by Rodney Bloor of Sports Motors as part of the sponsorship deal. My first job was to go with Gerry to Brabham to help build the car. We went up in an old coachbuilt van which had come from Brian Hart when he had been sponsored by the actor, Peter Sellers in Formula Three. It was in a bit of a state. I think Ronnie Grant painted it."

Ronnie Grant is a name that will reappear in the years ahead. He was based in his famous Clapham North Garage which was just around the corner from the infamous North Street complex from where Gerry would run both the Brabham and his business selling Avon competition tyres. The occupants of North Street were a real who's who of motorsport. Davrian, Palliser, Nomad and Gropa were the most famous, who along with many more motorsport-related companies, made the place a real hive of activity. Many people would pass through North Street on their way to long careers in racing.

It seems that Gerry the racing driver was also becoming Gerry the businessman. The lessons learned from his father and brother were now being put to good use. The aforementioned tyre supply business was the main one, with a couple of other smaller operations adding to the coffers.

"Gerry and Harvey had laid a completely flat patch of concrete so they could do car set-up work," continues Catt. "I got involved with that to keep the business going to give him a little bit of extra money. We had quite a few people from Formula Ford come along and I'd set them up. If it was a Merlyn, having worked on them, I was in my element."

Another sideline was to enter a car for a former rival in this ever-expanding category. "I had raced against Gerry the previous season in FF at some of the European races," recalled the late Tony Dron, who was not just famous for his skills behind the wheel, but also for being equally adept at putting pen to paper. "In qualifying for one of the races, he had been impressed by the way I had overtaken him and Syd Fox to end up on the front row with James Hunt, whom I had pipped by a thousandth of a second.

"A few months later Gerry approached me and said 'I can fix up a deal for you to run a Crosslé 16F, that Avon had bought, and you can share my workshop in Clapham'. Now, I imagine that his real motivation for doing the deal was not just the thought I was wonderful. I suspect that half the rent was paid by the Avon rubber company. Maybe even all of it. If Gerry was anything, he was a good wheeler-dealer.

"He was a very switched-on guy. Very business-like and efficient. Very positive. He always seemed to have a smile on his face.

"I remember having dinner with him and Margaret in Richmond a couple of times and Gerry came down to my parents' house and saw us there. He was always so busy so I didn't get to spend as much time with him as I would have liked. All in all, a really charming, good bloke."

In among all the preparations, Gerry found time to go back to his roots with a couple of engagements north of the border.

Both were in connection with that most famous of Scottish race teams, Ecurie Ecosse. First up was their annual dinner dance and awards ceremony at the North Bridge Hotel in Edinburgh, where the highlight of the evening was the presentation of the Ron Flockhart Trophy for the best up-and-coming Scottish driver. Gerry's name already adorned the aforementioned trophy, as he'd been the recipient two years earlier.

The second get together was the glamorously titled 'Grand Prix Night with Jackie Stewart' at the Dominion Theatre in Edinburgh where Gerry would be joined on the panel by the man himself, his brother Graham, and March designer Robin Herd. Chairing the panel and keeping them all in check was Graham Gauld, like Jackie another old acquaintance. All proceeds would go towards the Ecurie Ecosse Racing Fund.

Before the commencement of his hectic Formula Three campaign Gerry took time out to compete at the Race of Champions meeting at Brands Hatch in the Group 2 Saloon Car race, in a Hillman Imp entered by Jeremy Nightingale. It must have brought back some memories. In the end he didn't start the race due to a multitude of problems in practice, mainly in the braking department.

Finally, a week later, after a brief shakedown of the car, it was to Snetterton on Good Friday to make his F3 debut in the opening round of the Shell-sponsored British F3 Championship.

In the second of two qualifying heats a third-place finish behind the two Lotuses of Dave Walker and Brazilian newcomer, Carlos Pace, was a fine effort.

The final was an altogether different story and a short one at that. On the second lap while in a dice with fellow Scot Richard Scott and Pace, Scott got it all wrong and spun, leaving Pace with nowhere to go but to collide with him. Gerry went flying over the Brazilian's Lotus, dislodging his own nosecone. He did continue but called it a day late in the race. Both Scott and Pace had been instant retirements.

This was also the first occasion when Gerry had raced with one of the new full-face crash helmets. "He had to get the largest size available and had to have a hair cut to get the helmet on because he had a big head," remembers Catt with a wry smile.

Margaret recalls how Gerry came up with the patriotic design. "He was sat there one night and said, 'Jackie's got the tartan, so I need to do something different'. He sprayed it blue and then made the white cross with masking tape. He got a thistle sticker from somewhere and put it on the front above the visor."

Alongside Robin Herd at the Dominion Theatre in Edinburgh, waiting for the start of the Q&A at the Jackie Stewart Grand Prix Night. ***(SMRC/Graham Gauld)***

Next up was a trip to the streets of Pau in the south of France, a somewhat more glamorous location than Snetterton. A high-quality entry of 40 drivers would fight it out for places on the grid and with only 18 allowed to start, it was tough. Gerry was the first non-qualifier in 19th position.

"That was a disaster for us," recalls Catt. "He hadn't got used to the more neutral characteristics of a Formula Three car, having come from Formula Fords which were more prone to an oversteer. Unfortunately, he just wasn't quick enough."

It was back to the familiar surroundings of Brands Hatch the week after, but certainly not in a familiar machine. Gerry would make his world sportscar G5/G6 debut in the BOAC 1000km driving the Gropa with the car's owner, Andrew Mylius.

"I first met Gerry at the infamous North Street complex where I built my Gropa cars in the unit next to his," recalls Mylius. "The Gropa was a Chevron B8 with the roof removed and with some redesigned sills to regain its structural strength. The body was designed by myself and Bob Curl, who also worked at North Street for Mark Konig who built the Nomads.

"I'd see Gerry most days and have many a cup of tea throughout the day. The dividing wall between our two units was only made of hardboard, so it was pretty flimsy. I could hear what Gerry was up to and vice versa.

"Originally I had asked Hugh Dibley – another North Street resident who owned Palliser and was an accomplished driver – to share the car, feeling that he had a good track record in that form of racing. Unfortunately, Hugh was taken ill with the flu so was unfit to drive.

"It seems silly now that I didn't ask Gerry in the first place. He was doing well in F3. He was a nice guy and he was a fellow Scot.

"We needed a couple of mechanics, so Gerry asked John Catt to help out. I asked Julian Pratt, who worked for Mark Konig. He'd had a bit of a falling-out with Mark, so when I asked he jumped at the chance."

Exiting Druids in the Gropa behind the Nomad of Brands Hatch expert Tony Lanfranchi. *(Pete Austin)*

"Obviously, I knew Gerry with him being across the road from us at Nomad," recalls Pratt. "I got to know him very well because he was one of those guys that you could see had all this potential, and the brains to go with it. He was clearly going to make it and more importantly, he wasn't going to hurt himself."

With only a minor club race at Snetterton with Mylius at the wheel and a brief test at Brands Hatch prior to the event, expectations were pretty low.

Gerry qualified the car in midfield among the other Group 6, 2.0-litre runners and was by no means outclassed in the dry practice sessions. The weather changed come race day, as torrential rain greeted the competitors at the start time.

"The plan was for Gerry to start and finish the race and I would do the middle stint," remembers Mylius.

Despite suffering from the usual myriad problems associated with races run in such conditions, a fine 15th overall was achieved, with victory in the 2.0-litre class.

"The car basically ran like a dream more or less straight out of the box. I would like to think that the result gave his career a bit of a boost," concludes Mylius.

The next four consecutive weekends would see Gerry back in Formula Three, this sequence culminating with the 'blue ribbon' event of the year, the support race to the Monaco Grand Prix. An impressive string of results began with an encouraging third place at Paul Ricard, achieved despite making an appalling start which saw him drop right down the field.

The start of a typical Formula Three encounter at Magny-Cours. Gerry is second from the left. *(Unknown)*

He would go one better at Barcelona's majestic Montjuïc Park with a fine second place behind the dominant Chevron of Jurg Dubler. He was right in contention all weekend, qualifying in third position, his immaculate Brabham now sporting front and rear wings, unlike the majority of the opposition who were still sans them.

"The Brabham was designed to run with wings," recalls Catt. "It was very much dependent on the circuit. The use of wings was still in its infancy having only been introduced two years before in F1."

From Montjuïc en route to Monte Carlo Gerry took in a round of the French Formula Three Championship at Magny-Cours, where he encountered a strong British contingent all making their way south to the principality.

A dominant flag-to-flag win in his heat saw him secure pole for the final. Completing the front row was heat-two winner, Tony Trimmer, and local favourite Jean-Pierre Jaussaud. Trimmer led from the start until his retirement after eight of the 35 laps, which left Gerry to fight for victory with Jaussaud and Jean Max, who were both in Tecnos. He would end up a frustrated third with the fastest lap after he had been held up by the untidy and rather wild second-place finisher Max.

Joining Gerry, and the two Johns, Catt and Stanton, on many of the European travels was Margaret, as and when her work commitments allowed.

"By that time I was friendly with James Hunt's girlfriend, Taormina Rieck. We all knew her by her nickname 'Ping'," recalls Margaret. "I would pick her up from GKN where she worked on a Friday, and off we'd go.

"We took John Stanton with us to Magny-Cours, who had a wheel and tyre in the back for company. Plus, we had an engine in the boot. We met up with Gerry, James and the rest of the boys at the circuit. It was just like the year before in Formula Ford, all travelling together but by now with the amount of money being spent it was getting more serious. At least, on the track. Off-track it was even more fun!

"We followed them to Monte Carlo. By this time, James was giving 'Ping' a hard time – just James being James. She said to me that she'd enough of him. I suggested we go and look for some 'talent'. Gerry and John Catt were up to their elbows in oil and what-have-you, so we left the paddock and almost immediately, we bumped into three guys from London. One of them was called Peter but had the nickname 'Pong'. It was too good to be true! 'Ping' and 'Pong'. They are still together all these years later.

"The two of us had such fun together. We were young and a little crazy at times. We are still great friends."

The highly impressive run of results was ideal preparation for the race of the year around the streets of the principality. Gerry's on-track preparations may well have gone according to plan but seemingly things off-track were not quite so good according to Simon Taylor's *Autosport* report: 'Gerry Birrell found that his entry had not been accepted, apparently because the RAC had mixed him up with his sister-in-law Jenny, but hasty cables to Belgrave Square saw him take over Norman Foulds' entry.'

Not exactly the ideal preparation for the his first experience of the daunting streets. The fastest 40 cars in practice would qualify for the heats and Gerry was comfortably in among that number. He would line up in heat two and in a typical, incident-packed race would stay out of trouble and finish runner-up to Jean-Pierre Cassegrain, who was also in a Brabham BT28.

The second heat had been the faster of the two so Cassegrain would start on pole in the final with Gerry tucked in behind him in third. He would lose a place at the start to the eventual winner, Trimmer, but was still well in contention until a missed gear at Tabac, under pressure from Scott, resulted in a spin at around half-distance. This lost him three places to Jimmy Mieusset, Jean-Pierre Jarier, and Scott.

He was soon back in recovery mode and would repass the three of them before the conclusion of 24 frantic laps to end up with an impressive fourth-place finish. This was a fine achievement considering he didn't even have an entry on arrival!

Gerry had run his car with wings on the front and back. The victor, Trimmer, explains why he choose a different route. "In practice, I tried wings on my BT28 but took them off for the race, unlike Gerry. I found that I could not slide the rear of the car on the tight corners with the wings fitted. It all worked out well for me."

While matters on track had gone rather well, away from it, it was not so. Firstly, there was a slight disagreement over who was to blame for fusing the lights and, secondly, an embarrassing and uncomfortable moment for John Catt.

"The lights in our hotel room went out and I got the blame," remembers Margaret. "They said it was my Carmen rollers that did it, but it wasn't that, it was them charging the race car battery that blew the fuse."

Carmen rollers were the 'thing' in the '70s for styling ladies' hair.

"I remember it very well," says Catt. "We didn't stay in Monte Carlo because it was too expensive. We stayed out of town and I slept on a camp bed in the same room as Gerry and Margaret to save money.

"The electrics did leave a lot to be desired but it was Margaret's rollers that blew the fuse because a little battery charger wouldn't have enough power to do such a thing.

"I'll tell you something else that went on in that room. I was woken up in the middle of the night by Gerry being a bit fruity with Margaret. I thought, 'This is getting embarrassing'. I remember Margaret saying 'Stop it, you'll wake John up,' So I thought, 'How can I do this?'

"I started to pretend to talk in my sleep, saying things like how many gallons in a litre, how many miles in a kilometre and so on.

"What seemed like ages later, they stopped. They weren't sure whether I was awake or not. The rule was you didn't have 'nookie' the night before the race. Obviously, James [Hunt] did!

"Gerry mentioned the incident sometime later and I started to laugh.

"Margaret picked up on it and said, 'You were awake, weren't you?'

Entering Tabac Corner on his way to an impressive fourth-place on the streets of Monaco. *(Eric Bryce)*

"'Umm, yes. I didn't want to stop you, but it was embarrassing.'

"'You were very diplomatic.'

"'Well, I did my best'."

Having been away on frequent continental travels since the start of the season it was back to home soil for the British Empire Trophy race at Oulton Park on Bank Holiday Monday. Gerry had been at the circuit for much of the week before, getting in some serious testing. It certainly looked to have paid off when he annexed pole position by nearly a second from his closely packed pursuers.

After a dry qualifying in the morning, a brief rain shower before the first heat meant that an extra warming-up lap was granted by the organisers. Gerry had removed the wings he had been using on the last couple of outings, the nature of this parkland circuit suiting the car better without the appendages. With the change in the weather, he was offered the use of the wings at the last minute by John Stanton, but rejected them.

It didn't seem to matter either way as Gerry led into Old Hall for the first time from Trimmer, Walker, and Scott. It was a typical closely fought encounter with much weaving occurring along Top Straight. The inevitable happened on lap four when Trimmer tried to go through on the inside of Gerry at Knickerbrook. Oblivious of the challenge, Gerry took his normal line, they touched wheels and Gerry's car was heading for the bank at high-speed, overturning in the process. A somewhat shocked and stiff Gerry climbed out from his completely wrecked machine and was miraculously unharmed.

"That incident was the result of a typical F3 slipstreaming group ending in a pincer at the corner with wheels inside wheels," says Tony. "It certainly wasn't intentional on my part. Gerry was always a clean and fair driver. Plus, a very genuine guy."

Such accidents at Knickerbrook usually resulted in serious injury or worse, so he was indeed a lucky man though not a happy one.

"He was a bit peeved about that, as was I," reflects Catt. "We had been so quick all meeting so that was a lost opportunity. It was most unlike Tony. He was always very clean. They were two closely matched quick drivers who knew each other well from their battles in Formula Ford the previous year.

"No way, I'm a racing driver but I've sat in a few single-seaters and you can't always see properly. I was lucky enough to take it around the circuit after we won at Brands Hatch. I couldn't see a bloody thing and of course, you have to rev it because there's no torque. It was good fun, though!"

The next stop on the agenda – Gerry going pretty much straight from Oulton Park – was the magnificent Nürburgring set in the Eifel mountains of Germany. It was back to teaming up with Andrew Mylius to share the Gropa in the 1000km world manufactures championship encounter.

This time out the pair would endure a torrid weekend when a front wishbone broke while Gerry was at the wheel in practice, leaving the car stranded out on the circuit which severely restricted their track time. And a far more serious fate

Leading Trimmer, Walker and Scott into Lodge Corner at Oulton Park before the coming-together with Tony later in the race. *(Peter McFadyen)*

awaited them in the race.

"I started the race, meaning Gerry would take the flag," remembers Mylius. "The car had gone really well again and we had climbed up through the field to be second in class, I think.

"At the final driver change/refuelling stop Gerry got in and after only a couple of laps was overdue. We'd just received a message in the pits that he'd stopped when I saw a plume of smoke in the distance. I thought, 'Oh no'. I was so relieved to find out he was OK, which was more than could be said of the car."

It is believed that some fuel was spilt on to the car's undertray at the pitstop which had then found its way onto the exhaust and had caused the car to catch light.

"Gerry told me afterwards that he had seen smoke coming out of the intakes," recalls Mylius. "He had the presence of mind to drive to a marshals' post but unfortunately the extinguishers didn't work. The other problem was that at scrutineering one of the scrutineers had pressed the extinguisher button on the dashboard and had sprayed powder over the cockpit and engine. He had no idea what it was for. We were one of the first people to run with one of the plumbed-in Graviner systems that had just come out. With it being so new, nobody had any spare bottles, so we had no choice but to run it the way it was.

"Obviously Gerry knew this, hence him driving to a marshals' post. The car was just left to more or less burn itself out. It was completely destroyed.

"That was the last straw for me. I never drove again. I'd had a couple of narrow escapes with a couple of Chevrons catching fire. One was my own car, the other was when I drove one at Villa Real. Both times I got out without any problems. After Gerry's lucky escape, that was enough for me. I concentrated on building more Gropas to sell.

"We built them at North Street so I still saw Gerry. We kept in touch even when he had moved on."

Germany's other circuit of grand prix standard, Hockenheim, would see Gerry appearing in yet another different category of racing when he would make his Formula Two debut in a Brabham BT30. The car was part of the Sports Motors stable and was usually driven by Gerry's good friend, Tim Schenken. With Tim being away at Le Mans that weekend driving for Matra, it was Gerry who Rodney Bloor turned to for this one-off outing to partner regular driver, Francois Mazet.

The deal was done at the very last minute, meaning that Gerry had only the briefest of acclimatisation runs at Oulton Park before leaving for Germany.

Just how brief it was can be verified with the meticulous records kept by one of the Sports Motors mechanics, Derrick Worthington. His records of the test state that Gerry did 20 laps in total with the best lap time of 1min 34.2sec compared to Tim, who also did twenty laps with a best lap of 1min 32.8sec.

Gerry wouldn't be the only Birrell in the field at Hockenheim; his brother, Graham, was also out in the Ecurie Ecosse Brabham BT30. This must have seemed a far cry from their early days back in Scotland at places such as

Charterhall, Evanton, and of course, Ingliston.

It was Gerry who bagged the family bragging rights in practice by qualifying in the midfield, slightly ahead of Graham.

A demon start saw Gerry up to seventh in the race's early stages and part of the leading bunch of cars who were swapping places continuously at a track famous for its slipstreaming battles. By half-distance he was up to third and right in contention for the win on his F2 debut.

Disappointingly, his race would end with only six laps remaining with a broken valve spring. By that time he had slipped down the field slightly and out of the leading bunch after a spin avoiding Vittorio Brambilla, who had seemingly braked hard and early for the Sachs Curve.

Paul Watson, the F2 correspondent for *Autosport*, was full of praise, using phrases such as 'extremely impressive' and 'F2 newcomer Gerry Birrell drove a great race before retiring.'

While Watson seemed to have been impressed, Worthington from his diary notes was somewhat brief in his appraisal of events:

Friday practice – Francois slow
Saturday practice – Francois slower
Sunday race – Francois 9th. G Birrell classified 12th after a good race.
It seems from the diary that the team also had some trouble getting back to base in Manchester:

Monday 15 June – Went to Ostend. Missed the 7:30pm boat. Got 01:30am boat to Dover

Tuesday 16 June – Dover to London. Dropped Gerry off and went to Didsbury via Luke's for a cheque.
Again according to Derrick's diary notes before Gerry's F3 and the Sports Motors F2 team's next outings at Rouen, the schedule was:
23 June Tuesday – Set off early for Rouen. Went Manchester – Silverstone for testing. Stayed at Gerry's. (Note: We went out for a pub meal to a place near his home and Gerry treated us. I believe the pub was on the A30 in the Sunningdale/Ascot area.

The life of drivers and mechanics back in those days was certainly no trip to Paris. Or should that be Rouen, Imola, Hockenheim...?

It seems that while Gerry was away at Hockenheim, John Catt was hard at work making some modifications to the rear radius rod pick-up points on the rebuilt BT28, which when tested at Silverstone Gerry found gave the car greater stability out of corners. That was an essential requirement for the trip to Rouen.

A strong practice showing, on his first visit to the daunting, scarily fast French circuit, resulted in a second row starting position for the race. Unsurprisingly, it soon turned into a typical slipstreaming battle involving Hunt, Mike Beuttler, Wilson Fittipaldi, Jean-Luc Salomon and another half a dozen of the usual suspects, which included Gerry, all trying to out-manoeuvre each other to gain an advantage as the closing stages approached.

On the final lap coming down the home straight, there was a major calamity just after Hunt, Fittipaldi and Beuttler had crossed the line. It seems it was triggered by Frenchman Salomon, who seemingly tried to find a way past the bunch of cars in front of him and ended up being launched on to the car of Freddy Kottulinsky. Chaos broke out behind with cars going everywhere to avoid the mêlée. Gerry's car touched those of Scott and Cyd Williams and ended up in a ditch. Again, he would step out unhurt, which sadly was not the case for Salomon. Many drivers, including Gerry, went to try and rescue him from his Martini, but he died from head injuries and a broken neck.

In an earlier incident fellow countryman, Denis Dayan suffered a suspension failure at well over 100mph and suffered severe leg breakages, a broken arm and other injuries from which he would pass away a few days later.

When Gerry returned to Rouen the following year, John Catt remembers an incident relating to the Salomon accident. "We were in our hotel and a detective started questioning Gerry about his involvement. Gerry spoke a little French.

"I was afraid he would drop himself in it inadvertently and suggested that he go and get John Stanton who had lived with his granny in Switzerland and spoke several languages, including French.

"John was a nice enough bloke but could easily say the wrong thing unintentionally. I still thought it preferable but did suggest to Gerry that he may wish to be with him when he spoke to the detective or he may be hanged next week," concludes Catt with his tongue firmly in his cheek.

The following month of July saw Gerry string together an impressive sequence of results, culminating in taking his long overdue maiden victory.

It began at Croft with a second place in his heat behind Walker's Lotus. With their heat being the faster of the two, Walker started on pole with Gerry alongside for what promised to be a hotly-contested final. They didn't disappoint.

It was 30 laps of some of the best F3 racing of the season so far. In a race of changing fortunes and places, Gerry came home in fourth place, just over three seconds behind the first three of Pace, Dubler and Beuttler.

The recipe was just the same at Brands Hatch a week later but this time on a bigger stage, the support race to the British Grand Prix.

A cautious, safe run – if that was possible in F3 – to fourth place in his heat ensured Gerry qualified for the final. While he was in the mix throughout the final, he never looked like he would ultimately hit the front. He would end up in what would seem an outclassed seventh place at the chequered flag, but when you examine the results he was only three seconds behind the victorious Beuttler. That was yet further evidence of just how competitive the formula was.

Probably the most significant thing that happened during that weekend was the appearance of a Coca-Cola sticker on both Gerry's and James Hunt's cars. This was very much a case of the soda company exploring the motor racing scene for the first time. The deal had been put together by an emergent John Hogan. John, who sadly passed away in early 2021, would go on to be one of the leading PR and marketing people involved in Formula One, particularly, with Philip Morris and their Marlboro brand.

At that time he had become friends with Gerry and James and was doing all he could to promote them and find sponsorship. He would also socialise with the pair, who by now had formed an unlikely friendship. The closeness of their respective partners, Margaret and 'Ping' – or in James's case his on/off partner but still good friend – would have been a factor.

"They were chalk and cheese," offers Margaret. "James was such an eccentric. Gerry used to wind him up all the time. Before a race, he would say to him, if you're in front of me just let me through. No point in trying to stop me because you'll end up in the Armco. And he did, as well. James would almost jump out of his way. He was only saying it for a laugh.

"Then at breakfast, Gerry would say something like, 'Someone was having a great time in one of the rooms last night'. James would sit there chuckling and come out with, 'My room, was it?'

"He once had a shunt at Brands Hatch and refused to go in the ambulance to the hospital to be checked out. We were convinced he had a concussion, so Gerry, myself and 'Ping' took him back to his parents' house in Surrey. They were watching the TV and didn't seem that interested, just saying that he was away playing at being a silly racing driver again. We asked his brother Peter to keep an eye on him and if he was sick to take him to the hospital.

"James and 'Hogie' were part of our social scene. More often than not, we would all end up at the White Horse pub in Shere, near Guildford, after meetings at Brands Hatch. It was 'the' place to go and was full of racing people. We used to play bar football and if memory serves me right, we used to have pheasant and chips in the basket – a posh version of chicken in the basket, which was the 'in' thing at the time.

"I seem to remember James splitting his tight trousers but don't quote me on that. It's funny the things you remember. They were good days!"

Other regular attendees were Anthony Hussey and the renowned motor racing photographer, Michael Cooper. "We had some notable evenings in there," recalls Hussey with great affection many years later. "It was interesting to be in the company of Gerry and James. I always thought that Gerry had the Jackie Stewart approach to racing, while James had more of a Jochen Rindt type of approach. It's so ironic the way it turned out.

"Gerry was quite clinical and very methodical about not just his racing, but all aspects of his life. An example I have

Gerry lags slightly behind polesitter Beuttler's Brabham and Walker's Lotus at the start of the F3 final at Croft. ***(Unknown)***

is of when he fixed the clutch of a friend's Hillman Imp one evening. He just got down and got on with it. He was very practical. A first-class mechanic who could set up his own cars, and a bloody quick driver too!

"I would see them at the races in the UK. On one occasion at Snetterton I was sitting with Margaret in the pits while she did the timekeeping. Gerry suddenly stopped coming around and there was no news coming through from the commentator. It wasn't until the end of the race and Gerry brought the car back that he explained that when it had broken down, he had broken the wire to the commentary box. I realised then what it must be like to be a racing driver's wife.

"Also, Gerry and Margaret came to my mother's house at the top of Kingston Hill, which had a tennis court. On Sunday afternoons we used to have tennis parties – I don't think they turned up to play tennis – followed by afternoon tea. The tea parties were famous for Mother's homemade cream cakes.

"A vivid memory is of one of my sisters asking Margaret, 'How could you marry a racing driver?' Margaret just looked at her and said, 'I married Gerry Birrell,' which I thought was a great answer. Margaret was extremely entertaining and a capable lady."

"I can't remember saying that to his sister," says Margaret. "Me and my big mouth. I do remember the delicious afternoon tea at his mum's humongous house!

"Hussey is a great guy. We all had good fun together."

The aforementioned maiden win came at Paul Ricard, in dominant fashion. Gerry's winning margin of 12 seconds was huge by F3 standards and didn't go down too well with the organisers nor the runner-up, local hero Jean-Pierre Jaussaud.

"In the preceding Formula Two race one of the French Pygmée cars had dropped a load of oil," remembers John Catt." This seemed to make our F1 compound Dunlops really sticky and Gerry just drove off into the distance.

"Of course, the French couldn't have that so I think Jaussaud or maybe another Frenchman tried to say we were underweight. I had topped up the fluids as you were allowed to do, then there was some uncertainty about the weighbridge having a certificate of conformity, so they couldn't pursue that option.

"So then, at the prize-giving, they didn't credit Gerry with the fastest lap which he had clearly done and gave it to Jaussaud, who took the cheque and in his best French-English says, 'I didn't do the fastest lap but if someone wants to give me 1500 francs, then...' He was saying all this while he was running off the stage and disappearing into the distance. Gerry just turned to me and said, 'It's not worth it'."

While not wishing to diminish Gerry's excellent drive, the F1 compound tyres referred to by John Catt were surely a factor. Gerry was given the honour of being the first, and only, driver to try the new Dunlop tyre. It was the first tyre the Birmingham-based firm had produced since early 1968. Reportedly, it used the compound of the wet F1 tyres in an F3 casing with the usual tread pattern. To the naked eye, just the same as the existing tyre.

Why was Gerry given exclusive use? Could it be the influence of Jackie Stewart who had a long-standing arrangement with the company, pulling some strings in the background? Who knows?

What's that old saying? It's not what you know but who you know. You certainly can't blame Gerry for using everything and everyone at his disposal to steal a march on his rivals.

"We had a good working relationship with Dunlop," states Catt. "There was a lot of mutual respect and trust. They would always be probing the tyres with their temperature needles, then asking what camber we were running. Depending on the readings, I would alter the camber accordingly to get an even temperature across the width of the tyre."

Returning to UK soil, Brands Hatch was the next venue in Gerry's hectic schedule – the fifth race in six weekends. For the first time this year, a Holbay-tuned engine would replace his reportedly tired Lucas-tuned example. It was no surprise that it was tired after a season of hard racing, but that wasn't the only reason for the switch.

"We thought with the Holbay powering the majority of the winners so far, we should give it a try," recalls Catt. "Personally, I think the Holbay had a little more torque, that's if you could have torque from a 1000cc screamer. It was a case of horses for courses. On the tighter circuits, the Holbay seemed to have the edge but on the faster circuits, like Thruxton and Silverstone, you would want more top-end, so maybe the Lucas had the edge. We are talking tiny, tiny differences here.

"Gerry had been keen to carry on his association with Brian Hart and Brian had built him an engine, his first attempt at such a thing. Personally, I think he should have preserved with Brian's engine a bit more but in the beginning, he had come from using the more torquey Formula Ford engine and had to adapt his driving style to the different characteristics of an F3 engine. To help him adapt, maybe, he felt he needed one of the established tuners. I can't recall having any discussions about it."

One man who can shed some light on whether Gerry found any difference between the Holbay and the Lucas engines is Julian Pratt. "I remember him changing his engine after practice at one of the Brands Hatch meetings. I'm not 100 percent certain it was at that particular meeting. Anyway, he was moaning a bit about the one he had, so he swapped his Lucas for a Holbay. After I asked him what he thought, he said it was exactly the same. 'No difference at all. I feel such an arse.' I thought it was so honest and typical of Gerry."

The meeting had got off to an uncomfortable start with Gerry having to intervene when things got heated between John Catt and one of the marshals. "The guy was being a jobsworth," recalls Catt, anger still simmering anger even after all these years. "We had been told to park our van in a certain bay. The paddock in those days had some lean-to sheds. The trouble was our box van wouldn't fit under the canopy. He was going on and on, giving it some. I went to the paddock office to try and resolve the situation but felt quite threatened once the guy had got his mates in tow, but I managed to keep my cool.

"Gerry was away with Margaret, probably doing some PR or something. When he came back and I told him what had gone on, he went straight up to the paddock office and threatened to go home if there was any further trouble. With him being one of the star attractions, they sent someone more senior down to smooth things over. I think, in the end, the guy got his collar felt."

Matters on track didn't get any easier when, ironically, he was beaten by the narrowest of margins by the Holbay-engined Lotus of Wilson Fittipaldi after a close, fierce battle. It seems on this occasion even using the 'demon' Dunlop tyres weren't sufficient to help him overcome his rival.

"Wilson Fittipaldi was the world's greatest roadblock going that day," says Catt. "Gerry said afterwards, 'I could have passed him, but it would have been balls-out.' In the end, he wasn't prepared to damage the car and settled for second. But the crowd certainly loved it."

Yet further proof of what Pratt alluded to. You suspect the likes of Beuttler, Hunt, and a good few more, wouldn't have been quite so circumspect. There was nothing wrong with either approach, but Gerry was always thinking about tomorrow or the next race, not just the present one.

While the vast majority of the British regulars headed to Thruxton the following weekend he, together with fellow Brits Hunt, David Purley, Andy Sutcliffe and Peter Hanson, made the long trek to Karlskoga in Sweden, their decision no doubt influenced by the lure of a share of the prize money totalling over £2000 for anyone making the final.

Gerry would come back with a decent share of the pot with a victory in his heat and a second place in the final behind Hanson.

The schedule showed no signs of easing – it was still only mid-August – with a trip to Oulton Park for the prestigious Gold Cup meeting followed a week later by another traditional fixture on the UK calendar, the Bank Holiday meeting at Brands Hatch.

A very wet Oulton Park awaited the high-quality large entry for the only practice session that counted for grid positions. Ian Titchmarsh reporting for *Autosport* was in no doubt who the victor would be if the conditions remained wet for the final the following day: 'Birrell, with a fully sorted, well set-up car and F1 compound Dunlops, was a clear two seconds faster than anyone else. Other fast drivers, on normal Firestone equipment, just couldn't stay with the Scot either on braking or cornering.'

Unfortunately, the weather was dry for the 19-lap final which meant some guesswork on settings. Gerry, with a reportedly vast selection of tyres to choose from, elected to use some low-profile Dunlops which, Titchmarsh reported, 'Made the handling twitchy and Birrell was having to work hard to stay with the leaders.'

That proved to be the case with a disappointing fifth the best he could achieve after such promise.

Unbelievably, he very nearly ended up being awarded victory after the first four cars home were checked by the eligibility scrutineers and were found to be under weight. In concluding his report Titchmarsh was scathingly critical. 'The ludicrous prospect of awarding the race to the car placed fifth on the road was averted when it was pointed out that the smart new weighbridge didn't have a certificate affirming its accuracy. It seems almost criminal that drivers should be allowed to risk their lives for 19 laps only to be told afterwards that their cars are nine pounds too light and must be disqualified when this could have been ascertained and remedied beforehand. Do the RAC and some of their scrutineers really have any idea what motor racing is about?'

Different times. So very different times.

Another off-track incident again involving John Catt, who seemed to have his fair share, is still ingrained in his memory. The life of a race mechanic is never easy.

"Jackie Stewart was racing that day in the F1 non-championship Gold Cup," recalls Catt. Gerry and I were going to get some lunch and, on the way, we came across him in the paddock. He says to Gerry, while looking at me, do we need him?

"Before Gerry could answer, I said something like I've things to do and diplomatically made my excuses. When Gerry came back he apologised. I told him not to worry about it.

"These people sometimes get above their station. It doesn't faze me at all. I understood Gerry had to talk to him about his progression. I didn't need to be there, it didn't matter. For ages afterwards, he felt rotten that Stewart had said that. That shows you what sort of guy Gerry was. He was a nice bloke. He wouldn't pull a fast one. I think that's why we got on. He treated people properly. There's an awful lot of drivers who don't. He was always fair to me, that's why we stayed together for as long as we did."

'Birrell Speeds to a Dunlop win' was the headline to accompany Justin Haler's report from Brands Hatch in *Autosport*. This seems to imply that the victory was achieved due to Gerry being Dunlop's chosen man. Admittedly, they had brought some demon intermediate tyres for him to try which according to Haler's report: 'Birrell was delighted with, although he reported that when their high adhesion limit had been reached the breakaway came remarkably quickly.'

While, admittedly, Gerry had been the first one to have the use of the Dunlops and therefore had fine-tuned his car to suit, some of his rivals, the likes of Beuttler and Hanson, had chosen to try them at this meeting. Beuttler, in particular, wasn't convinced of their potential.

To achieve wins in both his heat and the final, by two and four seconds respectively from such high-class opposition is not solely down to the tyres you have fitted. Surely it is a result of a driver gaining confidence. Of teamwork from Messrs Stanton, Bloore and Catt and the ability to fine-tune the car to its absolute maximum. All of which Gerry seemed to have in abundance.

To celebrate such a fine performance, a meal was planned at a place on the Embankment in London. John Catt offers an amusing tale about how he and Gerry got there well before the other invited guests. "Gerry came with me in the truck while the others, Tim Schenken, James Hunt, 'Ping' and Margaret, all left before us.

"Funnily enough the restaurant wasn't far from where I'd worked previously so I knew the way plus I knew from having worked at Brands Hatch, pre-Gerry, that to try and go out via the main road was pointless, so I knew to use all the back roads.

"We arrive at this posh restaurant with me still in my working gear and no sign of Schenken and co. We must have waited about half an hour before they walk in and Schenken is incredulous, 'how the hell you get here? We left before you.'"

"We have a man with local knowledge," offered Gerry with a broad smile.

"Even at the end of the night they were still couldn't believe how we'd got there so quick."

The following month of September would see Gerry racing on every weekend – not for the first time – with varying degrees of success.

His final overseas foray of the year would be to Belgium and the Zolder circuit. In both his heat and the final he was right in among the leading pack and in contention for victory, but would ultimately come away with fifth- and fourth-place finishes.

Dominating both his heat and the final at Brands Hatch over the August Bank Holiday. Some weekends he was just unstoppable. ***(Pete Austin)***

The following weekend was a double-header with the first visits of the season to Crystal Palace on Saturday, followed by Cadwell Park on Sunday. What a weekend of contrasts it would turn out to be.

At the South London venue in ridiculously dangerous, ultra-wet conditions Gerry would spin off along with Sutcliffe and Purley at North Tower, and was lucky to emerge unhurt. The resulting damage would mean a busy time ahead for the team and the long trip northwards to the picturesque Cadwell Park.

With a hastily repaired but still immaculate car at his disposal Gerry wasted no time in getting to grips with the undulations of the Lincolnshire circuit and qualified on the third row for his heat. A steady run netted him a fourth-place finish and another third-row starting position for the final.

By the time the final was due to commence the weather had turned decidedly wet. In contrast to him going off the previous day, this time aided by his low-profile Dunlops, he was quickly in among the leaders and on laps six and seven had passed first Trimmer, then Hunt to take the lead which seemed his for the duration. But, disappointingly after another four laps, he ground to a halt at the bottom of the Mountain due to a broken rocker in the engine.

Thruxton the weekend after would finally bring a change of fortune when Gerry drove his best race of the season to date. The event was the 40-lap European Cup which not only brought probably the best entry to these shores thus far, but featured the drivers forming small teams to represent their respective nations. Gerry would be in the Great Britain second team with fellow Scot, Richard Scott. The other two planned team members, Trimmer and Cyd Williams, had been involved in incidents the previous day at Oulton Park so they were unable to take part.

Gerry had switched back to his Lucas engine due to the problems at Cadwell with his Holbay unit, and discarded the front and rear wings he tended to prefer, reasoning that a car minus appendages would be ideally suited to the fast sweeps of Thruxton.

From the start it was Jean-Pierre Jarier who led the screaming pack of Scott, Hunt, Torsten Palm, Jaussaud, Dubler, Sten Gunnarsson and Bev Bond, with Gerry right in among them. By around one-third distance he had made his intentions clear by hitting the front after a few incidents had seen the demise of one or two of the fancied runners. He would gradually pull away by sometimes up to two seconds a lap, aided in no small part to the large group of followers all falling over each other in their efforts to stay on terms.

By the chequered flag, after the marathon 40 laps, he had pulled out nearly 20 seconds on runner-up, Gunnarsson. Gerry's victory and Scott's ninth-place finish after a spin, meant that they were runners-up to the Swedish 'A' team in the team awards.

The Europa Cup race at Thruxton saw Gerry dominant again. This was the first lap, and from then on he just ran away with proceedings. ***(Unknown)***

Eager to read of his exploits, Gerry was seen heading into Paddington Station on Tuesday afternoon by rival Brendan McInerney. "WHSmith used to get a load of *Autosport*s in early, which were bound for the West Country. I spotted him driving in as I was walking out with my copy. I wagged a knowing finger at him and he gave an uncharacteristically bashful smile in response."

Gerry's drive also earned praise from Team Lotus F1 team manager, Peter Warr, who was in attendance with the 'works' Lotus F3 team.

"I was holding out the pit board when he came up to me," remembers Catt. "He showed me the lap times and said 'Your man is very consistent'. He'd noticed for the past 10 or 12 laps that Gerry's lap times had all been within two-tenths of a second, which was impressive at a place like Thruxton. It didn't surprise me, but it showed him his capabilities."

While his on-track performance was drawing praise from the right people, one person distinctly not impressed was Monsieur Arnold, the entrant of promising Frenchman Jarier. According to Pit & Paddock in *Autosport*: 'He became suspicious when Jarier began to drop back and Birrell pulled away to win, so he ordered Birrell's engine to be stripped and checked for capacity. Naturally, the engine was completely legal, and away went a rather unhappy Monsieur Arnold.'

"That wasn't the only time our engine legality had been questioned," offers Catt. "Wilson Fittipaldi protested at one of the Brands Hatch meetings. We had to take the head off so they could measure the bore and they also checked the air restrictor. Both were found to be perfectly legal.

"This caused us all sorts of problems because Gerry had qualified for one of the other F3 races and we needed to get the car back together. The Clerk of the Course, Nick Syrett, was going ballistic, not at us, but Wilson. He did offer to delay the start of the race. He did everything he could to help."

Having impressed on his Formula Two debut, Gerry was invited back for another outing, this time at Imola. On this occasion, he would take over Mazet's car, who was away competing in the Tour de France, and would partner good friend Schenken.

Both cars suffered their fair share of woes in practice, Gerry being delayed with a fuel leak and then an oil leak due to a sheared nut on the cam cover. All things considered, to qualify less than a second slower than the more experienced Schenken was a good effort.

The two heats yielded 12th and 10th place finishes resulting in an aggregate result of eighth overall, just pipping his team-mate who had been delayed in the first heat with a lengthy pit stop. All in all, a pretty mediocre outing for Gerry and the Sports Motors team.

A couple more outings back in Formula Three would round off the busy season. Firstly, it was back to Crystal Palace where he secured pole position for his heat. He lost out at the start to run fourth in the early stages behind the leading trio of Bond, Hunt and Beuttler. Bond's retirement promoted him to third and a chance to redeem things in the final.

Unfortunately, Gerry would finish one place lower after being involved in one of the classic F3 battles of all time. This was, of course, the infamous televised encounter that ended with the coming-together across the finishing line of Hunt and Dave Morgan, the conclusion of which saw Morgan on the end of an impressive right hook from hot-tempered Hunt.

Brands Hatch promised much of the same with a pole position and victory in his heat. But, again, fourth place was all Gerry could manage after Trimmer took the lead and established a gap, leaving him embroiled in a race-long scrap with Hunt, Pace, Ashley and Colin Vandervell.

It had been quite a season and was summed up succinctly by Justin Haler in his review of the season in *Autosport*: 'In contrast to the aforementioned pair of Beuttler and Walker, Gerry Birrell was very reluctant to get involved in the big slipstreaming dices that were the feature of so many races. Birrell, however, was a great thinker and planner, and when the conditions were right and the pack was behind him managed to get the works Sports Motors-John Stanton Brabham far off into the distance, as was seen at the August Brands and European Cup Thruxton meetings in particular.'

"That's such a true assessment," states Julian Pratt, "Some drivers were prepared to go out on a limb to win races, while the more sensible guys like Gerry and Emerson [Fittipaldi], just weren't prepared to take those risks. They – Gerry and Emerson – appeared to be safe as houses and actually were. That's why, in my opinion, Gerry struggled a bit at times in F3."

Pratt, while not directly involved in Gerry's F3 campaign, would often go and spectate and talk frequently with Gerry back at North Street, so is well qualified to offer an insight.

The most qualified to offer an accurate assessment of the season, however, was Catt, the man who worked closely with Gerry as his hard-working and dedicated mechanic.

Gerry, in untypical tail-out mode, fending off the advances of Hunt and Vandervell. ***(David Marshall)***

"We spent a great deal of time together both at the circuits and driving the many hours in the van to all points of the UK and Europe. We were getting to know each other. We got along fine straight away.

"Gerry used to give me snippets when we were driving. He used to talk about when he worked at Claud Hamiltons which was near Ibrox, the home of Rangers FC, and they used to climb up poles to try and get in for nothing. Hooligans!

"When he went to Northern Ireland to meet the Crosslé people one of the first questions he was asked, was he a protestant or a catholic? Crosslé were protestant, so was Gerry. He was sure if he had been catholic he wouldn't have got the drive.

"The results were good. Thruxton, in the big European race, was a highlight. He just disappeared. He treated the car well, didn't abuse it.

"From what I know, Gerry had been more hands-on previously but he did very little, leaving me to get on with it. He had more commitments by then.

"It was hard work, especially the travelling. I was self-employed, so if I worked sixteen hours one day, I could take the next day off. Not that I got many days off.

"I was single at the time, didn't even have a girlfriend. I enjoyed it."

It had been a long season and since there was never any intention to concentrate on a particular championship either in the UK or in Europe he missed out on being highly placed in any of them, but he did manage to claim some honours when the French newspaper *L'Equipe* published its own championship based on the results from all the major international races. Gerry had a total of 90 points to Tony Trimmer's 88, so claimed a title of sorts.

In all, it was a most satisfactory and impressive first season in this highly competitive formula where nobody ever dominated for sustained periods. Gerry had beaten some of the very best and accomplished everything he could have hoped for. It was time to make the move up to Formula Two, where he would align himself with one of the most famous names in motor racing to aid his progress.

But it wasn't just in the category one step below Formula One that he would seek to further his career. The signing of a contract with a certain global car manufacturer with a strong competition heritage to be a part not just of their saloon car plans, but also their research and development programme, was yet another endorsement that the right people in the right places were beginning to appreciate the myriad range of skills he had to offer.

This was getting more and more serious, which was just the way he wanted it.

The first outing as a works Ford driver was in the Boreham-entered Capri at the Race of Champions meeting at Brands Hatch. Two third-place finishes in his heats resulted in third overall on aggregate. *(Tim Marshall)*

CHAPTER SIX

FORMULA TWO AND MUCH MORE

The revealing of Gerry's plans for the year ahead came in the specialist journals in February when John Stanton announced an expansion of his involvement with an ambitious programme of all the major Formula Two races in a Lotus 69. In addition, he would also provide a Formula Three version of the 69 with works assistance in certain international races, including the support races at the International Trophy at Silverstone, the Race of Champions at Brands Hatch and the races supporting the British and Monaco Grand Prix. Sponsorship for the Formula Three campaign would be on a race-by-race basis. The increase in Stanton's financial outlay was vital in keeping Gerry's career trajectory on the upward curve. The previous year's principal backer, Rodney Bloor's Sports Motors, would run their own Formula Two programme.

The preparation and maintenance of both Lotuses would be the sole responsibility of John Catt, who would stay loyal to Gerry despite another offer.

"At the beginning of the year Tim Schenken mentioned that they were looking for mechanics at Brabhams," recalls Catt. "He did say that I'd probably be better off staying with Gerry. I was never tempted. But Gerry got to hear that Schenken had spoken to me, so he offered me a 100 percent increase from £20 per week to £40 per week. Thank you, Tim!"

While this was, in itself, big news, it paled into insignificance compared to the announcement from Ford that Gerry would drive a works 2.6-litre Ford Capri run by their competition

From left to right: John Catt working away, as usual, while Gerry, John Stanton and John Reynolds pose for the camera. Reynolds worked in the car accessories/ racing spares shops owned by Stanton. ***(Chris Walker/Kartpix)***

department at Boreham in the British Touring Car Championship. Other selected European forays for the car giant's competition department based in Cologne, Germany, would be undertaken, subject to Gerry's availability.

His duties for Ford didn't end there. When not representing them on track he would also carry out many, many miles of road car test and development work at their Boreham test facility. Dovetailing both racing campaigns and work at Boreham would be a challenge but one which Gerry relished. A day not behind the wheel of a car was a wasted day in his world, a mantra he had long advocated and one he would continue to follow.

The top man at Boreham was Peter Ashcroft, who was responsible for Gerry's appointment. Sadly, Peter passed away in 2008, so we are unable to hear first-hand from a man synonymous with the Ford name, but we can hear from Ford's European Director of Motorsport, Stuart Turner, to whom he was answerable and who endorsed Gerry's appointment wholeheartedly.

"There must be something in the water up there," says Turner, in reference to Gerry's Scottish roots and his illustrious predecessors Jim Clark and Jackie Stewart, both of whom had strong Ford connections.

"I always felt in motorsport you need three things, you need a car, you need a driver and you need a team. The interplay between those three ingredients is one of the keys to success. With Gerry having come from a motoring background, he understood his cars, but unlike some drivers, if he'd got some ideas on how to improve an area of the car, he was able to communicate with the engineers/mechanics, which is why he was a highly successful car developer.

"I had a good working relationship with him. I'm far from technical, but he was understanding enough to allow for that when he was explaining to me what he was doing. He was highly articulate and such an amiable character, but not a pushover. He'd got a personality and was just a very nice guy."

One of Gerry's first tasks was to help with the development of Ford's new mid-engined sports car, the GT70. Working with the car's designer, Len Bailey, who had been responsible for both the GT40 and F3L sports racers, Gerry would spend many miles pounding around the Boreham test track in trying to make the car into a viable rallying replacement for the Escort which, while still competitive on the loose, gravel rallies, was struggling on the tarmac events against the Alpine-Renaults and Porsches.

The initial engine in the prototype was a 2.6-litre V6, which although powerful enough, was leading to problems in the handling department. This was something Gerry very quickly brought to the attention of the Ford technicians.

"One of the Ford designers asked what would improve the handling," recalls journalist Jeremy Walton. "Burying the centre of gravity six feet in the ground might help," Gerry said solemnly, before the laughter broke out. "He was truly very witty," says Walton. "Very sharp, and a quick brain."

Gerry applies a touch of correction exiting Shaw's hairpin in his first F2 outing of the year at Mallory Park. Behind, in typical full opposite lock mode is Ronnie Peterson. ***(Chris Walker/Kartpix)***

Jeremy Walton was then writing for *Motoring News* but would work for a time as Ford's motorsport press officer during Gerry's time with them. Now he's a prolific, leading author on a wide range of motoring and motor racing subjects.

A similar memory is offered by Turner: "I was talking to the mechanic involved in the building and development of the GT70. After only five miles in the car, Gerry said you have to change the engine for something less heavy."

Despite the many hours of work undertaken, the whole project was canned before the car became close to being competitive. It would seem that the powers-that-be at Ford were listening.

There is no doubt that the deal with Ford was big, but in no way did it distract Gerry from his single-seater aspirations. The goal was still Formula One. But being associated with such an illustrious, worldwide brand certainly helped raise his profile. It was final confirmation, if any were needed, that here was a man to watch and people of the calibre of Ken Tyrrell, a renowned talent-spotter, seemed to be one of those watching closely.

In the issue of *Motoring News* dated 21 January 1971, Tyrrell said of the upcoming Formula Ford European Championship: 'There seems no doubt that Formula Ford has in the last three years produced some remarkable talent. I'm always on the lookout for new talent. If this year's series produces someone of the calibre of Tim Schenken, Gerry Birrell, Claude Bourgoignie or Colin Vandervell, I shall be very pleased.'

Another vitally important part of the Ford deal was that, for the first time, Gerry would earn some decent money. "That's how we managed to live," recalls Margaret. "They were very good because they gave you X amount of money on paper which enabled us a get a mortgage. Gerry was like a consultant with his non-racing work and helping with their rally programmes. Ford were very good to him."

In between his Ford commitments, Gerry had found time to fit in a couple of test sessions with his Formula Two Lotus at Snetterton and Lotus's adjacent test track Hethel, and had reportedly expressed himself very pleased with the car after completing about 90 laps. This was ideal preparation for the first race outing of the year, a non-championship encounter at Mallory Park in mid-March.

Despite its status, a quality entry assembled at the Leicestershire venue. Ronnie Peterson, Niki Lauda, Carlos Reutemann, Derek Bell, John Watson, Henri Pescarolo, Mike Beuttler, Jo Siffert and Tom Walkinshaw were all names who would play a significant part in motorsport in the years ahead.

Gerry was by no means overawed by such illustrious company and impressed every time he took to the track in what was just his third Formula Two outing. He qualified on the outside of the front row alongside Pescarolo and polesitter Peterson, who were both in the latest March. The result was to be taken from the aggregate of two 40-lap heats.

Gerry would come home as runner-up to Pescarolo in both of the heats which resulted in him being placed second overall. He had run third in the first heat but had benefited from the huge accident involving Peterson, who had suffered a seized steering balljoint and almost gone into the crowd at the Esses. In the second heat Gerry had led in the early stages until being passed by Pescarolo at Shaw's Hairpin.

His highly impressive performance earned him the BP Man of the Meeting award and praise from Alan Henry of *Motoring News* and Simon Taylor of *Autosport*. Each man would go on to be recognised as leading motor racing writers.

Henry, in particular, was effusive in his praise filling his report with comments such as 'Scottish revelation.' 'Impeccably driven Lotus,' 'Looking absolutely confident and unruffled, Birrell continued to lead,' and 'Drove an outstanding race in both heats'.

Taylor wrote in a similar vein: 'The extremely impressive Gerry Birrell,' 'Impressive display of polished driving,' and 'An excellent drive by the young Scot in only his second [sic] F2 race'.

The good form continued the week after at the Race of Champions meeting, the annual non-championship F1

First time out on the F3 Lotus 69, Gerry scored an impressive third place. *(Tim Marshall)*

At the first round of the European F2 series at Hockenheim the car looks bare without its wings. Loyal mechanic John Catt is alongside. ***(Jutta Fausel)***

encounter at Brands Hatch. On this occasion, Gerry would be having his first outings in the Formula Three Lotus and the V6 Ford Capri.

In F3 he took pole position by quite a margin from Colin Vandervell's Brabham. Both practice sessions were run in the wet, allowing Gerry once again to show his undoubted prowess in those conditions. He couldn't quite repeat his domination come the race, which was run in the dry. He came home a close third behind the duelling pair of winner Vandervell (the son of Vanwall's founder) and Bev Bond in the new Ensign.

The outing in the Capri in the opening round of the British Saloon Car Championship (BSCC) run to Group 2 regulations yielded a trio of third-place finishes (two heats and the final). Gerry commented with much enthusiasm about the power of the V6 motor, and suggested that once the handling and braking had been sorted he would have backed a winner.

It wasn't just on the track that he was kept busy. Away from it he attended the Jackie Stewart Speed Show held at the Kelvin Hall in Glasgow where he was due to join, on one of the days, a forum sponsored by Goodyear which was panelled by Stuart Turner and Ken Tyrrell. He was certainly mixing with the right people in the right environment. The man lending his name to the show would be in attendance a couple of days later once he had returned from the Ontario F1 race.

Gerry's first foray overseas was to Hockenheim for the first round of the European F2 series. Up against the cream of international opposition, he found things tougher than Mallory, qualifying in 12th position before a 10th-place finish in the first heat followed by a sixth place in the second yielded sixth overall on aggregate.. Due to second-placed Graham Hill being a graded driver and thus ineligible to score points, Gerry scored points for fifth. Considering that he was reportedly uncomfortable in the slipstreaming battles associated with circuits like Hockenheim, preferring venues where some flair would pay dividends, it was a good result.

A busy Easter weekend should have begun with a Capri outing at Snetterton on Good Friday but after only a few laps of practice the engine broke a valve spring and rendered him a non-starter. The valve springs were an experimental type from America, so as replacements were unavailable the Capri was also a no-show at Thruxton on Easter Monday. That at least would enable Gerry to focus his efforts on the Formula Two feature race, round two of the European series.

An advert from Autosport. ***(Reproduced with kind permission of Autosport Media UK Ltd)***

Continuing his good form, he qualified an impressive fourth for his heat, despite a rear suspension that was bottoming so hard that the driveshaft doughnut bolts were scrapping the gearbox sideplates. To end up only a second slower than the polesitter, the flying Peterson, was encouraging.

With the rear suspension stiffened up to alleviate the bottoming, a neat and tidy drive in the first heat netted a fourth-place finish that earned him a place on the third row of the grid for the final. Disappointingly, after a good start that saw him running in fourth in the early stages, he had to retire with a broken exhaust manifold.

A significant development away from the track saw a topping-up of the budget with the addition of Coca-Cola stickers

A one-off outing for Gerry in the Ecurie Ecosse March 712M at the Nürburgring. *(Jutta Fausel)*

Gerry on (or over) the limit of adhesion on the slippery streets of Pau. *(John Stanton)*

adorning the car. The deal – which also included backing James Hunt, who had stayed in F3 for another season – had again been arranged by John Hogan.

Motor Sport provided some background from that time via a feature in 2004 by respected journalist Adam Cooper. 'I had met James, who was keen to find out about sponsorship,' Hogan recalled. 'At that time I was working on the Coca-Cola account and it was James who introduced me to Gerry. They both carried modest Coke logos on their cars, while I continued to search for funds to top up their budgets. We soon became close friends.

'Even then James had an eye for a good driver, and he said Gerry was really good. Talk about two people who were chalk and cheese, but they had tremendous respect for each other. James liked a drink, I liked a drink, Gerry didn't. Gerry was in awe of James's ability to drive at 10/10ths the whole time, while James regarded Gerry highly because he was a lot quicker than he looked.'

The reference by Hogan of his quest for further funds was a part of his involvement with Guaranteed Promotions (Motor Sport) Ltd, which was another part of the John Stanton empire. The company looked after race entries/travel arrangements, insurance and so on for drivers who had signed on their books. 'Hogie' was responsible for the promotional activities, while Norma Robb, who had experience with Surtees, McLaren and Frank Williams, looked after the admin side. Obviously Gerry was on the books, along with James and Kiwi Graham 'Cassius' McRae, who was making a name for himself in F5000.

Before the next outing, a non-championship encounter at Pau in less than two weeks, John Catt had been hard at work trying to cure some of the issues from Thruxton. "The exhaust had broken due to bottoming on the lower radius rod, so I'd made up a new one and altered it to prevent it from happening again," he recalls.

"The driveshaft yokes had been damaged and had to be replaced. New front and rear anti-roll bars were made and fitted and Gerry had reported experiencing some rear bump steer, so the rear pick-up points for the top link had been altered."

Upon arrival in Southern France, the weather wasn't too kind in helping to see if the modifications had been a success. The first practice session was run in diabolical conditions. Gerry ventured out, unlike some, and as usual in such conditions, lapped competitively.

The final practice session began in wet conditions but gradually dried just as the session concluded. Gerry qualified on the fifth row, emerging as the fastest Lotus runner and beating the works car of Emerson Fittipaldi and the London International Racing Association (LIRA) version of Reine Wisell, both notable F1 scalps. At that time Fittipaldi was the number one at Team Lotus, following Jochen Rindt's death at Monza the previous September, and had scored his maiden Grand Prix victory in the United States that October to confirm the Austrian's posthumous World Championship. Wisell had joined the Brazilian on the podium with third place.

Come race day the weather had improved considerably, but the same couldn't be said of Gerry's fortunes. He would end his race in the unyielding barriers after a safety peg had fallen out of a rear tyre, resulting in a sudden deflation. Thankfully, he was unhurt, the car less so, with two corners torn off. The streets of Pau were certainly not his happy hunting ground. Adding further to his disappointment was that Wisell took victory, having started behind him.

With only a week to the third round of the European Championship at the Nürburgring, it was almost certain that Gerry would have to miss it due to insufficient time to effect repairs to the damaged Lotus. Fortunately, he was thrown a lifeline at the eleventh hour when his old friends from Ecurie Ecosse contacted him to stand in for their regular pilot, Tom Walkinshaw. Walkinshaw and his mechanic had been involved in a road accident on their way to the circuit, and with injuries to his eye and foot Tom would be unfit to take part.

At least Gerry had some experience of the daunting Nürburgring but not of the car he was due to drive, the March 712M. But he wasn't complaining because on paper it was the pace-setting car of the season so far, especially in Peterson's hands.

Considering that he missed the whole of Friday practice while he made his way from the UK, Gerry impressed many onlookers with a time just over 10 seconds off the pole time of Derek Bell's Frank Williams-entered March, and lined up on the sixth row. Gerry said that he found the March much more forgiving than his regular mount.

An impressive ninth-place finish in the race behind such luminaries as Niki Lauda, Graham Hill, Carlos Reutemann, the Fittipaldi brothers, a shade over two minutes behind the eventual victor, Francois Cevert, after 10 laps or 140 miles of the tortuous circuit, highlights just what a fine job he'd done in the unfamiliar car.

Next on the agenda was another outing in the Capri at Silverstone in the fourth round of the BSCC which was on the support card for the non-championship F1 International Trophy. Since its last troubled outing, the car had undergone improvements to its fuel-injection system, the fitting of a front spoiler, an increase in wheel sizes and, most importantly, an increase in engine size to 2.94 litres from the previous 2.6 and 2.8 variants. This was very much part of Gerry's job remit, the test and development of the Group 2 machine which was just one of the many Fords whose future specification he would influence.

All the work seemed to have paid off, enabling Gerry to be the fastest Ford qualifier in third place. A frantic scrap in the race with the Chevrolet Camaro of Martin Thomas was resolved in Gerry's favour when Thomas spun the lap after Gerry had lost ground after a huge grassy moment of his own. An eventual fifth-place finish was only just achieved due to fading brakes. Gerry would finish only two places in front of brother Graham, who was out in his Wylie's Escort in the 2.0-litre class and had come from the back of the grid.

With his Lotus now back in fine fettle, Gerry having helped John Catt straighten things out, it was off to Spain and the Jarama circuit for another Formula Two Championship outing. But as John Catt explains, it almost didn't happen: "Gerry missed all of Friday practice when we were delayed at the Spanish customs. They were just being awkward. I think the Williams team just turned around and went home. I think Gerry had to go and find a lawyer to help out and assure the customs we weren't importing the car, or something like that. Typical Latin temperament.

"Basically, they wanted some money, some stickers or signed photos. You would think customs officials would be above wanting stickers and the like. Whether they had a market for that sort of thing, who knows? It wasn't just the Spanish; the French, Germans and Italians were just the same. All were troublesome. You couldn't imagine a British customs official wanting stickers."

They didn't arrive until late on Friday night, Gerry only managing a couple of hours sleep in the back of the team's truck before going out to practice on Saturday. A good effort scraped him on to the last row of the grid.

It was always going to be a struggle from so far back in such a competitive field, and the best he could achieve was a respectable eighth-place finish.

After a promising start to the Formula Two campaign, things had become a bit of a struggle. Trying to run your own show up against works-supported cars is always difficult. It didn't help that the other principal Lotus runners, Fittipaldi in the Team Lotus Bardahl-backed car and Wisell at LIRA both recently scored victories. Old adversary Wilson Fittipaldi in the sister Team Bardahl car had consistently out-paced Gerry in the races and it appeared he was struggling to keep up with the ever-increasing competitiveness of not just his fellow Lotus users, but also the newer cars from March, Tecno and Brabham. Money certainly wasn't the problem, as John Stanton, Coca-Cola and assorted trade suppliers were providing ample funds. The choice of car seemed to be the biggest single factor.

"The Lotus was a heap of rubbish," states Catt emphatically. "After we'd stripped it down after the accident at Pau we realised it was too heavy. It was supposed to be a semi-monocoque, but it wasn't. It had tubes running through the centre section.

"I'd have preferred to stay running a Brabham. We had a lot of spares from the BT28 F3 car which was interchangeable. They [Gerry and John Stanton] could have had Rodney Bloor's Brabham BT30 which had the later bodywork and it had only done one race, so it was virtually brand new. Gerry and Stanton wanted a semi-works deal, so went away and talked to Lotus Racing and got the deal they wanted. It wasn't a semi-works deal at all and then, of course, later on, Lotus Racing went bust.

"I sensed we would have problems before the season had started when I had to go up to the Lotus factory to build the car. It was supposed to be built by them, but Gerry had told them that he'd supply his own mechanic. I had to correct a lot of things which they had already done."

Gerry was in for his busiest weekend thus far over the May Bank Holiday with races at Brands Hatch and Crystal Palace. He would commute between the venues over the three days.

First up on Saturday was practice at 'the Palace' for both Formula Two and the BSCC. A far more competitive performance in F2 practice saw him qualify fifth for his heat. Catt had been hard at work on the rear suspension fitting spacers under the wishbones in an effort to raise the roll centre, and on other detailed improvements. You certainly couldn't knock the effort being put in, both in and out of the cockpit. Despite the strenuous efforts they still found themselves a second shy of polesitter, Peterson. It was the same margin as at Thruxton near on two months earlier.

The following day at Brands Hatch he was greeted by

A busy man at Crystal Palace in May. Another outing in the Capri resulted in a non-finish. While... *(Tim Marshall)*

...Better fortunes were had in the F2 race with sixth-place finishes in both his heat and the final. *(Chris Walker/Kartpix)*

torrential rain. At least in both outings, he would have a roof over his head. The first appearance was in his usual Capri in a mixed race for all types of Ford saloons. A second place to Dave Brodie's prodigiously fast and well driven 'Run Baby Run' Escort was the end result.

The second outing would be an altogether different encounter, a race for fifteen identical, standard Ford Cortina 2000GTs. The opposition was a real who's who of motorsport, ranging from former World Champions John Surtees and Graham Hill to motoring journalists Simon Taylor and Michael Bowler. Add in seasoned racers Tim Schenken, Frank Gardner, Tony Trimmer, Jody Scheckter, John Fitzpatrick, Chris Craft and top man rally man, Roger Clark, and you had a recipe for disaster. The wet weather played its part as well.

The grid was decided by drawing lots. Gerry got lucky and drew third place alongside Schenken and Gardner. Needless to say, a close, fraught race ensued with Gerry having a race-long battle with Surtees, only losing out on second place to the former champion when he took to the grass on the exit of Paddock Bend to pass him. The leading pair of Gardner and Schenken eventually had the inevitable coming together which resulted in the latter dropping to fourth place behind Gerry leaving Gardner to claim the spoils.

Thankfully, drier weather greeted Gerry on Monday back at Crystal Palace. In the F2 Championship race solid drives to sixth in both his heat and final earned him a confidence-boosting point.

The Capri outing ended in retirement with no oil pressure. Ironically, Gerry was happy with the engine performance but less so with the handling, feeling there was still work to be done in that area. Overall it had been some weekend, just like the old days at Ingliston.

A somewhat less hectic schedule was around the corner with only a couple of outings in June. Another failure to start after an engine/head gasket issue at Silverstone in the Capri was followed by a non-finish in the final at Rouen in the F2 Championship encounter after a fourth-place finish in his heat had promised much. The race at Rouen would be the last outing in F2 for several weeks, but that didn't mean Gerry would be any less busy.

The almost forgotten F3 Lotus 69 was wheeled out for its second outing of the season at Paul Ricard for the support race to the French Grand Prix. Gerry, no doubt, trying to impress the assembled F1 talent-spotters at a circuit where he had performed well in the past, unfortunately had a problem with the wheel balance weights and a flat tyre brought about his retirement before he had the chance to show well.

Due to his tireless work at Boreham, he was rewarded with the offer of a drive outside of his usual UK commitments with a drive in the Nürburgring Six Hours which was a round of the European Touring Car Championship (ETCC). He would partner quick Belgian Yvette Fontaine in a BP-backed, Belgian-entered Ford Escort RS1600. A reliable run brought them fourth place.

"We achieved an excellent result," remembers Fontaine, all these years later. "Gerry was a very nice person and a very good driver. It was a pleasure to have him as my co-driver."

Another supporting role to a grand prix was next on the agenda, this time in the Capri at Silverstone at the British Grand Prix meeting. A much-improved machine enjoyed a mostly reliable outing, work on the engine and the handling leaving Gerry far happier than of late.

This was evident in the race where he battled with the Camaros of Brian Muir and his nemesis, Martin Thomas. Despite his best efforts to relieve Thomas of second place, Gerry had to be content with a fine third place.

A visit to one of the classic race tracks was next up – as Gerry paid his first visit to Spa-Francorchamps for the annual 24-hour classic for Touring cars. In a series of firsts, he would partner Jochen Mass, drive a 24-hour race and drive a Cologne-prepared Capri. In the future, Gerry would become synonymous with all three.

The two Cologne Capris of Gerry and Mass, and Dieter

Glemser and Alex Soler-Roig, pretty much dominated proceedings for the first 12 hours as they traded first and second places constantly depending on pitstops. Gerry held his own impressively in such capable and experienced company. Disaster struck with dawn approaching when, while in the lead, the car stopped with a suspected broken crankshaft when Gerry was at the wheel.

While it was still just past the mid-point of the season, there was real momentum in Gerry's career at this time. The work with Ford was proof – if any were needed – that he was heading for the very top. He was certainly putting in the work, not just behind the wheel, but behind the scenes, forming close relationships with the management and technicians at Boreham. You don't get the opportunities that were coming his way, at that level, without showing a high degree of professionalism and dedication to the cause. The top people in such organisations are not easily impressed.

Impressed they must have been, as Gerry was offered another opportunity to represent the Cologne department a few weeks later at another enduro, this time the double Six Hours event at Paul Ricard. This event would also see him pitted against two former World Champions, Graham Hill and John Surtees. They would be out in Gerry's regular BSCC Boreham-prepared car which was equipped with many TV cameras to record their participation for posterity.

Gerry and Margaret had quite an adventure getting there, as she recalls. "Ford had given us tickets to fly there. It was probably going to be the last meeting I went to, as I was quite pregnant by then. We get to Heathrow to discover we had the wrong tickets. They were for the day before or the day after, I can't remember. Eventually, we go stand-by to Paris, then from there, we had to get to Marseilles. The problem was there was only one seat left. Luckily for me, there was this really nice German journalist who gave up his seat for me. By this time we were running late and Gerry was supposed to be there by two o'clock to start testing.

"We got to Marseilles and Ford had sent a single-engined plane that looked like a WW2 Spitfire. I had to sit in the front because there wasn't enough room in the back for me and my bump, so Gerry sat in the back with our case. The pilot arrives and puts his briefcase on the wing and got in. He starts the thing up and the briefcase falls off the wing. I was thinking 'What else has he forgotten?' Another thing was that it was rather intimidating taking off among the Air France commercial airliners.

"The pilot couldn't speak any English and he was sweating like a pig. Believe it or not, he took the plane down to read the signposts and then came back up again. Before that, he turned to me and asked, "*La mer?*" I knew he meant the sea, but I hadn't a clue what he was asking me for, so I shrugged my shoulders, just like the French! I don't know who was more relieved, him or us, when we flew over the tree line and saw the circuit. He blurts out, "*Ah, Le Ricard*," and landed the plane.

A quizzical look from Gerry, as 'SuperSwede' larks about for the accomplished lenswoman Jutta Fausel, who was a regular on the F2 circuit. ***(Jutta Fausel)***

"On more than one occasion, I honestly thought that was it, the end. Gerry didn't tell me until afterwards, that the pilot had the radio on and the sound of the radio added to the engine noise made it sound like the engine was packing in.

"Having endured all that, there was no way I was going back in that plane with him. We were telling Graham Hill about it all and he said, "Come with me, when I fly across the Channel it's like, *Tora! Tora! Tora!* This was the American/Japanese 'in' film at that time about Pearl Harbour. After hearing that, I wasn't going with him either. I was going to try and chat up the Dunlop boys and go back with them in the back of the van if I have to. I didn't care.

"I was speaking to someone afterwards and they told me that our guy had got his pilot's license from the local club or something. I thought, 'Thank you, Ford!'"

The ordeal didn't seem to affect Gerry's performance on the track when he and his partner on this occasion, Rolf Stommelen, not only out-qualified the two World Champions, but also the rest of the field to annexe pole position by nearly a second from the sister car of Glemser and Soler-Roig. None too shabby!

The race turned quickly into a question of which Capri would win. The three aforementioned pairings swapped the lead constantly, until Stommelen blotted his copybook with an off causing damage to both the bodywork and the suspension. Once repairs had been effected, Gerry was sent out to try to recover lost ground. The many assembled Ford VIPs were apparently not that impressed by the German's performance. With Gerry reportedly doing the lion's share of the driving, a recovery was achieved, climbing from 17th place at the three-hour half-distance mark to an eventual fourth by the end.

With a 12-hour break before the next race, the Ford mechanics worked tirelessly on all three machines, Gerry's car receiving a new gearbox and rebuilt front suspension. The second race saw no dramas for him and Stommelen as they won pretty comfortably from the Glemser/Soler-Roig sister car. Unfortunately for Gerry, they had finished runner-up on both occasions so claimed overall honours on aggregate, just pipping him to the spoils. But he had certainly enhanced his reputation more than did his team-mate, who would not be seen behind the wheel of a works Ford again until 1974.

In between the two Capri outings, Gerry had twice been to Sweden for Formula Two meetings. A sixth-place finish in the championship round at Mantorp Park was followed by fifth in the non-championship race at Kinnekullering. By that stage of the season, those were the sort of results that both car and driver could realistically achieve.

It was back closer to home for the busy August Bank Holiday meeting at Brands Hatch, where Gerry would run in both the F2 and BSCC races.

Another fifth place was achieved in the F2 encounter despite the car having undergone further modifications to the rear suspension and new brakes on all four corners. It seemed that, no matter what Gerry and John Catt tried, the car had just simply run out of development.

The latest modifications had been carried out by Catt after a brief flirtation with the recently formed Group Racing Services (GRS). "When Lotus Racing pulled out, we knew we were on our own," recalls Catt. "We were trying everything to keep up. A lot of the ex-Lotus people had formed GRS, so we took the car up to their place in Norfolk to see if they could help. It was no better. I think Gerry was getting a bit demoralised by this time. I wouldn't say he gave up. I just think he knew he was on a losing wicket with that car."

Now that's how to take a corner in a Capri! ***(Jeff Bloxham)***

In an interview with journalist and friend Graham Gauld, Gerry offered his thoughts on the closure of Lotus Racing and its subsequent knock-on effects. "I had a contract with Lotus Racing to carry out all the development on my F2 car and that's why the F2 didn't develop. The contract I had with them for F3 was really good money, as well. Then, of course, I did the one race and that was the end of that, Lotus Racing closes down and stops trading.

"All we had was our spares, so it was a case of, 'it's up to you, mate'. I was very open about what I thought of Lotus Racing. With all this going on, Stanton was getting a bit concerned. It was really a case of knowing that if I wrote the thing off, that was the end of F2 for the season, so I had to be slightly careful.

"I actually got compensation out of Chapman when Lotus Racing closed down. I actually think Chapman's a good guy, but you've got to be careful because he's not. He's a fantastic con-man. I don't think he particularly rates me because Fittipaldi doesn't rate me either," concludes Gerry, with his tongue firmly in his cheek.

While his Formula Two fortunes were on a seemingly downward slope, things were looking up on the Capri front with further improvements in the handling department pleasing Gerry, and enabling him to qualify on the outside of the front row for the BSCC race alongside season-long rivals, John Fitzpatrick and Brian Muir. The first corner promised to be interesting, and indeed it was. Gerry made the best start of the three and was almost into Paddock Bend when he was nudged in the rear end and sent spinning by Muir. Chaos ensued as Gerry was facing the wrong way with the pack screaming towards him. Luckily they all missed him and he was able to limp around to the pits for repairs. He did restart, but a gearbox oil leak would bring about his retirement.

With the season drawing to its conclusion, all that was left on the F2 schedule was another three overseas races. None of them were notable for any performances on the track, but memories are still pretty vivid for a couple of team members and a journalist covering his first F2 race.

The trip to Albi in France for a championship round resulted in Gerry failing to qualify due to running out of fuel in practice. "That was down to me," offers Catt. "In fact, it is something I'd like to forget. Thanks for reminding me!

"In my defence, we were misinformed. We were told that the session would last for 30 minutes when, in fact, they carried on for 40 minutes. Because the car was so heavy, we had discussed running with the minimum amount of fuel to save weight. By the time the 30 minutes were up I was getting worried, then Gerry failed to come round. He was a bit pissed off, understandably. That was the one time when, I suppose, I let him down.

"I do remember Ron Dennis, who was at Rondel Racing at the time, being very good that day. He invited me to their pits, seeing how annoyed and upset I was."

Paul Watson's report in *Autosport* backs up John's story by describing practice as being 'disgracefully organised'.

The next F2 race was a non-championship affair at Hockenheim. A second-row starting position was achieved not only by Gerry's driving but also by a clever little tweak by his faithful mechanic. "When we were in F3 we used to filter all the rubbish out of the petrol through a leather cloth," reflects Catt. "It was unbelievable what rubbish we used to collect. Even the Shell guys couldn't believe it.

"Due to it being so hot in practice the majority of the runners were suffering from misfires at the top end. I remembered something Brian Hart had told me about removing some of the filters from the mechanical and electric fuel pumps, and also from the inside of the metering unit on very hot days because they created air bubbles. But to be able to do that, you had to have fuel that was spotless, hence the cloth came out again.

"It worked like a dream. Most of the runners were getting to the end of the straights and the engine would start going, *brrp, brrp, brrp*, and Gerry would go past them sounding sweet. By the end of practice, I had loads of mechanics coming up to me and asking why our engine wasn't misfiring like theirs.

"Gerry and I decided to have a little fun at their expense and came up with a plan. I had an old water hose from the Transit, you know, one of the elbows. I stuck it with tank tape to the side of the tub so that the air would rush in through the bend in the hose and blow over the mechanical fuel pump. It didn't take long for cars to start appearing with scoops and all sorts, copying our 'tweak' The thing was, much to our amusement, they were still misfiring and they couldn't understand it. Surprise, surprise.

"This is the best part. We were on the grid and just before I had to leave Gerry gives me the nod and I pull off the rubber hose. Everyone's looking going, *what the...?* We were killing ourselves laughing by then. Gerry really enjoyed that."

Come the race, a most bizarre reason caused him to have to pit early on. The opposition, who had failed to see the funny side of the joke with the hose, might have called this some sort of justice. "Unfortunately, for some reason, Gerry had turned on the red light at the back and it started to short out," remembers Catt. "The aluminium bracket holding the light had broken with all the vibration and was shorting out on the gearbox and was causing a misfire. Typical, we'd cured the misfire and now this. He came into the pits. I noticed what had happened, wrenched it off, leant in the cockpit and said something like 'It's a problem with the light. Go!'

"By this time, he was a lap down. But he carried on racing with the leading bunch until he eventually backed off. I think he ended up in seventh place."

Reporting on the race for *Motoring News* was the now well-known, prolific author, Ian Wagstaff. He recalls how that came to be: "It was my first year at *Motor Sport/Motoring News* and I was due to report on a Silverstone clubbie. On Friday lunchtime Alan Henry, who covered the majority of F2 races, fell ill so I was told to take his place reporting on the race at Hockenheim.

"My only previous trips abroad had been with school to Paris but that evening, still wearing the clothes I had gone to work in and with just a pen, notebook and new passport, I found myself on the last PanAm flight of the day to Frankfurt. I eventually found my hotel at about three in the morning.

"Later that morning I went down to breakfast, not knowing even how I would find the track. Sitting in the corner of the breakfast room were a couple of chaps, one much larger than the other. The smaller of the two I recognised as Gerry Birrell from his photos. I tentatively approached them, said who I was and asked how to get to the track.

"From then on Gerry and the other chap, his entrant John Stanton, were kindness itself and helped me through the weekend. I first followed them to the circuit – not easy. I was in a knackered hire car, a VW Beetle, Gerry in a 3.0-litre Ford-tuned Capri.

"After practice they insisted on driving around the countryside with me (cramped in the back of the Capri) to try and find somewhere I could buy toothpaste etc – not easy in those days on a Saturday afternoon in Germany. I distinctly recall at one point Gerry clasped the steering wheel between his legs and proceeded to don his seatbelt. 'Lookout!' warned John Stanton. 'Birrell's about to drive fast.'

"Another memory of Gerry from that meeting is of him telling me after the race that at one point he had found himself behind Wilson Fittipaldi and Dieter Quester, who were contesting second place, and that they were bouncing off each other like saloon car drivers around the very fast, outer part of the circuit.

"I never saw Gerry again, but John became a lifelong friend."

The final words on the eventful time at Hockenheim belong to Gerry's large friend. "When Gerry was driving the Capri with Ian in the back, he was so relaxed," recalls Stanton. "It just confirmed what I already knew. He was one hell of a driver. The downside to that journey was that I knew that when we stopped, I was going to be ill. I got out pretty sharpish and found the nearest loo and was indeed violently sick."

A rather long trip to Vallelunga was the last stop on the F2 trail and one that didn't go according to plan, as Margaret recalls. "John Catt was taken ill and had to come home. The problem was that Gerry had his car out there, so he asked me to fly out and bring his car back, while he brought the transporter back.

"Another problem was that when I got to the airport they wouldn't let me fly because I was then six months pregnant. I remember grabbing one of the journalists and asking him to sign this form saying he was my husband. He did seem a little shocked, but signed it anyway.

"I got out there and followed him back in the car. I think we stopped at Mont Blanc, and then went on to Calais. Another

At the October Brands Hatch meeting marred by the tragic death of Jo Siffert, Gerry claimed his first win in the Capri after a difficult season beset by mechanical issues. ***(Peter Carey)***

one of the crazy things we did. We just got on with it. My mother didn't know half of what was going on. Just as well, really!"

While Gerry may have had problems off-track, at least his performance was an improvement on recent outings. A fifth-place finish brought the curtain down on what had been a long, frustrating, and for the most part, hugely disappointing F2 campaign. There had certainly been lessons learned, all of which would for sure be put to good use in the future.

"I didn't enjoy '71 with the Lotus," offers Catt. "It was hard work."

The outing at Vallelunga would see the end of John Stanton's two-year involvement with Gerry, but there wasn't any falling out.

"Many people have asked me why did I spend all that money," offers Stanton. "That's so easy to answer. They were the best two years of my life. It was so worthwhile to spend that money. I could have bought some property and made some money, but that's boring.

"I was never a hands-on sponsor. My knowledge was very limited. Why would I interfere and say why are you running those tyre pressures or what have you? Both Gerry and John Catt knew what they were doing. You put your trust in the right people. John Catt was a great guy. His workload was enormous.

"All my dealings with Gerry were straightforward. His honesty and integrity were beyond reproach. I had complete trust in him. He never once let me down. He was a super guy.

"The only reason I stopped was that I had spent so much and couldn't go on the way I had been doing. F2 was expensive and would only get more and more expensive in the years ahead. I have absolutely no regrets. Like I said, the best two years of my life."

One more outing in the Capri would close this long season for Gerry. It would be at Brands Hatch as support to the non-championship F1 race organised to honour the World Championship success of both Jackie Stewart and Ken Tyrrell. Sadly, what was billed as a celebration turned out to be one of the saddest days ever at the circuit when the likeable and supremely talented Jo Siffert perished after his car burst into flames after a high-speed accident while approaching Hawthorn's Bend.

"We could see loads of smoke from where we were in the pit lane," remembers Margaret. "It was like a bomb had gone off. My first thought was that someone had died in that.

"And then, everyone just sat around and waited for the next race. It was weird. How can you go out and race when somebody's been killed? Different times..."

The saloon car race involving Gerry was to follow the Formula One race. After a lengthy delay following the clean-up operation after the accident, the race got under way.

While a subdued affair might have been expected, when the three front runners were Gerry, Frank Gardner and John Fitzpatrick, that was never going to be the case. They put on a cracking show for the spectators that had remained, until the inevitable happened at half distance.

Reporting on the race for *Motoring News* was Jeremy Walton. "I, like the crowd and media, was enthralled as the race unfolded. Gerry hung on grimly to the fiercest scrap seen all year between John Fitzpatrick's comparatively diminutive but fabulously agile Broadspeed 1700 Escort RS and Frank Gardner's enormous SCA freight Chevrolet Camaro. 'Fitz' kept harrying the leading big Chevrolet until, as Gerry recalled to me immediately after the race: 'They just started bangin' inta each other. I couldn't believe my eyes...John was actually trying to out-barge Frank in that big yank tank!' Suddenly cars were cartwheelin' everywhere. I didna know if I was the wrong way up, or they were right, or the other way about!' While Gerry was telling me all of this he was grinning from ear to ear, in convulsions of laughter."

The cause of the accident was that Fitzpatrick and Gardner had made contact at Stirling's Bend which had taken a chunk out of one of Gardner's wheels. When the pair were side by side heading towards Clearways, the tyre came off the damaged wheel and spun Gardner into Fitzpatrick's car. Fitzpatrick ended up cartwheeling down the track while Gardner hit the bridge parapet. While all this was going on, Gerry somehow threaded his way through the carnage. The Fitzpatrick and Gardner wrecks blocked the track, resulting in the rest of the field having to wait until a path was cleared. All this left Gerry with a huge lead, one that he would retain to the chequered flag.

As far as racing was concerned that was it after another super-busy year. If there had been a championship for sheer effort, time behind the wheel and involvement in racing on an everyday basis, then Gerry would surely have taken its crown.

The Birrells at home. The lampshade is so '70s. Margaret remembers they had orange velvet curtains to match! ***(Unknown)***

The season on the whole was a disappointing and frustrating one, with only two victories, well below Gerry's usual tally. But he never seemed to lose that innate enthusiasm and sheer dedication at any stage through the long campaign. The comments from his close-knit team, friends and rivals are a testament to a temperament that never went to the extremes of tantrums and sheer elation, but just seemed to stay on an even keel. It's often said that nice guys, ultimately, don't get to the top of their chosen profession. It seems that one, Gerry Birrell Esq, was out to prove that the nice guy can sometimes go all the way to the very top.

Helping him behind the scenes in his quest to reach the summit was Stuart Turner, who paid a visit to a modest lock-up garage in Romford that was a hive of activity. Taking shape inside was an ambitious new Formula One challenger which was the work of former Surtees designer Peter Connew. "Stuart came to see towards the end of '71," recalls Connew. "He was very pro-Gerry. He said he couldn't help us out money-wise, but could help out with parts. I did need a couple of the latest Escort steering racks, so I was straight down there. Boreham wasn't that far. We ended up making our own casings for the rack and pinion to go in.

"Gerry came down soon after, but we were looking for a driver with money/sponsorship and he didn't have any, unfortunately. He would have been the ideal driver to help us develop the car."

With that door seemingly closed, another one swung open, albeit, only slightly. Robin Herd and Max Mosley of March were scouting around for potential drivers to partner their star man Peterson. Gerry's Formula Two performances in inferior machinery against the works March of 'SuperSwede' had reportedly not gone unnoticed. Disappointingly, as before, money was the issue. More so when a certain young Austrian appeared with a bag full of schillings courtesy of an Austrian bank, and took the drive. Whatever happened to him?

In an interview with Graham Gauld in early 1972, Gerry makes no mention of the above opportunities, but does offer the opinion that the only Formula One drive worth considering is in a car painted blue!

While most of his rivals thought of sunnier climes by jetting off to Brazil for the Temporada series in November and December, Gerry would be found in the forests of the UK doing recce work for Ford on the RAC Rally. He would run about three hours ahead, assessing conditions in the area. His job was to see what it was like on the entry and exit to the stages, ask marshals what they thought about the conditions, and then report back. Sounds like glamorous work!

Another far more important reason for him to be at home or, at least, near home, was to support Margaret, who was due to give birth to their first child early in the new year. But Gerry's idea of support was different to that of most of the world's male population. As we would hear in his venture into journalism in the first weeks of January, he was hardly ever at home.

CHAPTER SEVEN

CONSOLIDATION AND PROGRESSION

Part One

For 1972 Gerry would again be seen in Formula Two, this time with the latest offering from March, and he would continue his association with the Ford Motor Company. The Ford deal, in particular, was the one that would keep him away from home for the longest periods. With an expanded race programme involving more races on the continent that also included rally reconnaissance work, promotional work, fitness training camps and the main development driving role for the new RS2000 Escort. Throw in driving a Ford Transit van at Monza for 24 hours, and you could probably count the number of days he would spend at home on the fingers of one hand and still have digits to spare!

If that wasn't enough, he would write a regular column – ghost-written by journalist Chris Witty – for the new racing magazine *Competition Car*. The first of the 11 columns appeared in the March issue of '72, the last in May '73. To be able to quote first-hand from Gerry gives a unique insight into the mind of a racing driver at that time. No apology is made for the extensive use of the content contained in the short-lived magazine. The columns give detailed and comprehensive coverage on a whole manner of topics, some of which are quite revealing and controversial. He certainly wasn't afraid to speak his mind on subjects close to his heart. They were just another example of Gerry, the complete professional, not missing a trick to publicise not just his career, but also his sponsors, to give them maximum exposure. As in the past, one could sense the influence of Jackie Stewart.

The first highlight of the year was most certainly not racing related. Gerry had become a proud father of two girls after Margaret gave birth in late January.

Kara and Maija were not typical names for girls in Scotland, or anywhere else, at that time. "Maija was named after a Latvian girl I worked with in the States and with whom I'm still friends," explains Margaret. "Gerry and I had hung out with her and her husband, Aviars, when Gerry came across to visit me for my 21st birthday in '68. We also hung out with them when we went to Sebring for a race meeting after we were married and went back to Boston to visit them before going home. Kara was a Dutch version of Claire. My mother pointed out if we ever returned to Glasgow she would be called 'Clayerrr', pronounced with a Glasgow accent!"

Three attempts aren't necessary to guess where Gerry was.

"The twins were born on 27 January," recalls Margaret. "They came three weeks early, and Gerry was in Monte Carlo doing a recce for Ford for the upcoming rally. They kindly sent him back the following day, or it could have been the day after, for 24 hours to see them. I was surprised to see him as I wasn't forewarned. He announced to me then he'd give me time to recuperate and then we'd have a boy. My sense of humour failed me at that point. You can imagine my answer! They kept you in hospital for seven days in that era.

"Males in my generation were not expected to do so much with the kids as they are now. He soon found out when we all got home what was required. Plus, we had the three-day working week then so electricity was only on for three hours at a time. Such joy! I'm sure he was delighted to get back to racing once the season started."

In *Competition Car*, Gerry's only mention of the happy event was in the last paragraph of a lengthy two-page piece: 'Oh, yes. My wife Margaret also gave birth to twin girls, so it was quite an eventful start to the new year!'

Before the mention of becoming a father, he seemed more interested in telling the readers what he'd been up to since the start of that January.

'I had great fun in Monte Carlo doing ice notes for Ford for the upcoming rally. I was partnered up with Gunnar Palm, co-driver of the winning car on the London-Mexico rally. We got kitted up with a very basic Escort Sport belonging to Ford France, equipped with Dunlop snow tyres with 600 studs per wheel!

'My ambition through the whole week was to try to get rubber on the road because the car just sat up on the spikes! Our first job was to go and have a look at a stage up near Monte, where I had my first taste of having pace notes read to me.

'Well, I reckon this rally driving's all a con. They go on about race drivers knowing what's around the corner. Well, these guys have got a bloke who tells them and what's more he

A delighted couple holding their new arrivals. Gerry is holding Maija. *(Ford Motor Company)*

tells them when there are little bits of snow and little bits of ice as well! We don't get told if there's a patch of oil around the corner, we've got to rely on some guy with a flag to wave it at us!'

Either Gerry had forgotten all about his rallying exploits in the past, both behind the wheel, or in the passenger seat or he'd got his tongue very firmly in his cheek. Probably the latter.

Palm had obviously worked with the very best, Ove Andersson, Timo Mäkinen and Hannu Mikkola, the pick of them. Plus, he had won the 'Monte' in 1963 alongside the great Swede, Erik Carlsson, so was not easily impressed despite Gerry's attempts to do so.

'We'd gone over this one particular stage up near Grenoble nearly three or four times,' Gerry, continued in *Competition Car*. 'The road was covered with snow and I was having a real go, sliding the car from side to side and me thinking I'm getting good at this. Because we'd been over the stage so many times, Gunnar wasn't reading any pace notes. Towards the end of the stage, I turned to Gunnar to ask him what he thought and he was sound asleep! That really knocked the wind out of my sails. Every so often he would wake up and say, "Watch the right-handers, watch the right-handers." Then he'd go back to sleep.'

While Palm didn't seem that impressed with Gerry's driving abilities, Gerry was clearly impressed with Palm's pace note reading skills, as he continued: 'It was a terrific experience to be with someone like Gunnar. He just knew when to read the pace notes at the right time, just when the corner was coming up. If there was a long straight, he wouldn't say a word until the point where I was having to start to think about positioning the car. It was surprising how a really good co-driver could speed up a driver.'

After having had what seemed a great time, the conclusion to their time left Gerry a tad disgruntled as he concluded: 'We were taking it easy on one of the back roads coming down the hill into Monte Carlo, when this guy in a Triumph Spitfire gets all tweaked up, as Spitfires do, comes skating across the road, and his rear-end smashes us into a wall. There was very nearly a punch-up with this irate Frenchman. The car didn't survive much longer though because one of the mechanics flipped it end-over-end in Paris on the way home.'

Upon his return from his French adventures, it was time to start planning for the season ahead. First up were his Formula Two plans, which he outlined exclusively in a recorded interview with trusted journalist Graham Gauld. "We are guaranteed £3500 from Coca-Cola with another £500 through the year. We've got £1750 from Castrol and I can get £1500 from Sports Motors if I want it. We'll be running under the Sports Motors name, but running our own show. The illustrious John Catt is on board for another year, and I'm looking to find someone to give him a hand.

The other side to being an up-and-coming racing driver. It's a dirty job, but... *(Ford Motor Company)*

"I've got a deal with Brian Hart for my engines. Brian, as far as I'm concerned, is the only person I would go to for an engine. I don't have to buy the engines, just hire them. The engines are going to be so important this year. It's not just a case of everyone running an FVA, like last year. Hopefully, Brian's development alloy block engine will be homologated by mid-season. You can only get them from him because he owns all the castings etc. The alloy one will be the one to have, so I've made sure I'm in there.

"I've got a deal with March to buy the prototype first chassis. It will be all rebuilt before the start of the season with some improvements we've found. I was quietly hired by them to do some testing while everyone else was away in Brazil at the Temporada. As soon as I drove it for the first time, it made me think again that perhaps it wasn't me after all last year. Maybe the reason I couldn't go quickly in Formula Two was that I just didn't suit the Lotus. The March is frighteningly quick already. Far, far better than the Lotus. It puts the power on the road so well, it's a different driving style altogether.

"It looks as though March has got me a deal with Goodyear. I've been trying really hard with the Dunlop racing department to get the directors to change their minds to produce tyres for Formula Two, but they won't back me up. I can't waste my time with them."

After outlining his Formula Two plans, Gerry continued excitedly to talk about a small part of his Ford programme: "The new Escort thing. Which is an absolute device of the first degree. What a machine. You name it, it's got it."

On the limit in the highly-modified Escort. *(Christian Sandler)*

To hear Gerry talk on tape is an absolute delight. Back then, unlike today, you very rarely heard drivers talk. The TV coverage was minimal. If any races – mainly the British Grand Prix – were shown, you just saw highlights of the race, never any pre- or post-race interviews. And the coverage wouldn't always be kept for posterity due to the high costs of the film. Journalists such as Graham Gauld would record interviews that would be used for magazine or book purposes,

Graham Gauld's son, Lance, sits at the controls of the go-kart built for him by Gerry. ***(Graham Gauld/SMRC)***

Trying it out. ***(Graham Gauld/SMRC)***

but would never be aired in public. Again, as with Gerry's written columns, the recordings give a unique insight.

Graham's name crops up on a regular basis because he'd been around, seemingly, forever. He's most famous for his friendship with the incomparable Jim Clark. But he has done so much more. The author of numerous books, he has travelled the world unearthing racing stories, helped out at Ingliston, and is one of the stalwarts, not just of Scottish motorsport, but of motorsport worldwide.

He enjoyed a close friendship with Gerry and would hang out with him, and the other assorted members of the Scottish motor racing scene, on a fairly regular basis at the many dinners and sporting club get-togethers which were prevalent at that time.

From his many memories, one in particular stands out involving Graham's young son, Lance. "Gerry was a very nice guy and he used to come over to the house when we lived in Pollokshields, which is in the southside of Glasgow.

"Lance, who was about six years old at the time, had one of those carts with foot pedals but the wheels were too small and too weak to use on the rough grassy patches around where we lived. So Gerry stiffened it up, modified it with a pair of full-size pram wheels for the rear, which would have come from Graham, who was the agent for Royale Baby Carriages. He fitted a pair of industrial barrow wheels for the front. The finishing touch was a piece of aluminium for streamlining. Lance and I used to set up a ramp on a bit of rough ground near us and he would shoot down the hill, and off the ramp. Gerry was so good with Lance."

It certainly seemed like all the ingredients were in place for an even busier year, if that was possible.

As Margaret has alluded to earlier, Gerry wasted no time in leaving her with their new arrivals when he was off again to the South of France to begin testing his new potent Escort at Paul Ricard. The choice of venue was chosen not just for it being an ideal test track to shake down new machinery, but also for the climate. But this time the latter let him down. It more or less rained for the entire duration of the test, rendering it unproductive mainly because the car was so new that the team didn't have any wet tyres to fit the new larger wheels.

Gerry did do some laps on slicks when the track was still a bit on the damp side and found that, due to the new compounds, he was able to lap a couple of seconds off the pace of the Cologne Capris on wets. After the usual new car niggles, the test was finally curtailed when a gasket blew on the oil pump which spewed oil on to the track. That caused an overreaction from the inexperienced marshals, as Gerry recounted in *Competition Car*. 'The marshals they have there, for which we were paying all this money to hire the track, are not really that bright. I think they must have shipped them in from Morocco or somewhere! There were dozens of them. They'd obviously heard that what you do is put cement, or is it sand, or something like that, down on the oil. So anyhow, these guys go out and promptly shovelled, literally, about half a hundredweight of sand onto the oil which completely ruined the track.'

An alternative venue was sought but things didn't go to plan, as Gerry explained further. 'Len Bailey, one of the design brains behind our Escort, had been paddling about down at Ricard, as he does, complaining that it never rains at Goodwood. So we arranged to set off for some more testing and yes, you've guessed it, we sat there and watched the puddles fill up!'

Yet more testing woes were encountered after John Coombs, the legendary entrant and proprietor of Coombs of Guildford, asked Gerry to give their new F2 March a run at Silverstone. He explains in *Competition Car* how the day came to an expensive end. 'It was a damp, nasty morning. The track was drying and with about 20 minutes to go before they stopped for lunch, John asked me to give it a run until they stopped me. I was taking it very gingerly, but John thought I was going a bit too quick too soon, so he signalled from the pits for me to slow down. I looked up at him and then looked

The works contracted Ford drivers for 1972 gather in St Moritz, the venue for the first fitness training camp. From left to right: Larrousse, Mass, Gerry, Stuck, Team Manager Neerpasch, fitness instructor Traub, Bourgoignie, Soler-Roig and Glemser. ***(Ford Motor Company)***

A soaked Gerry climbs out of his March at Oulton Park. Typical Good Friday weather. ***(John McTavish)***

down again to see – no oil pressure! So I promptly abandoned everything. Alas, the oil pump had stopped rotating and that was the end of that.

'Brian Hart has always said that you've got three seconds to switch off an FVA or FVC when it's revving or that's it. I didn't hear a bang, but unfortunately I don't think I caught it in time before the crank and rods were damaged.' The joys of being a racing driver, or a team owner.

After all the aforementioned testing problems, Gerry would have been looking forward to going racing. The first outing would be the opening round of the European F2 Championship at Mallory Park in mid-March. But as he recounted in *Competition Car* he would fail to attend when something supposedly to his benefit rendered him hors de combat: 'Just before Mallory Park, I went over to St Moritz in Switzerland where Ford of Germany was organising a keep-fit session for their drivers. It was all very well for people like Dieter Glemser, Hans Stuck, Jochen Mass and all the other Germans, but I wasn't used to the altitude and, within two days, I was back home feeling dreadful. It transpired that I had caught some sort of bug and my temperature had gone right off the clock!"

The fitness camps at St Moritz were a ground-breaking initiative in motorsport from, firstly, Ford of Germany, instigated by the team manager Jochen Neerpasch (who left shortly afterwards to take up a similar position at rival BMW, who soon followed suit with their own training camps) and his inner circle and were overseen by the then world ice skating champion Gunther Traub. They encompassed an in-depth look not just at the fitness, but also the diets of all the contracted Ford drivers.

"The diet thing was ridiculous," recalls Margaret. "He came back with a list of things he couldn't eat and at the top of the list was eggs. I started laughing and said something like, "For God's sake, you're going out dicing with death every weekend and you can't eat an egg."

The perception is that such matters were something that is associated with modern racing. The fact that these important elements of a driver's performance were being monitored nearly 50 years ago is extremely impressive on the part of the global car manufacturer.

Fully recovered, Gerry headed to Monza for Ford duties with the debut of the Escort in the opening round of the European Touring Car Championship (ETCC). In the four-hour race he shared the car with the Belgian Claude Bourgoignie, a new Ford recruit but an old adversary he knew from their days together in FF1600 and F3.

They seemed to make an evenly matched pairing, coming home a fine third overall and first in class despite a puncture in the closing stages that dropped them from second. They had put on a terrific show up against the more powerful 2.8-litre BMWs and 2.9-litre Capris. It helped that they had one of Brian Hart's F2 1860cc Ford BDAs under the bonnet, which, to quote Gerry from *Competition Car*, 'Was an absolute flyer.'

He finally got his F2 campaign underway with a busy double-header over the long Easter weekend. Oulton Park on Good Friday for the opening round of the British Championship was followed by Thruxton on Saturday and Monday for Round 2 of the European.

At Oulton Park, whether it was dry, damp or very wet, Gerry was mixing it with the likes of Lauda, Schenken, Surtees et al. Contrary to what he'd said in pre-season about Dunlops not being interested, he'd managed to talk them into bringing along some of their 'demon' wets that he'd used on the Capri the previous year.

The start of the race was delayed a while everyone had to change to wet tyres following a sudden downpour on the

Now that's how to take the Parabolica at Monza. The first time out in the Group 2 Escort brought a third-place finish overall and a first in class. *(Josef Mayrhofer)*

warming-up laps. With the late arrival of the rain, most runners had to run with a compromised set-up. In Gerry's case, that was dry settings with wet Dunlops.

In *Competition Car* he revealed: 'I made a complete boob of the start by starting in third. I was so mad that I had passed four cars between the first and second corners, to lie fifth.'

That wouldn't be the only time during the race he would manage that misdemeanour. He also spun at Island Bend, after he again selected third gear instead of the intended first. Add in a visor that kept misting up due to him not having cleaned it with a demisting cloth due to the panic with the tyres, and it was an eventful outing.

Despite all the dramas, a good recovery drive earned him a second-place finish, albeit a long way behind Lauda's March. His cause was helped with many of the other fancied runners having problems in the dreadful conditions, notably Schenken whose Brabham he passed for the runner-up spot with a couple of laps remaining. In *Competition Car* he said: 'When I saw it was Schenken ahead, it gave me a real incentive. Passing him turned out to be no great feat, he'd got a puncture.' There was no time to celebrate the decent result, however, as a long trek to Thruxton was necessary immediately after the race with the first practice session being held the next morning.

Having tested there earlier in the season Gerry had a good set-up on the car and wound up second quickest behind Reutemann in qualifying for his heat. This was despite doing a limited number of laps in a bid to save engine mileage. While obviously delighted with his performance against such illustrious names, his joy was short-lived when according to Ian Phillips in *Autosport*: 'Gerry was none too pleased after he saw the times from the other heat because he was so much slower than Peterson.' It was no disgrace being slower than the flying 'SuperSwede', who was over two seconds quicker than everybody. Needless to say, he would carry that advantage forward by winning both his heat and the final comfortably.

Gerry started from pole position following the serious ankle-breaking accident that befell Reutemann at the end of qualifying that rendered him a non-starter. Gerry led initially from Lauda and Carlos Pace's Pygmée but was soon suffering from excessive oversteer caused by a defective shock absorber, and one of his Firestone tyres began to shred badly. They both overtook, but Pace's retirement promoted him to an eventual second position.

Frantic work ensued to cure the handling issues in time for the final. The Firestones were swapped for Goodyears and the Armstrong shock absorbers to Konis. Drastic problems call for drastic remedies. Initially, all seemed well but then the oversteer returned, as there had been insufficient time to change the suspension settings to suit the different tyres. Despite this, Gerry maintained a creditable fourth place behind the flying Peterson, Cevert and Lauda, all of whom were in March 722s.

Disappointingly, his race would end in retirement on lap 38 of the 50 when the water temperature began to climb to the danger zone. Wisely, he switched off to save engine damage. Adding to his disappointment was that had he managed to come home fourth, he would have been rewarded with the nine points for the win, being the first non-graded driver home. The F2 rules at the time prevented 'graded' drivers, such as Peterson, Cevert and Lauda who all had F1 experience, from scoring championship points.

A somewhat unusual diversion was next up when Gerry found himself down at Monza driving a Ford Transit for a week! Well, not exactly for the whole week. He was part of a crew of drivers who were doing stints conducting reliability tests on the new van and engine. Ford certainly kept him busy as he went from the sublime – racing and developing Escorts – to the ridiculous – thrashing Transit vans around the decrepit Monza banking.

To relieve the boredom, when the two vans were circulating together they would end up racing one another, much to the dismay of the assembled Ford personnel and the FIA officials. These were supposed to be reliability tests, after all. But get any racing driver behind the wheel of anything and he will go balls out! The task of keeping to a sensible speed was made all but impossible with the presence of, to quote Gerry in *Competition Car*: 'A certain young German driver, Hans Stuck, who while passing a van on the banking, was waving madly out of the side window. To the horror of the other driver, me, as the van gradually eased past I saw Stuck waving out of the back window having climbed over the large fuel tank in the back. By this time he was at least 15 feet from the steering wheel!' Racing drivers...

After all that joviality, it was back to serious racing with the F2 car at the contrasting venues of the Nürburgring and Pau. Both outings brought more engine problems.

At the Nürburgring a camshaft broke, destroying the top half of the engine, after only a few laps of practice. With no spare engine and with nobody willing to hire them a replacement, despite the valiant attempts of Gerry and John Catt, it was left to Gerry to head back to England and to Brian Hart's, to try to fix the problem while John headed off to Pau. With only a week between races, it was going to take a superhuman effort to be ready in time for practice around the French streets.

The fact that the car was ready to go in time for the first practice session is a testament to what a formidable pairing Gerry and John were. It looked like all the hard work would be rewarded when Gerry showed a good turn of speed in the rebuilt car in his heat by coming home in third place behind Lauda and runaway victor, Patrick Depailler.

Gerry leads the similar March of Niki Lauda into the chicane during his impressive showing. ***(Chris Walker/Kartpix)***

In the final, though, there was yet another headgasket problem. This occurred quite a way before half-distance, which was when money for completing half the race and the starting money and expenses was paid out. So to claim much-needed funds, Gerry motored slowly around and completed enough laps – 48 of the 70 – to collect the French Francs.

While in previous seasons the sole responsibility of preparing and transporting the car to all corners of the UK and Europe had been Catt's, with the occasional assistance from Gerry, this year due to Gerry's extra commitments with Ford and matters at home, he had, as promised, hired an extra pair of hands.

"I got the job with Gerry despite having no qualifications as a mechanic," remembers John McTavish. "In my favour was that my younger brother, Bruce, had worked with Gerry on his Formula Vee and FF1600 cars and I was at a bit of a loose end at the time. My role was very much that of a 'gofer'. A car came with the job, an old, worn-out Ford Anglia. This may even have seen prior service as one of Gerry's race cars.

"I guess most young men would have given their right arm to be doing what I was doing, something Ronnie Grant wasn't shy in letting me know as he told me how lucky I was. Because I had just completed National Service as an army officer and had spent a winter in Switzerland skiing, then my true passion, I wasn't shy in making it clear I thought luck had nothing to do with it. However, we must have got on well because I recall being his gofer on a couple of occasions when he was racing. We were based some of the time in Ronnie's railway arch in Clapham which was the base for his taxi business. Ronnie was a character!"

Describing Grant thus is akin to describing Jim Clark as someone who could drive a bit. There is insufficient space here to do the man justice. If you have a keen interest in what it was like to go motor racing in the '60s, '70s and '80s as a privateer and in someone who has lived a life and a half, use a search engine of your choice to check out the great man.

"I first met Gerry when we were both doing Formula Vee," remembers Ronnie. "He went off to do FF1600 and F3 and kept the car in North Street, Clapham, while I stayed in Vee and Super Vee. When I was winning in Vee, he used to say, 'You're winning more bloody races than me!'

"He asked if he could garage the F2 car with me at Clapham North. I had the truck, which we painted, and the car in the middle arch. We made a concrete flat patch so they (Gerry and John Catt) could set the cars up. He would come around with Margaret. Sometimes with other people. I remember Tim Schenken being one of them. James Hunt had a little Mini we used to look after.

"I had an engine hoist and I can remember Gerry standing on it, sort of, rocking on it, arguing with Margaret about who was going to pay for lunch in the Bedford Arms, which was across the road from the garage. It was typical of those two. They would argue who was going to pay for this, etc... Typical Scots. Margaret is a very strong lady. Very black and white."

"As for us arguing about who was paying for lunch... I can't remember that," she offers in response. "It was more like banter as I was the one earning a salary and must have been keeping Gerry on his toes until he had a salary on paper so we could get a mortgage. We were still renting in those days. So Ronnie's probably right about me being headstrong! And, yes, I am black and white.

"Gerry and I stayed with Ronnie for a short time after we got married while we were looking for another flat to rent. That was while Gerry was building the Crosslé Formula Fords at Woolers."

Another member of the Grant family who has fond memories of Gerry and Margaret is Ronnie's son, George. "I knew Gerry from when I was about eight years old, which would have been in 1969," he recalls. "I was just a little kid and I was sort of in awe of him.

"He was incredibly close to dad and I could see that as I was growing up. It's a very sensitive time in a kid's life, you are very impressionable at that age. To me, he was a very, very special person. I don't know why, but he had this incredible calmness about him. As a kid, he was almost like, next to your dad, of course, a young superman.

"There are lots of things I can remember specifically. I had a fantastic poster of Gerry on my bedroom wall. Either, Gerry or dad got it for me, it was a lovely thing. We would play with my Scalextric. He also gave me a beautiful Garrard watch, which had 'Gerry Birrell – GT Commander's Cup' engraved on the rear. I have no idea what that was. I took it to school and I broke it. I never saw it again. That is a big regret. I wish, in one respect, he'd never given it to me or dad had kept it and just put it away. That's life, I suppose.

"Gerry was the first professional sportsman I met. When he came to the Bedford Arms for lunch, dad would say, 'Gerry, doesn't drink because he's a professional racing driver.' He used to drink Coca-Cola. In those days, it was the sort of drink that was fashionable. When he was sponsored by Coca-Cola, somehow he got hold of a load of material. It just appeared. A friend of ours made me a suit. Jacket and trousers. I only remember the trousers, which were flared. They were the loudest looking trousers ever. Just imagine a white background with Coco-Cola all over it. It was like something out of a psychedelic '60s movie. I thought I was the bees-knees in them. Dad would take me to Crystal Palace and Brands Hatch to watch him race and when I was walking in the paddock everyone was looking at me. I loved it, absolutely loved it.

"From my point of view as a young kid, I was very impressionable. Gerry was always kind and considerate. I thought he was a lovely guy.

"Also, Margaret was a gorgeous young woman. Blonde. Very bubbly. Very vivacious. They were just a brilliant couple. That's what it felt like to me."

After the troubled Formula Two outings, Gerry's fortunes improved considerably in both his Escort outings. The two-hour race at the Salzburgring saw him driving solo for a change. After practice it looked like another easy class after he and the sister car of Han Akersloot had been much faster than their Division 2 opposition, which consisted of Alfa Romeos and BMWs. Then it snowed for the race! The BMW of Harald Ertl beat Gerry easily to finish seventh overall and claim Division 2 honours. Gerry came home eighth overall, second in class.

Better weather greeted everyone when they arrived in Czechoslovakia to race around the streets of Brno. On this occasion, in dry conditions, Gerry would score a resounding win in his class by five minutes and finish fourth overall, beaten only by the two Cologne Capris of Glemser and Mass and the BMW of Fitzpatrick after two hours of racing.

While he would have enjoyed his performance, Brno was not to his tastes, as he recalled in *Competition Car*. 'The town of Brno is a very dull and dreary place – in fact, the whole of Czechoslovakia, I'm afraid, is definitely not for me. The food was pretty grotty, while certain women were plentiful, cheap, but not very beautiful. I don't speak from experience, but I have spoken to people who have experienced, and they seemed fairly pleased with what they got!

'I'd better not say anymore because if there is a race next year, I'll probably not get a visa to enter the country.'

Somehow in among his ridiculously busy schedule – six races on five consecutive weekends – Gerry found time to return home to Scotland, and to Ingliston, for his first appearance there in well over two years. The meeting was on the weekend between Pau and Brno, so you would have thought after all the travelling and problems, he would have preferred some time off. But not Gerry. A weekend not racing was a wasted weekend. Back home, Margaret probably wasn't thinking that.

Unsurprisingly, Gerry received a hero's welcome. People celebrated the homecoming of one of their own, who had learnt his trade on this short and twisty circuit, and had gone on to attain international recognition. He was seen, by the partisan crowd, to be Scotland's next World Champion. And it wasn't just the crowd that seemed to have been won over.

"When I presented the car for scrutineering," recalls John Catt, "it was a case of, 'it's Gerry's car, it's perfect'. I wouldn't say they tugged their forelock to him, but...

"I did insist on them checking it properly, saying to them, 'I'm only human'. We had a bit of friendly banter. I'd learnt a fair bit of what I would call Scottish-English by then. Gerry had a name for just about everything. We had a small notebook with all the set-up information in. That was 'the wee bookie'. I wondered what the hell he was on about at first."

Gerry had brought along his March 722 with the help of Coca-Cola, who were using the event for promotional purposes. In addition to sponsoring the Formula Libre event Gerry was entered in, Coca-Cola had quite a presence around the circuit.

Unsurprisingly, he romped home an easy winner after his only real opposition, Brian Nelson in a Crosslé 22F powered by one of Brian Hart's F2 engines, had crashed out on the opening lap. Another aim of the visit was to try to break the outright lap record, which Gerry accomplished with a stunning lap of 47.7sec, making him the first man, officially, to lap under 48sec.

In *Competition Car* he summarised it thus: 'The first thing I noticed was how bumpy the track was; the last time I raced there was in 1969 in a Formula Ford. The car literally hopped from bounce to bounce. Having 280bhp behind you from one of Brian's engines was pretty horrifying – so quick! It made for some very short straights and some very busy laps.'

Before embarking on a busy May Bank Holiday weekend, which entailed visits to both Brands Hatch and Crystal Palace, he managed to find time to fly to Germany to carry out some testing of the German works Capri at the Nürburgring. Then it was straight over to Belfast to renew his relationship with Crosslé.

'When testing the Capri I had a very hairy experience of hitting a rain shower near the Flugplatz while on slick tyres,' he revealed in *Competition Car*. 'Fortunately I didn't hit anything solid, but it took an awfully long time to slow down because the tyres just rode up over the water.

'I went to test the Crosslé 22F F2 car with a view to using it in the Rothmans 50,000 race at Brands Hatch on the August Bank Holiday weekend instead of the March. Although I think the March will be very good, I don't want to hack it about and modify it.'

The Rothmans 50,000 was open to all large single-seaters, including F1, F5000 and F2. In essence, it was an international Formula Libre race.

'I have a great deal of faith in Crosslé and they're willing to make me a car especially for this event to use with a 2.0-litre alloy BDA engine. It will have to be a good car to match the March!'

Never one to forget his roots, Gerry took the March to Ingliston in May, and unsurprisingly, took Formula Libre honours. In front of the packed grandstands, he poses with his trophy. Formula Ford winner, Don MacLeod waits his turn behind. ***(Eric Bryce)***

Back to the racing. That Bank Holiday was a weekend of very mixed fortunes. It had begun with a light-hearted outing at the Fordsport meeting at Brands Hatch in a race for standard Ford Capris. The idea was a two-part team race for drivers and entrants. Gerry would be partnered by Rodney Bloor of Sports Motors. Gerry set the second-fastest time behind Dave Brodie for his race, but it was rendered worthless when it was decided that grid positions would be decided by drawing lots from a barrel. This system saw him on the back row alongside Emerson Fittipaldi and Niki Lauda. At least he was in good company.

In *Competition Car* he wrote: 'You couldn't get past anybody without touching, but I made it up to sixth place at the end of the first part of the race, keeping Emerson and Lauda firmly in my mirrors.'

The starting order for the entrant's race was the finishing order of the driver's race, so Rodney Bloor was up at the sharp end, but he would slip slowly down the order, beaten by the likes of Frank Williams, Colin Chapman, Frank Gardner (an entrant?), and a good few more. It will come as no surprise that the team prize was claimed by Gardner and Cevert. Some pairing.

The more serious outing in the F2 race at Crystal Palace was a disaster after Gerry was involved in a startline shunt in his heat. In *Competition Car* he said: 'I was on the second row alongside Graham Hill. When the flag dropped Jean Pierre Beltoise made a better start from the middle of the front row than Surtees and Depailler, who were alongside him. Graham went for the gap behind Beltoise just a fraction in front of me, but I couldn't move out of the way because (I reckon) Lauda had jumped the start from the row behind and was already alongside me. Anyway, Graham's rear wheel touched my front and slewed his car across my bows. I was launched right over the top of him before totalling my Coke can into the wall.'

The end result was two very badly damaged cars and a trip to the hospital for Graham for a check-up after Gerry's car had clipped his helmet when flying over the top of him.

At least better fortunes awaited him in the Group 2 race. On this occasion he was out in yet another variant of a Ford Capri – you could easily lose track of just how many there were – this one a '71 spec car entered by the Frans Lubins Frami Racing Team and looking stunning in the gold and white livery of Kent Cigarettes. Despite being up against the more powerful and latest-spec Capri of Brian 'Yogi' Muir, Gerry hounded him for the majority of the race until being forced to slow with fading brakes in the latter stages. He was sufficiently in front of the rest of the field to finish runner-up to Muir in both his class and the overall placings, which made a fine end to a traumatic couple of days.

With Gerry's participation in the Le Mans 24-hour driving the works Cologne Capri preventing him from attending the next F2 championship round at Hockenheim, it had been planned to install Brian Hart in the March for a one-off outing, but after a close examination the damage was extensive, as Gerry recounted in *Competition Car*. 'The whole job took about three weeks in the end – in fact, I now call it my new March 722. All but the rear bulkhead and dashboard of the monocoque was scrap – even the engine cylinder block was cracked. The body was scrap and every wishbone, bar one, was bent. The amount of damage is no reflection on March whatsoever – you're not supposed to low-fly in the cars!

'Anyhow, I escaped very lightly and set off for Le Mans, leaving John Catt with all those problems.'

The assault on Le Mans by the works Cologne Capris was a serious one with three cars. Gerry would partner Claude Bourgoignie. The other pairings were Mass/Stuck and Glemser/Soler-Roig. Surprisingly, like Gerry neither Mass or Stuck had previously driven at Le Mans.

In *Competition Car* he gave a unique insight into the team's preparations for the event, some of which seem well ahead of their time in their thoroughness. He also showed his humorous take on various situations which came his way. 'We had to arrive very early because we had our resident keep-fit man there, Olympic trainer Gunther Traub. We "assembled", as the Germans put it: they like to keep all their team drivers together getting to know each other.

'The next day we drove to the circuit to go through the ridiculous rigmarole of signing on and getting the cars scrutineered. The palaver is almost laughable. What was really impressive was seeing the cars going on the weighbridge and coming out pretty well exactly on the listed weight. I don't think the French knew quite what to do about that, they were just so accurate. When the Germans have regulations to work to, they work to them very, very closely indeed.

'After a great deal of fuss – and entertainment from our boisterous German mechanics, who mucked the various officials about something rotten – we returned to our hotel for the first part of our physical training. This, believe it or not, was a 12km run – well, walk as far as G Birrell was concerned. For this they strapped on to the drivers a little bleep box thing which made sure that we didn't under- or over-exert ourselves. It works off the pulse rate: It emits a single bleep at under 120 and a double bleep at over 160, and you have to do your running bit without it making a noise. Gunther Traub was running alongside me and would tell me when to slow down or speed up – usually speed up! We then had our massage from him, which was done with a thing which I am quite sure was just a floor sander (with no sandpaper on it, thank goodness).

'Breakfast the next (and every) morning consisted of fizzy water with vitamins, then our tea (we're not allowed coffee), stirred up like porridge. Then we had our orange juice and a boiled egg with a lot of salt. This revolting stuff took about an hour to get down, but I must say I for one felt a lot better for it.

'Every day we went to a local gym for an hour to do all our physical jerks including yoga – standing on our heads relaxing, meditating or just generally trying to stay up, which was a bit difficult with Hans Stuck running around pushing everybody over. He always has a great sense of humour, does Stuck. Mind you, you need one with this sort of thing, otherwise you might get all fanatical about the whole business.'

You can't help but smile when you read Gerry's comments on physical exercise, the old 'Excuse boots Birrell', coming to the fore once more after lying dormant for several years.

After that exhaustive and, at times, light-hearted preparation it was now time to get on with the serious stuff, a chance to sample the delights of Tertre Rouge, the Mulsanne Straight, White House, and all the other famous twists and turns of this historic circuit.

It was while doing a few laps to bed in the brakes that Gerry came close to turning all of France against him when nearly accounted for the demise – through no fault of his own – of their favoured one, Francois Cevert, who was part of the state-funded works Matra squad. He told of his narrow escape in *Competition Car*. 'What I didn't realise was that we had a sticking throttle. With this problem, the car obviously tends to run on into the corners, but I thought this was because the brakes were new. I came up to one of the new corners and saw a lot of yellow flags, so I backed off. I came over a brow, and the circuit was just a sheet of water after a sudden freak rain shower. They were waving the flags because Cevert was off the road, with his Matra's tail stuck in the wire fence; he was desperately spinning the rear wheels trying to get the car out. I put on the brakes – nothing happened. So I turned to the right – nothing happened because the sticking throttle was pushing the Capri straight on. I just heading for the Matra – you should have seen Cevert's face as this Capri came straight at him! Somehow I managed to stop about three feet away

He may have been smooth in single-seaters but, if required Gerry, could wring the neck of his saloon cars. ***(Peter Carey)***

from him, and the marshals then straightened us both out and sent us on our way.'

The historic accord that existed between Scotland and France would surely have been severely tested if Dame Fortune hadn't been on Gerry's side.

When it came to the serious part of getting the Capri qualified, the feeling by the team hierarchy was that there was no great need to go that quickly, just a matter of doing the minimum number of laps to guarantee a start, but Gerry and one of his team-mates had other ideas as he explained in *Competition Car*. 'I felt I needed a few extra laps due to my lack of experience of the circuit, so without telling the Germans I thought I'd stick a quick lap in. It was while entering the Esses on that lap going at a safe speed considering my lack of laps that I saw these six lights flashing in my mirrors. Expecting a Matra or something I moved over, and then with a sudden roar and screaming of tyres Stuck went by on opposite lock, through the Esses scuffing the banks, way off down to Tertre Rouge, which he took in classic style with one wheel in the air and the tail out... just fantastic. You just can't slow the guy down – that's his way of practising for a 24-hour race, and I thought I was disobeying team orders!'

Other dramas happened both on- and off-track when Bourgoignie had a slight off causing slight damage to the front of the car, and to be on the safe side the engine that had given trouble the day before was changed for one chosen by Gerry after he had been taken to the transporter by the mechanics to select one of three – that way he couldn't complain about its performance, having chosen it himself!

The off-track incident involved Glemser, who suffered injuries to his ribs during an unofficial game of basketball which Gerry described as more like a game of rugby. Boys will be boys.

"Gerry is mistaken, the basketball game where I injured my ribs a little was in St Moritz, not at Le Mans," recalls Glemser, nearly 50 years later. "I had a bit of body contact and I think I bumped into Jochen Mass, which led to the incident. Gerry was there but from what I remember he wasn't directly involved.

"In the world of car racing, the training camps were completely new – but they were fantastic and so much fun. Gerry was out of his depth trying to do cross-country skiing. In the beginning, he just wasn't much of an athlete and didn't have a priority on fitness. Still, he tried hard and we had such a good time together getting to know each other.

"Jochen Mass, Hans Stuck and I were probably a lot fitter than Gerry when we went there. From St. Moritz we went straight to the season-opener at Monza and we continued doing exercises every day before we left for the track. As I said before, Gerry wasn't too fit early on. But he started to do more and more training, lost some weight and later on was becoming quite fit. He definitely benefited a lot from Gunther Traub's programme.

"We only did the one race together at Jarama. I was usually paired with Alex Soler-Roig, then later with Jackie Stewart and Jochen Mass. The driver allocation was chosen by the team principals, Jochen Neerpasch and then his replacement Mike Kranefuss.

"The competition between the drivers was very civilized. Of course, no-one wanted to be left behind and the older, experienced guys were well aware of the challenge coming from the young guns. But there were no silly games that I was aware of. There was a sense of camaraderie with a very healthy spirit of competition – unlike a couple of years later when Zakspeed ran the Group 5 version of the Capri in the German DRM series and Klaus Ludwig and Hans Heyer started their little private war within the Ford team. But the years when I was driving for Ford it was a great and fair team of works drivers. Everyone tried to be quicker than the other, but there was no major controversy that I knew of."

Displaying the famed German efficiency, all three cars were given a set lap time to adhere to. Gerry did the first stint and lapped in convoy with the other two cars driven by Glemser and Mass. Apart from the usual routine maintenance/refuelling stops, the only serious problem was with the windscreen wipers that decided to start fighting with each other in the middle of the screen when Gerry was at the wheel.

The Mass/Stuck car fell by the wayside after seemingly Stuck ignored team orders and firstly, wore out the brakes and tyres. Then, secondly, the engine blew. The two remaining cars continued to circulate in convoy with Gerry's car coming home 10th overall and winner of their class with the Glemser/Soler-Roig car three laps in arrears in 11th. To have achieved such a result on his first appearance – it was his team-mate's second, having raced a VDS Alfa Romeo in 1969 – was highly impressive and his biggest win on the global stage. And it would cement his burgeoning relationship with the German division of the Ford motorsport empire.

In *Competition Car* Gerry offered his overall impressions of his first 24-hour enduro and how he had already felt the benefit of the keep-fit sessions. 'Even though I was pleased with the result, I didn't find the race very satisfying from a driver's point of view. Long-distance racing is a totally different sport and it requires different skills. I felt that I hadn't won the class because I was quick. But it is a type of racing that is useful to learn.

'It was amusing to be able to pass the 2.0-litre sports prototypes along the straights – the fastest Capri was measured at 171mph compared to the 150mph or so of the prototypes. Later, I had a marvellous time passing three Matras and one Alfa in one lap in the pouring rain. They had been screaming past us all night, so it gave me tremendous satisfaction and brightened up the whole event.

'I found that the keep-fit business had done me tremendous good; between stints, I was getting as much as 80 minutes sleep in a 110-minute stop. Gunther Traub did a terrific job. We'd get out of the car and he'd take us to the food caravan. Then over to our own caravan where we would dry off and be completely relaxed with this electric massager thing. Then we just went off to sleep – it was really good. When we woke up we were given tea with the vitamin stuff which, although not a drug or any sort of stimulant, woke us up and generally refreshed us, and then straight to the pits where inevitably the car would appear almost immediately. No time wasted whatsoever. Sometimes it seemed they almost cut things too fine – on one occasion I got up and was in the car and halfway to the Esses before I realised I was out of bed!'

From the glamour of racing at one of the iconic events, the next stop on Gerry's busy itinerary was Snetterton to test the rebuilt March and to continue his work for Ford. The time behind the wheel of the March went well enough for the car to be loaded into the van and John Catt dispatched off to catch the ferry – Gerry would join him later – to Rouen. But, unfortunately, Gerry never made it. Instead, he was on his way to Norwich General Hospital with a dislocated clavicle after having an accident in a car he shouldn't even have been driving. The intended pilot, Gillian Fortescue-Thomas, takes up the story: "The accident should have been mine. That's why I'm grateful and guilty.

"I was racing a 3.0-litre Capri in the BSCC and was getting beaten by the Camaros. I could keep up through the corners but got left behind on the straights. I kept asking for more power. Ford quite rightly decided it would be a good idea to have a Mach1 Mustang and a standard road car came over from the States. I was supposed to go up to Snetterton but had just moved down to Dorset and I knew Gerry was there, so... It just needed a few laps to shake it down and then it would go back to Boreham to be fitted with a roll-cage, seat and to be stiffened up, to end up a Group 1 racer.

"Gerry took it out and did some modest laps. After

Heading to 10th overall and a class victory at Le Mans. ***(Motorsport Images)***

leathering it down the long Norfolk Straight he put his foot on the brake and the pedal went to the floor. He thought never mind, it's not a problem, I'll just turn it on to the infield to slow it down. The problem was the farmer had dug a drainage ditch and basically it rolled itself into a ball. How he got out of it, I don't know. It was the only time I saw the Mustang, it ended up about three feet high. I did take a picture of it up at Boreham. I'm sorry he had my accident. He did nothing wrong, it was just that nobody knew about the drainage ditch, normally you could pull up on the infield and spin it around.

"Our paths crossed frequently when on duties for Ford. Gerry was there with Dave Matthews the day I got my Ford contract. After doing so well against the likes of Gerry Marshall, Barrie Williams, and a whole load of more idiots, I ended up at a test at Silverstone. In the Group 2 car, Gerry and I were about the same but I just pipped his time in the Group 1 car, which he was a bit pissed off about. He wanted to go out again but they said no, that's it, if you go again, she has to go again and on it goes.

"Gerry was a lovely guy. Very much a family man. He was someone I was very comfortable with. He was like a brother. He wasn't the chatting-you-up sort. I would have been nervous with some of the others, as nice as they were. He was open, honest and genuine. I always thought what you saw was what you got."

The injury meant that he would miss not just the aforementioned outing at Rouen, but also another at the Österreichring. Instead, he was sent to Cyprus to recuperate courtesy of Ford.

"We went out for about 10 days," remembers Margaret. "It wasn't a holiday, Gerry was to recce the Cyprus Rally for Ford. We left the twins, who were about six months old, with my mother."

Once he was recovered, the second half of the season would begin in earnest with another 24-hour enduro at Spa-Francorchamps. It wasn't exactly a leisurely way to play yourself back in after injury.

Part Two

Upon his return from his working holiday, Gerry headed straight off to Southern Germany for another work-out courtesy of Gunther Traub. In *Competition Car* he told of his fitness – or the lack of it – and the exploits of Hans Stuck (again): 'I went over with fellow saloon ace Dave Matthews who had just joined the Boreham squad, so they could how fit he was. Anyhow, he's obviously a sneaky trainer because there's nothing wrong with him.

'Once again, yours truly was bottom of the unfit brigade which numbered three. Hans Stuck, Dave and myself. It all took place at Gunther Traub's parents' home, which was fantastic: swimming and sailing in the lakes; running around. All good fun!

'From there, we were heading straight to Spa-Francorchamps for the 24 hours. Dave and I were in a hire car, while 'Stucky' was in his company RS2600 Capri. We set off with Dave driving, almost immediately 'Stucky' pulled into a filling station for fuel. I sort of warned Dave to keep an eye in the mirror for the dreaded Stuck appearing and, sure enough, about 15 minutes later, there was a great flash of lights and sounding of horns when he came past at about a million miles an hour and disappeared into the distance. I turned to Dave and said: "Be careful, keep an eye open on the road for the con-rods!" After all, we didn't want to get a puncture!

'It's quite funny just how true that story became because we got up to Spa, checked in at our hotel, to find no sign of of 'Stucky'. Around midnight, Jochen Mass arrives with him in his car after picking him up. Apparently, he had turned off to go to Cologne and well and truly blew his engine. Lucky for us it didn't happen in front of us.'

"I first met Gerry at the Green Man Pub near Silverstone," remembers Dave Matthews. "I had been invited to test with some other UK and European racers at Silverstone and Oulton Park. The weather was changeable. Wet at Oulton, dry at Silverstone. Gerry set some marker times in one of the European championship BDA-engined Escorts. The test went OK for me. My main drive was in the British Championship, in a Group 2 Escort.

"I did the occasional race in Europe with Ford but was usually paired with German drivers in the lower class. Gerry was in the senior squad in the Capris. We did travel and spend together. We shared a love of fruity yoghurts which seemed to be kicking off in choice and popularity in the early '70s.

"He had a great relationship with Peter Ashcroft. Peter would guess/bet what Gerry's lap time would be on his third lap of first practice, whether on a circuit new to him or one he had raced on before; he was rarely more than a few tenths out. They were both a pleasure to be with for a new guy like me. Gerry was always kind, cheerful and knowledgeable too; a great guy and unselfish, too."

For the Spa 24 hours Gerry would have local ace Bourgoignie as his partner for their first outing together in a Capri. The car would run in the green and yellow colours of BP Belgium but was still a works Cologne car.

As per the usual meticulous planning of the Cologne department led by Mike Kranefuss, a limited number of laps was completed in qualifying. Gerry qualified on the second row behind the sister cars of Stuck/Mass and Glemser/Soler-Roig. Stuck, in his normal fashion, put in a lap at breakneck speed on only his second lap, which had Gerry and Mass a bit concerned, Gerry commenting, 'Oh well, Stuck isn't that much quicker, or we hoped he wasn't!'

For the race, the team elected Gerry's car to be the hare, to try to break the threat from their main rivals, BMW. The sister cars would hold back and help out when necessary. Given the normal changeable weather conditions in the Ardennes region and with help from his team-mate's local knowledge, Gerry, along with Stuck, changed to intermediate tyres, while the Glemser/Soler-Roig car and the BMWs remained on slicks.

For the first couple of laps the Capris and BMWs circulated together, then Gerry put his plan into action and with the help of a slipstream down the Masta Straight from Glemser, moved from fifth to first on one lap. He soon opened up a 10sec lead but the BMWs weren't taking the bait. As predicted before the end of his first stint, it began to rain slightly, so Gerry ran at a reduced, safe pace to maintain his lead before handing the car to his team-mate.

The threat of BMW disappeared due to a multitude of reliability issues, leaving the three Capris to circulate for the majority of the race in formation. Gerry's car had lost the lead among the many scheduled pit stops and ran in second and third places throughout, the Mass/Stuck car having opened up an advantage. The only problem encountered by Gerry's car was a faulty alternator light.

In *Competition Car* he described the final laps: 'At the end it was a bit conceited the way we drove around for about the last six laps really rubbing it into the opposition, either in formation, or line astern, or three abreast, eventually crossing the line with one lap to go three abreast so that people could get photographs! On the final approach to the finish line, the three cars – I was in the middle in second place – went very slowly. It was a tremendous feat that the Capris were going just as well at the end. In fact, I'm sure the three of them would have done another 24 hours. That was the end of that and we all made a bit of money. Quite chuffed.'

The two strong showings in both of the classic 24-hour races had certainly enhanced Gerry's growing reputation in the works Cologne ranks, which could only lead to more and more outings. Unfortunately, the outcome of his next Ford outing was the opposite of the Spa result.

Originally, for the next round (sixth) of the ETCC, Gerry was to partner Dutchman Han Akersloot and new recruit Matthews in the Sony Racing/Ford of Holland Escort RS1600 in the Division 2 class (the Capris ran in Division 1). His place had been put in doubt when Glemser was injured on the Olympia Rally and Gerry was put on standby to take his place in the Cologne Capri if he was still unfit. In the end, after much deliberation on Glemser's part, he decided he was fit, so Gerry was in the Escort after all. A few hours later, he'd wished he hadn't bothered.

In *Competition Car* he described the events in detail, which make for harrowing reading: 'After only a couple of laps while going very quickly around the back of the circuit, I turned the steering wheel to the right but the car decided it was going straight on. A ball-pin had sheared in the front end and I was heading for the Armco flat-out in fifth gear. It hit so hard I must admit that I thought it was "lights out" as far as I was concerned. I did manage to turn the car slightly to prevent it from going in head-on.

'The car, according to an eye-witness, nose-dived (thank goodness) into the Armco. It corkscrewed the top layer of the Armco, but luckily it didn't give way because behind it was a bridge parapet. We managed to break away a bit of the parapet but the barrier stayed firm. The car then flicked onto its roof and went along the track for about 200 yds, wearing away the roll-over bar and then started to do fairly normal (!) rolls, ending up another 500 yards down the road from the initial impact, on the right and through a fence.

'The few things I remember are going along upside down with sparks, stones and all bits of glass flying through. I remember seeing the red of all the sparks. I must have the real answer to all boy-racers; stone chips on the back of my helmet! The car eventually came to rest on its wheels, in control all the way! I always end them up on their wheels! The driver's door wouldn't open, so I climbed out of the left-hand side which was now a fairly large hole.

'It's at times like these that you're glad that the car is built at Boreham, where a great deal of the lessons learned in rallying come into the construction. It was fantastic how well everything stayed in the car. It didn't disintegrate. The battery stayed in place, as did the fuel tank. Not a drop of fuel leaked out from the special quick-fill aircraft spec equipment and all the electrics stayed in place. Nothing caught fire, fused or anything. It's then that you are thankful you're driving a works car that's properly prepared with proper seatbelts and a solid roll-over bar. I climbed out of it with literally just a bruise on my arm, which was very lucky, to say the least.

'The course car took me back to the pits. I think they were a bit surprised to see me all in one piece but checked me over and I felt alright. At this point, Frans Lubin of Frami Racing rushed up and told me to get into his Kent-sponsored Capri.

Gerry turning into La Source on his way to second place overall and second in class. ***(Ferdi Kräling)***

So I zoomed out and did a quickie on my first lap. On my second lap around the back of the pits, I was confronted by what seemed like half of the Dutch RAC in the middle of the road waving red, black and chequered flags at me. I thought they must want me to stop. They gave me a little lecture and recommended that I should go home and have some rest before attempting to drive another car. Therefore, I wasn't allowed to do the five laps to qualify, so the next day I sat and watched the race.'

It certainly seems like Gerry was living a charmed life. Two huge saloon car accidents, only a few weeks apart, and a nasty F2 accident at Crystal Palace preceding them. Reading his comments from the time, he didn't seem overly concerned or affected by the incidents. The fact that he readily accepted the offer to drive the Kent Capri and went quickly confirms he was strong mentally.

"The danger wasn't something we talked about," recalls Margaret. "The only thing he was frightened of was fire. That's a clear memory."

In between his saloon car outings Gerry, typically, wasn't idle. A long trip to Mantorp Park for the 10th round of the European Formula Two Championship brought yet more single-seater disappointment. After qualifying on the third row for the first of the two heats, which made up the final classification, his race ended – after a demon start that saw him third at the first corner – when he selected third gear exiting the first turn and the car stopped dead. The transistor box had burned out. The non-finish meant that he started a lowly 15th in the second heat, which again resulted in retirement after a stone had entered the airbox, taking the protective mesh with it. The result was that the throttle stuck wide open. He certainly couldn't buy any luck at any price, as far as Formula Two was concerned. All the early season promise had failed to come to fruition, which was causing some frustration in the Birrell camp. He quipped in *Competition Car*: 'What do you do? Don't go Formula Two, is my answer.'

Thankfully, a long-overdue upturn in fortunes came in the next outing at Brands Hatch in the much-heralded Rothmans

The start of the huge accident at Zandvoort in the Sony Escort. ***(Dick Vergers)***

It's not finished yet. ***(Dick Vergers)***

50,000. As noted, it was a glorified Formula Libre race with a big prize money payout that the promoters had hoped would attract many Formula One teams. When it became apparent that they would be unable to go the full distance of 118 laps (more than 300 miles) without a pitstop, which was a political hot topic at that time, or substantial modifications to the car, many teams withdrew, leaving a meagre entry of nine Formula One cars, most of which were second-string entries. The obvious exception was Emerson Fittipaldi in his all-conquering JPS Lotus 72. The rest of the field consisted of a mix of F5000 and F2 cars, of which Gerry was one.

The initial idea mooted a few months earlier to use a specially built modified Crosslé F2 car came to nothing as several factors prevented it. Thus the March would be equipped with the latest high-specification refuelling system to enable it to complete the distance. The car had been taken back to the factory for March to modify the monocoque with larger fuel tanks. All the work was carried out to Formula One standards that greatly impressed Gerry and led to increased involvement from Brian Hart who was very much batting for Gerry in his usual methodical and understated way.

Gerry took up the story in *Competition Car*. 'I had arranged with Brian that, if he had his alloy development engine ready, we would use it. He became more interested when it became apparent about the lack of F1 cars appearing. We both felt that a good Formula Two – or an alloy-engined Formula Two – was definitely going to be in the money. We decided to take things more seriously and go about the whole thing in a professional manner.

'Brian gave us the engine to run and also did some calculations as to what lap time he thought we should do. He agreed to manage the whole day's racing.'

All the preparations seemed to have paid off, which included a good few test sessions adjusting the suspension to cope with the extra weight and fine-tuning the balance of the car when Gerry qualified sixth overall and fastest F2 runner with a minimum of fuss.

Before the start there were various parades and much fanfare to entertain the crowds, all of which was 'a real palava' according to Gerry in *Competition Car*. Doubtless he wouldn't have been so dismissive of the entertainment in the shape of the reigning Miss United Kingdom, Jennifer McAdam, all decked out courtesy of Coca-Cola, whom he had the pleasure of posing for photographs with on more than one occasion.

While he was involved in the glamorous side of promoting his sponsor's product, Margaret was seeing the more practical benefits: "Crates of Coca-Cola would arrive on our doorstep every Friday. It got me hooked on it!"

The race finally got underway from a rolling start with Gerry trying to stay out of any first-lap trouble and maintaining the agreed lap time until the scheduled pit stop on lap 65. The first part went according to plan as he enjoyed dices with the F1 BRM of Howden Ganley, who eventually waved him through, and the F2 Chevron of John Watson. With an eye very much on the bigger picture he left Watson to it, sticking religiously to the plan as his saloon car/long-distance racing experience came to the fore. The only problem he encountered was in the braking department.

"Gerry thought that he had a cracked wheel," recalls John Catt. "But it was the rubber from the front tyres, plus the marbles from all the other runners that were getting trapped between the brake caliper and the wheel. They were making horrible noises and sending shudders up the steering column, but he kept going.

"When he stopped at the end of the race, he didn't apply the brakes but just rolled to a halt. When we went to push it back up into the paddock, we couldn't move it. I had a get a screwdriver to pull all the rubber out."

That wasn't the end of Catt's troubles. The pit stop was a whole mixture of emotions, as he recalls: "We had a quick-fill system from Boreham and I'd rigged up an air system, a plastic bottle type thing with the top cut off, so when you attached that at the same time as the fuel filler, all the air was removed allowing a faster refuel. We added

20 gallons of fuel in just 22 seconds, which was the fastest of the race, apparently.

"We had discussed the stop at length and at first Gerry thought he would have to get out of the car when we refuelled, but with me on the fuel churn and John McTavish on the air-vent bottle, we got another chap to put this fire-resistant Draylon cloth (which came with a sofa and chairs Gerry's father had sent down from Scotland), over the roll-over bar and Gerry's head to protect him if any fuel was spilt.

"The refuelling couldn't have gone any better but when Gerry came to restart the engine it wouldn't fire up. The bloody starter motor was heat-soaked and was kicking backwards. I said, 'Keep going. Keep going. Don't panic.' Then suddenly it went, and he was off. I think if I had panicked, Gerry would have."

Once the pitstops had sorted themselves out, Gerry settled into a secure fourth place. At one stage the third-place runner, Henri Pescarolo in a Frank Williams-run March, pitted for a new front tyre but was able to maintain his position. Both he and Gerry would end up two laps down on the runaway victor Fittipaldi and runner-up Brian Redman in a McLaren.

Gerry's fine drive to fourth and first F2 car home was a great team effort, something he acknowledged in *Competition Car* while modestly playing down his part: 'The pitstop was very efficient, which is a tremendous credit to John Catt for his hard work in modifying the car to suit all these bits, and also for performing the stop in such a slick manner. This was the first time he'd ever been involved in such things, and as it worked out we were probably the quickest. In fact, that had a great deal more bearing on the result of the race than my performance!'

The ample prize money meant that Gerry came away with a whopping £4000 for his efforts, but he didn't take it all. Both his wife and mechanic have fond recollections of how they used their share.

"Gerry had said that if he won some money I could have a kitchen," recalls Margaret. "I was watching the race on the TV and willing him to keep going. I was thinking of my kitchen, which I got eventually. I was pretty chuffed with it."

"I got £400, which was a deposit for my house," offers Catt. "When we were driving home Gerry said that I was on a 10 percent bonus of the £4000. That was the first bonus I'd ever had in nearly three years. It was very welcome."

Catt has a story about Margaret's kitchen. "They had bought this house which required some attention. They went to this company who came and designed the kitchen. It spanned the entire width of the house. The idea was to put in as many cupboards as possible and then make a dining area, divided off with them.

"Ronnie Grant knew someone who supplied Indesit appliances. We actually went to the warehouse and took the fridges and washing machines off the truck that had come from Italy. The problem was that Gerry now had this metric fridge freezer and was trying to fit it into an imperial size gap,

On the grid at Brands Hatch before the Rothmans 50,000. Gerry points something out to Miss UK, Jennifer McAdam, while John Catt behind the rear wing and John McTavish with Ronnie Grant look on. ***(Ford Motor Company)***

A superb shot of Gerry on his way to a fine fourth overall and first F2 car home. ***(Ford Motor Company)***

and it wouldn't fit. Gerry asked them to modify one of the cupboards but they said they didn't do such things. So Gerry had to order a new cupboard which took nine months to turn up. They were both going to be away, so I was asked to be there. It was duly delivered and had to be paid for. Gerry hadn't left any money. I fluffed about a bit saying that I hadn't been left any money until, eventually, they left. I think they were pressing Gerry for the money and he told them that they had kept him waiting for nine months, they would have to wait for their money. Gerry thought I was brilliant because I got the cupboard without paying for it."

Again, that old saying: you can take the boy out of Scotland, but you can't take Scotland out of the boy...

Gerry made another return to Ingliston in September and won again in the March, setting a new outright lap record. ***(Colin Lourie)***

He also brought the Frami Racing Capri along. Again, the result was another victory. ***(Eric Bryce)***

With fellow race winner and friend Bill Dryden in the boot of a Vauxhall Firenza during a lap of honour. ***(Iain Nicolson)***

Being interviewed by commentator Jim McInnes after the Capri victory. ***(Eric Bryce)***

As far as Formula Two was concerned, the season petered out, with a couple of notable exceptions. Gerry ventured back to Ingliston the day after a disappointing race at Oulton Park. A resounding victory against meagre opposition was secured, and again he lowered the lap record. Since his last visit in May it had been bettered by Brian Nelson who set a new mark of 47.2sec. Now Gerry clipped another 0.6sec off that to become the first man to lap the track in under 47sec.

As well as the F2 car he took along the Frami Racing Kent Capri to break another class record, which he duly did on the way to an easy victory. And to give Scottish mechanics Gordon Horn and Ian Dawson a chance to return to their home city of Edinburgh. But the appearance didn't go down so well with sponsor Kent Cigarettes, as Horn recalls: "They went barmy when they found out that the car carried Kings stickers. They were a tarmac and road construction based in Glasgow and were sponsoring the meeting and the race for Special Saloons and Group 2 car, which we were competing in. I don't know who organised the stickers but they weren't supposed to be on the car. Kent decided which races we competed in.

"It was a big car for Ingliston, and pretty spectacular. Gerry was quick, against no great competition."

The last Formula Two outing had a notable twist. Gerry was not behind the wheel of his March but a Rondel Racing Brabham BT38 in the European round at Albi in France. In *Competition Car* he explained how it came about and how it went: 'I was supposed to be at Silverstone for the Tourist Trophy (TT) with the German Capris because Jochen Mass was due to go to Albi with the works F2 STP Marches. But they decided not to go, making Jochen available for the TT. When Ron Dennis, the Rondel supremo, got to the bottom of his list (!) he offered me a drive in Carlos Reutemann's car. I got in touch with Ford's Michael Kranefuss, who kindly excused me from pedalling a Capri.

'Chevron had also asked me earlier about driving for them at Albi, but I had thought I was still going to Silverstone.

'Anyhow, it was a bit difficult to climb into a totally new car

(I'd never driven an F2 Brabham), especially with Rondel's new front-radiator, wide-nose arrangement which they were trying for the first time. I finished third in my heat behind Mike Hailwood and Jean-Pierre Jaussaud. In the final I had a bit of a tussle with Dave Morgan in the Tui. After having a couple of wheel-touching sessions, I decided that I wasn't really getting anywhere in sixth place, so I decided to have a go! The only place I was going to get by was at the end of the straight, as Mister Morgan was driving very much on the right-hand side of the track! As I got around the outside, Dave wouldn't give way, and we got a bit tangled. I got sideways in the middle of the road and he drove over the lovely new Rondel nose with his back wheel. I ended up stationary in the middle of the road, and poor Dave and the Tui went and tested out the new Albi safety fences, which proved adequate for the job! All good stuff! After all, you've got to get by these guys because it's no good for me, or Rondel, coming in sixth.

'I may end up testing their new super-looking F2 car if it's ready before I leave for the Springbok series in South Africa.'

It seems despite a disappointing season in Formula Two Gerry's reputation hadn't been tarnished. Offers from Chevron and Rondel, two of the leading outfits, stood him in good stead for next season to finally crack his Formula Two jinx.

While taking some time off from his various driving duties Gerry met up with his former mechanic Bruce McTavish, who had moved on to greater things since working with him in '68 and and '69. "I paid Gerry and Margaret a visit after returning to England after working in the CanAm series for McLaren," recalls Bruce. "The twins weren't very old and we decided to take them for a walk. Margaret and the girls, along with my friend, went at a sedate pace to the marina, not far from their house. Meanwhile, we took the scenic route, rather quickly, through some narrow English country lanes to meet up with them. Fun or what?

"We were in a Capri that Gerry had the use of through his Ford contract. I don't know what state of tune it was in, but it was quick.

"I nearly ended up working with him again before that visit. I joined McLaren in late '69 to work on the Formula One team on Bruce's car. When Bruce was killed, the team drew up a shortlist of possible replacements. The two names were Reine Wisell and Gerry. Wisell actually got a test drive, but not Gerry. It would have been cool to have worked with him again."

"The quick Capri that Bruce mentions was hand-built in Germany, and the car that all the Ford-contracted drivers were given," offers Margaret. "It was like a race car with sports suspension. We had the kid's seats strapped in the back before such seats were compulsory. If they hadn't been strapped, in they would have been bouncing off the roof."

As Read prepares to climb aboard. Gerry, Gillian Fortescue-Thomas and Ken Tyrrell find something to laugh about. ***(Ford Motor Company)***

Gerry in the cockpit of an Elden Mk8 Formula Ford at Brands Hatch with the late motorcycle racer Phil Read, looking super cool in the shades. Gerry was in attendance to help/instruct Read, who was considering a switch to car racing. Reportedly, the test went well, but in the end, a lucrative new deal with MV Agusta kept Phil on two wheels. ***(Ford Motor Company)***

A one-off outing in the Rondel Racing Brabham BT38 at Albi. ***(Unknown)***

The Frami Racing set-up pictured at Ingliston featuring the transporter that was the scene of some high-jinks involving Gerry and the team. ***(Michael How)***

The last three Capri outings saw Gerry in three different variations, all of which he was familiar with. First up was another appearance in the Frami Racing example at Paul Ricard, partnered by Jean-Claude Franck. A somewhat surprising choice of team-mate given the opposition. Gerry would have pulled out all the stops to be present due to the added attraction of Tyrrell team-mates Jackie Stewart and Francois Cevert in an Elf-backed works Capri. Plus, Mass and Glemser in the leading Cologne machine. No doubt all the regular Capri pilots would be keen to get one over the 'star' pairing.

Gerry took first blood by upstaging the works cars by recording a tremendous time in the first two-hour session on Friday. It was difficult to get a fair comparison due to the complicated tyre contracts of the teams and drivers. Gerry and Franck were on Firestones. The works cars of Mass/Glemser and Larrousse/Soler-Roig were on Dunlops, while the Stewart/Cevert car was on Goodyears.

In his *Autosport* report Richard Feast offered a whole range of possibilities. 'Was it the light weight? It was alleged the Frami car was 40kg lighter than the works entries. Was it the Firestone tyres? Or was it Birrell, a bit of a Ricard specialist? Whatever, it wasn't until the last few minutes of Saturday's dry practice that Mass managed to snatch back pole position for the factory, while the Frami Racing example was stationary with a broken gearbox. Gerry did have the consolation of still beating the time set by Cevert – Stewart only appeared on Saturday – by just over half a second.'

Another factor in his favour was that he had been testing extensively at Ricard in the week leading up to the event. While the testing may have gone according to plan, matters away from the track didn't, as Horn recalls: "Gerry was staying with us in a house Frans Lubins had rented close to the circuit. It wasn't particularly great, to be honest. Gerry lasted just one night after he had to wear his Nomex suit all night because he was being eaten alive by the mosquitoes. He couldn't cope with that, so he moved out and went down to Bandol to stay with some other guys.

"We did get up to some hi-jinks when driving back to the circuit. We only had one vehicle, which was our transporter, a Transit cab with a low-loader ramp on the back. We had converted it in our workshop in southern Holland. We had four people crammed in this thing. I was driving, so I was in charge of the steering and brakes, while Gerry who was next to me, was in charge of the clutch and gearchange. We drove for about 30km like that.

"Gerry would test for us on a fairly regular basis through the offices of Ford. He was a pretty switched-on sort of a fella, which is why he did a lot of testing for them. He was always very fastidious about things, especially brakes. If he got the slightest vibration, he didn't like that. He was quite sensitive in that respect, that's why he was a good test and development driver. He was a bloody good driver with an excellent work-ethic, and was good fun."

Come the race, the tyres would play an important part in the outcome. Gerry's car suffered numerous wear issues

The patriotic helmet design. *(David Pearson/Roger Swann)*

throughout, to trail home a disappointing sixth overall. At least, he would have smiled wryly, that the Stewart/Cevert car was usurped by the privately-entered Capri of John Miles and Brian 'Yogi' Muir who claimed the spoils.

The outing in the Cologne car at Jarama, sharing with Hans Heyer for the first time, was a troubled one initially. Reportedly, Gerry was still suffering from the effects of his mammoth Zandvoort shunt a few months previously. It seems that what he thought was just heavy bruising on his right arm was also actually a pinched nerve. The plan was to see a specialist to get to the bottom of the problem. On this occasion, the lack of strength in his damaged arm prevented him from correcting a lurid slide with the heavy steering. The result was damage to the front wing and steering arm, all of which was easily fixed by his German mechanics.

The injury, which seemed to go as quickly as it flared up, didn't prevent Gerry from putting in his usual quota of stints alongside Heyer and they came home in second place behind the sister car of Mass/Larrousse/Soler-Roig.

The main focus of the ETCC was the manufacturer's championship honours, rather than the drivers. But in their championship, Gerry took third place overall behind winner Mass and runner-up Glemser.

The final outing of his European season was at the end-of-season Brands Hatch Victory meeting, whose main race -was again a non-championship F1 encounter. The Cologne team had taken over a last-minute cancelled entry and would run the car in the same BP livery as the car ran at the Spa 24 hours.

Gerry was competitive throughout up against his old adversary Frank Gardner. The Aussie had to wring his Chevrolet Camaro's neck in his efforts to stay in front. Gerry's challenge came to nought when, with just four laps remaining of the 20, his fire extinguisher unleashed itself on a non-existent fire and forced his retirement.

The late October chill of Brands Hatch was soon swapped for the sunnier climate of the Kyalami circuit in South Africa. Gerry had signed for the works Chevron team to contest the five-round Springbok series alongside his Ford of Germany team-mate Jochen Mass, the vastly-experienced Chevron favourite Peter Gethin and the defending champion from Rhodesia, John Love. It would turn out to be some trip on so many levels.

SPRINGBOK SERIES

Part Three

The eligible cars for the Springbok series were 2.0-litre sports racing cars, and various classes of saloon/sports from the popular and well-supported domestic South African scene to make up the grids.

Gerry had signed to partner his Ford colleague Jochen Mass in one of two Gunston-backed works Chevrons. While both Chevrons would be identical B21/23s – effectively the B23 was next year's car – the engines would differ. With the backing of Ford, Gerry and Jochen would use the 2.0-litre alloy-block engine developed by Brian Hart, which Gerry had used previously in the back of his F2 March at the Rothmans 50,000 race back in August. The sister car would be powered by the heavier and less powerful FVC.

Before setting out Gerry had encountered some minor problems on the domestic front, as his understanding and ever-supportive wife Margaret recalls: "We were trying to buy a house in Maidenhead, but at that time the gazumping was ridiculous. We had rented up until then because it was difficult to get a mortgage with Gerry being freelance. Being employed by Ford made it possible to get an endowment mortgage which enabled us to buy a house in Purleigh, in Essex. It was only about 10 miles from Boreham, so it suited Gerry. I ended up moving house with the twins while he was away. My mother came down to help. It was a nightmare.

Gerry took an impressive second overall partnered by Jochen Mass in a works Chevron B21 in the Kyalami Nine Hours. ***(David Pearson/Motorprint)***

"I remember going to the airport with him. He had too much baggage and he was running late because an interview he had done before had overrun. He started emptying the case and began throwing stuff at me. He took out the things he could get out in South Africa. I had the twins in a buggy, so I stuffed all his things into it, then had to go and buy a bag to put everything in. He had to carry his helmet on board."

The journey to South Africa, according to Gerry in *Competition Car*, 'Seemed like a week on a plane, the only entertainment was watching films – and Gethin and Mass trying to pull anything female between 16 and 40!'

The Castrol Springbok Series

Incorporating the Castrol Drivers Championship and the Castrol Manufacturers Championship

Castrol

Regulations for the 1972 South African International Endurance Races

Races Comprising the Series

The 15th Rand Daily Mail 9 Hour Race
Kyalami. 4th Nov.

3 Hour Endurance Race, Killarney, Cape Town. 18th Nov.

3 Hour Endurance Race, Lourenco Marques. 26th Nov.

Die Volksblad 3 Hour Endurance Race, Goldfields Raceway, Welkom. 2nd Dec.

The Natal Mercury 3 Hour Endurance Race, Roy Hesketh, Pietermaritzburg. 17th Dec.

The schedule for the series. ***(David Pearson/Motorprint)***

On arrival it was straight down to business the next day, sampling his mount for the first time in an unofficial practice session on the Wednesday in preparation for the traditional series opener. This was the Kyalami Nine Hours, which unlike the other four rounds of the series, was open to entries from 3.0-litre prototypes. Disappointingly only Ferrari took up the offer, sending two factory cars.

The pair of Ferraris were expected to romp away to victory; one did while the other retired. Gerry's focus was on beating the other 2.0-litre runners, of which the main threat – apart from the other Gunston Chevron – was the new March driven by local favourite Jody Scheckter and Niki Lauda. March supremo/designer Robin Herd was in attendance, so they were taking things seriously.

Gerry set a slightly better time than his team-mate to qualify third quickest, and fastest 2.0-litre runner, behind the two Ferraris. Reportedly, the only issue he and Jochen encountered was the usual one associated with long-distance racing, that of the seating position – a compromise was quickly reached between the pair, who were firm friends. And Jochen was happy with the selection of an extra half-inch wide front tyre that made a big difference, according to Gerry. His ever-sensitive skills were again coming to the fore.

The race got off to a chaotic start after Mass and Ickx in

At the prize-giving after the race, the successful pair enjoy the company of two admirers. *(David Pearson/Motorprint)*

the lead Ferrari looked for the starter on the left-hand side of the track, only for the flag to fall on the right. This dropped Jochen down to sixth place but he quickly regained ground before handing over to Gerry.

In a largely untroubled race, the pair overcame spasmodic pressure from the Lucky Strike-sponsored pairings of Scheckter/Lauda and Charlton/Hine, in March and Chevron respectively, to finish second overall behind the sole-surviving Ferrari of Merzario/Regazzoni. They scored maximum Springbok points but received no prize money, something Gerry made light of in *Competition Car*. 'To my horror, I discovered that we had raced for nine hours just to earn a trophy! Off to the pawn shop, I suppose!'

According to Chevron's Paul Owens, who was in charge of the Gunston team, the result should have been different. "That was an incredible race and truth be known Gerry and Jochen should have won it because we led it for a while and the Ferraris towards the end were in trouble. One had broken down and the other one in the last hour came in for the last pit stop and wouldn't start, it had no clutch," he remembered nearly 50 years later. "They push-started it and the rules in those days said that it had to start under its own power with no outside assistance. We protested it, meaning we would have won, but you know... Chevron wasn't Ferrari.

"We were told quite categorically by the organiser Alex Bignault that if we wanted to come back here again and compete we should withdraw our protest. I said, 'Well that's all well and good, Alex, but we're here now and we could win and you know we could win.' He said, 'You're right, but I've said you won't come here again if you don't withdraw your protest and that's it.' I said, 'We'd better do a deal now. What's the deal for next year then, Alex?' We virtually did a deal there and then for the following year, and withdrew the protest."

In *Competition Car* Gerry offered his recollections of events away from the track, in his usual entertaining way. 'During our stay, we went to a speedway/hot rod meeting at a stadium called Wembley, and the way the South Africans talk about it you would think the London one was named after the one here. Some V8 Midgets, using methanol fuel, proved to be great entertainment on the cinder track. The entertainment continued even after the racing had stopped, because two of the locals, suitably lubricated with beer, decided to settle an argument in the good old-fashioned way, and put on a really good punch-up.

'My lasting memory of the Klammy (Kyalami) race' – Gerry's tendency to have alternative/amusing names for things hadn't left him – 'was the smokescreens caused by the crowds grilling steaks on their barbecues, the various smells making the drivers feel sick or hungry. The crowds are very different from back in Europe. They all arrive very early and get sloshed before the race even starts!'

His driving partner has another lasting memory of a different nature. "We had an apartment in Johannesburg which was run like a hotel," recalls Mass. "We both slept in this big room. One morning I had gone to the bathroom and was stark naked. It was summer and I didn't give a hoot. I heard someone come in, which I thought would be the maid who came in about seven o'clock. She walked straight into the bathroom, looked at me and said, 'Good morning, massa.'

"I said, 'Excuse me, do you mind waiting outside.' I meant for her to go out of the apartment but she went out of the bathroom into the big room and started hoovering while Gerry was still sound asleep. I had to ask her to come back in an hour or so."

In *Competition Car* he regaled us with memories of the first road trip, to the next round. 'From Johannesburg, we set off for Cape Town (a distance of approx 1400km) in our genuine Ford 'Rumble-Rocket' Fairmont GTE Automatic for our next race at the twisty Killarney circuit, which was at the foot of Table Mountain.

'Jochen and I found that, if we drove above 3500 rpm, we couldn't make it between the two filling stations on the main road, which were about 140 miles apart. Unfortunately, we didn't suss this out until we were about halfway through having been driving at 4000 rpm. We had to go very slowly and easily for the next 60 miles! We learnt our lesson and were a bit careful after that because the thing consumed petrol at a vast rate, but also went at a helluva speed.'

"The Fairmont had a ram box on the hood," remembers Mass, laughing as the mention of the car brought back many happy memories. "It was a lovely, attractive car. We never did anything silly with it. Never got stopped by the police. We drove quickly because you could see there were none around. We just enjoyed it. It was super nice."

This was just the first of many adventures they encountered as they went back and forth across the vast country. They travelled in convoy in their 'Rumble Rocket' with the pairing of Peter Gethin and Paul Owens, who were travelling in a Ford Taunus V8. Both cars seem to have made a lasting impression on the occupants we can still hear from, in one form or another. Sadly, the versatile and extremely capable Gethin passed away in 2011.

With Kyalami out of the way, it was time for the series to continue with the regular competitors who would contest the remaining four rounds, all of which would last for three hours.

Killarney would end with a five-lap victory for Gerry and Jochen but was by no means straightforward. The pair had qualified second (Gerry setting a slightly faster time than his partner) behind the March of Scheckter, who was driving solo. Three hours in the Cape Town heat would be a tough ordeal for the young South African.

Gerry did the first stint lasting some 80 minutes and his battle for the lead with Scheckter was, according to Jeff Hutchinson in *Autosport*, 'becoming a classic one. Scheckter was really getting the March sliding around beautifully to stay ahead of Birrell, who was pressing him hard.'

The battle ended when Scheckter rolled into the pits with a broken throttle cable at the same time as Gerry handed over to Jochen. The now commanding lead was maintained

Just one of the many things Gerry got up to on his travels. ***(Unknown)***

by the German despite oil leaking from the gearbox, which eventually resulted in the loss of all but fourth and fifth. The win put the pair in the lead of the championship on 26 points.

In his now customary style in *Competition Car*, Gerry made only a brief mention of the race but offered a very detailed and entertaining account of his off-track activities before it and the lengthy journey (over 1800 miles) to the next round in Mozambique. 'A big factor in the Cape Town race was the tremendous heat. This was because there had been a heatwave for about a week, which helped Mass to top up his suntan, and for me to get a suntan! We had a fairly good time on the beach. The first day we went into the sea and everybody looked at us as though we were bloody mad. When we got into the sea we found out why; it was so cold it was untrue! We also went down to Cape Point (to look at the shipwrecks) and up the Table Mountain like good tourists.

'We left Cape Town on the Sunday after the race and set off on what the locals call the Garden Route. This is right along the south coast and up the east coast via Port Elizabeth, East London and Durban. The weather was so hot it was almost cooler to leave the windows closed because the air outside was stifling. Every so often we had to stop and refill our Thermos flasks with soda water or cold milk. But we did sort of drive as though we were in a permanent three-hour race, taking very little heed of the 110km/h signs (which we took as mph!).

'On the journey, we stopped at the Ford plant in Port Elizabeth, which is an incredible town consisting of one street about eight miles long! It was while cutting across the main roads to run up the east coast south of Durban that we nearly had a bit of an accident.

'We had been criss-crossing this railway line along a dirt road, and each time the railway crossed, there was a halt sign. Well, the first one we halted for. The second one, almost; the third one, we slowed for. The fourth one we lifted off for, and the fifth one we thought about. By the sixth one, we didn't even back off! This went on and on until about the 12th (or was it unlucky 13th?) time. We were just coming into town, and luckily Jochen had lifted off. By now it was dark. There was a vehicle coming the other way, which we noticed suddenly stopping in the middle of the road; we couldn't understand what for. Then we heard this funny hoot, and never thought anything of it before all of a sudden Jochen jumped on the anchors and a bloody train appeared out of the bushes pulling about 16 trucks in front of us and no lights. The only thing we could see was the glare from the fire within the cab appearing from behind a bush! I must admit it could have been a very nasty accident – from then on we listened for hooting noises!

'We stayed a couple of days near Durban and spent a day on the beach. The sea was incredibly rough and there was a lot of muck and dirt in it; we found it had been caused by an oil slick, and some detergent had been poured into it. The sea was unbelievable to swim in: you'd be swimming out, trying to clear these waves by diving through them, and the next you knew, you were upside down about six feet up the beach on dry land!

'When we were safely back in our hotel, we asked if the seas were normally as rough as that. The locals said that it was much rougher than usual, and inquired as to which area we were swimming in. We were then told that there were no shark nets there, as they had been washed away by rough weather, and that they had caught 50 sharks there the previous weekend!

'We moved out the next morning and drove across Swaziland, covering the 120 miles in about an hour and a half. Foot flat to the board over the dirt roads! We then had a bit of a problem: a customs officer didn't fancy Mr Mass leaving his country without a visa or 'visor' as he called it. Anyhow, he was rather a large kinda customs officer and we didn't really like to argue, especially as he threatened Jochen with three years in jail in Swaziland, which I wouldn't wish on anyone...

'Eventually, we arrived at yer actual mucky Mozambique, which has dirt roads twice as dirty and half as wide as the place we'd just come from. We proceeded onward to Lourenco Marques, where the next race was. I had been told about the prawns in this place and, needless to say, the first thing we did was to set out and find these prawns. Well, they told me there were big, but I would never have believed they were quite as big. When they arrived on my plate, they were about the size of my hand! Two nights of prawns were enough for me.'

Celebrating after clinching the championship at Welkom. ***(David Pearson)***

If all that wasn't enough, Gerry's travelling companion offers his memories of their quest to find some accommodation. "We were near the Mozambique channel coast and had to look for a hotel because there was nothing planned in that sense," recalls Mass. "We saw a hotel which looked attractive enough. It was very colonial. The ladies had long dresses etc... it was the evening by then.

"We went in having sat in the car for hours and hours and asked a lady, who must have been the owner, for a room. She gave us a funny look; you know, looked us over from head to toe. She said, "I only have a family room." I said, "That's no problem, we will pay for it." She replies, "How can I give a nice family room to two fellas like you." I said, "We could look a little better if you give us half a chance with a quick shower etc..." But she still wouldn't do it.

"So we got really miffed with her. We went back to the car and, having parked it facing the building, when I turned around, I floored it and showered the front with gravel. It put loads of pebbles into the hallway. My parting words were, 'That was a nice welcome to your country down here'.

"In the end, we found a beautiful place near the beach. A more modern building but it was lovely and the welcome was completely different. We were in the bar and I was having a little beer.

"A guy came in dressed in shorts and high stockings. He looked proper. He introduced himself and apologised for being so casual. I said, 'You must be joking, look at us.' This was so different. It was so nice.

"Together, we discovered these beautiful places. It was fantastic."

The life of a racing driver is never dull, is it? Joking apart, the distances covered between the races, and with some only being a week apart, was quite something. They ranged from anything from approximately 300 miles to over 1800 miles, in some cases heading virtually back the way you had come. No wonder they had to drive at the speeds described and take the associated risks. They probably found the racing safer, by comparison, though by all accounts, that wasn't the case come Lourenco Marques. A good number of errant saloon cars which made up the entry caused many problems and several were involved in numerous collisions during the race. Gerry was in one of them. Fortunately, he came off lightly compared to the leader Scheckter who hit about five. It was while his partner Dave Charlton was at the wheel that the race was decided in Gerry and Jochen's favour yet after another collision with yet another saloon delayed Charlton with just 15 minutes remaining. Mass swept by to win by two laps to claim a fortunate victory. The March duo had been quickest in practice and very much the fastest car in the race. Still, it meant it was three out of three for the Scottish/German pairing, to maintain their lead in the championship.

Once the celebrations were over the pair headed back to Johannesburg, according to Gerry in *Competition Car*: 'At breakneck speeds, setting a new record by road from Lourenco Marques to Johannesburg which will never be repeated for fear of instant arrest.'

For the next race at Welkom for the Goldfields Trophy, Gerry would be travelling and racing alone, Mass having flown back to Germany to be presented with the Sportsman of the Year award on German television. This was an important moment in the series, giving Gerry a chance to claim the title or, at least, put one hand on it. Typical of the thoroughness of his thinking and that of his close ally Brian Hart, the alloy-block engine that was still in the development stage but hadn't missed a beat in the extreme conditions, was flown back to the UK to undergo a rebuild. Amazingly, considering the races were only a week apart, it was back in time for Gerry and his travelling companions, Gethin and Owens, upon their arrival at Welkom.

While the engine had travelled thousands of miles, Gerry and his companions encountered a spot of bother on their own relatively short journey of 155 miles from Jo'burg to Welkom. 'Our troubles started when we entered the Free State or, as it transpired, the Police State,' he wrote in *Competition Car*. "We noticed a great deal of white and double-lining along the road, a lot of it pretty unnecessary. We were travelling in convoy with Ray Wardle, the team manager of March, and his boys. We came across this Mercedes doing about 20mph, so we all promptly passed it on the double white lines – only to be stopped half a mile further up by a policeman, who booked us all! He'd been watching us all the way. Could it have been a trap, methinks?'

"I've got a photo somewhere of Gerry being booked by the copper," offers Owens, with much amusement. "We were always playing games on the road, it helped pass the time while we were covering the huge distances."

The problems didn't stop there. 'The hotel proved a problem because only six of the rooms had air-conditioning, and mine wasn't one of them,' Gerry continued. 'So I moved in with Paul, only for the system to fail the following night! So we had to roast. You don't sweat because it's so dry.'

Thankfully, after all those trials and tribulations, the important part, the race itself, went considerably better. With Mass being away, Gethin joined Gerry in the lead car leaving Love driving solo in the other car, just in case Gerry had to join him if his own had any issues.

The race developed into the usual battle with the Scheckter/Charlton March, Gerry as usual doing the first stint. For the first hour, they swapped places constantly, always never more than a couple of seconds apart. Their domination was such, that within the first 13 laps, the two battling cars had lapped the entire field.

The complexion of the race changed when a backmarker spun in front of Charlton, who was leading at the time, allowing Gerry through. Surprisingly, Charlton fell back rapidly and pitted soon after suffering from exhaustion. Scheckter took up the chase and soon regained the initiative when Gerry was seen making signs to his pit that he was coming in. He was having trouble selecting gears. It turned out that the drain plug had fallen out of the gearbox and all the oil had seeped out. The plug was replaced, oil was added and the car was refuelled for Gethin to take over to resume the futile chase of Scheckter, who was nearly three minutes up the road.

Again, much to the disappointment of the March crew, the lead car began emitting an ominous trail of smoke, which ultimately became terminal in the closing stages. Gethin swept by to win by three laps from the Brian Robinson's Chevron, with the rest of the field some way behind.

One of those some way behind in fourth position was Love in the other Gunston car who had spun on the first lap and clouted the pit barrier, causing sufficient damage to delay the car. It finished 13 laps in arrears, so would have been a factor without that. Gerry had done the second stint and had according to *Autosport*: 'Underlined his long-distance stamina by a fine drive in this car as well.' It seems that the Ford training camps and having to wrestle his Capri around were paying off, especially when you consider how local ace Charlton suffered.

The victory, his fourth in a row, confirmed Gerry has the Springbok Champion. Mathematically, his total could still be equalled by the returning Mass at the final round at the Roy Hesketh circuit in Pietermaritzburg. As with Gerry at Welkom, Jochen would share two cars to give him the best possible chance of maximum points.

For the first time since the second round in Cape Town, the

teams and drivers were afforded a two-week break and only needed to cover the short distance of 300 miles to contest the final round a week before Christmas.

For once, it wasn't the extreme heat that would cause problems but the complete opposite, a steady drizzle and overcast skies greeting the entries come the start. Practice had been dry and saw the usual trio of cars at the sharp end. Scheckter, driving solo, on pole from Gerry and Jochen with Jochen's back-up Gethin car completing the front row.

Tyre choice proved to be critical in deciding the race and the championship. Mass elected to start on wet tyres in the car he was sharing with Gerry, which ultimately cost him the lead after 10 laps when he was passed by Scheckter's intermediate-shod car. Two laps later he was in for slicks, which cost him two laps and dropped him to 12th. He would have to pit again for wets after the rain began to fall heavily after around 30 laps.

Scheckter retired from the lead, yet again, handing the advantage to Gethin who was doing a sterling job keeping Mass's title hopes alive. After 85 laps he came in to hand over the car. Mass had done only eight laps, which included a spin on the straight in the ever-worsening conditions, when the race was halted after two of the three hours. It wasn't just because of the rain, but also a heavy mist which had descended across the circuit to make visibility nigh-on impossible.

The Mass/Gethin car was declared the winner, meaning maximum points for the German. And what of Gerry in the delayed sister car? After two tyre changes and a faulty ignition box, he recovered from a lowly 14th to finish in sixth overall and fifth in class, and had the race not been stopped he would have ended up much higher. Ultimately, it didn't matter, the two points that he scored were sufficient to make him the outright champion.

In celebration he decided to indulge in an alcoholic drink for the first time which, according to Margaret, ended up with him getting a bit carried away. "He always said that he would have his first drink when he won his first Grand Prix," recalls Margaret. "He must have decided in South Africa that he'd never win one, so he decided to drink a bottle of wine instead of the fizzy stuff, which he had threatened to drink if he became World Champion. He ended up dancing on the table. Many years later our daughter Kara, after over-indulging on the 'fizzy' stuff, ended up doing the same. It must be hereditary."

What a campaign it had been on all fronts. The fragile new March had been a serious threat but up against the combination of a robust and reliable Chevron overseen by the extremely capable and versatile Paul Owens and a bulletproof engine from engine wizard Brian Hart, they stood little chance.

Gerry and Jochen proved to be a perfect match, and it was remembered with much fondness by the latter. "We were very compatible in the car," offers Mass. "The speed was pretty much the same between us. There were fractions between us but it didn't matter in a long-distance race because you have to make sure you get to the finish line with a good car. You didn't want the guys who wanted to be heroes and superquick, which harmed the car. We never had any different views on things. We worked as a team.

The start of the Natal Three Hours at Roy Hesketh. Mass takes the first stint while Gerry stands alongside. ***(H Matheson Collection)***

"The whole series was terrific. It was a wonderful time to get to know your team partner very well. We talked about Margaret and the twins often. He regretted he wasn't with them. I don't think I had met Margaret by then. We travelled together. We stayed together, often in the same rooms. It was fantastic to be with him. There were forever smiles with Gerry. He was easygoing. We got on very well. It was super-nice.

"The whole bunch of us got on well. Mike Hailwood was around some of the time. Mike and Peter, those guys stirred up some stuff. Paul was clever and a good guy."

"I am sure I had met Jochen before they went to South Africa but obviously didn't make an impression on him!" says Margaret. "It was in Berlin, at the Kempinski hotel where Ford held a 'do' to, I think, announce the drivers for the next year. Not 100 percent sure if that was the reason but it was Ford hospitality at its best. Jochen was being very funny in the spa complex!"

With only seven days to go, once the series and celebrations had ended Gerry was heading back to the UK to spend time with Margaret and the twins for their first Christmas together. Then, in the New Year it would be Gerry Birrell racing driver, again, not Gerry Birrell family man. Exciting times lay ahead.

On the limit during pre-season testing at Hockenheim. *(Unknown)*

CHAPTER EIGHT

ON THE CUSP

The new year dawned with two works contracts safely trousered, both of which were a continuation of the deals from previous years.

The renewal of the Ford contract for a third year with more outings in Europe for the Cologne competition department was further confirmation – if any were needed – just how highly thought of Gerry was by the powers-that-be. It wasn't just in the motorsport arena that the car giant required his talents but also in the development of the Escort RS2000, a sports version of the market leader in the family car market. A mundane task but no less rewarding for Gerry, who just loved to be behind the wheel of anything motorised. Especially since, in this case, the car had undergone an extensive programme of research and development, of which Gerry was at the centre when it came to testing out the ideas of the engineers.

In his role of Ford's European Director of Motorsport Stuart Turner oversaw the project, along with many others. He remains full of praise for the time and effort Gerry put in to make the car a success. "A classic example of Gerry at his best is the work he did on the RS2000. We had a race track at Boreham where the competition department was based and he was a very good test driver, as well as a brilliant racing driver. I can still remember him coming in after one lap of Boreham with the prototype RS2000, looking at me and the engineer and saying, 'Is it too early in the morning to be rude?' And then he was amiable, not rude, but extremely critical. And because of his work with the engineers, the car became very, very successful. I don't know if anyone has done a detailed analysis, but my guess is that at either grass-roots, national and international level in both racing and rallying, more events have been won by what I would term as the 'clubman' in that car than any other in history, and the fact it was such a successful car you have to give full marks to Gerry.

"It was born out of needing a slightly bigger-engined car than the Mexico, which would be good for the clubman as well as being a useful road car. Ford had an Advanced Vehicle Operations (AVO) which was low volume, making specialised cars like the Escort Mexicos. The idea was to get the congestion and confusion out of the main plants at Halewood and Dagenham and have a special unit to build these cars."

On the single-seater front there was more equally good news. On the back of the successful Springbok campaign, Gerry had signed a deal to drive for the works Chevron be his third season in the formula, but the first one as a works driver. The opportunity just to focus on the driving,

Another works drive clinched. This time in F2 with Chevron. ***(John Leck)***

for once, must have been a welcome relief. And for once he didn't have to bring any money. Ford had agreed to supply free engines, which would be the alloy-blocked Hart, to facilitate the deal. The running costs would be taken care of by the usual trade suppliers.

The signing of the deal put an end to Gerry's partnership with mechanic John Catt. But, as Catt explains, it wasn't that straightforward: "When we stopped at the end of '72 Gerry said 'You keep all the tools because if we get to work together again, we'll need them. We never really split up. It was a case of I had to get a recognised job to get a mortgage, I was planning to get married at that time. I wasn't prepared to go up to Bolton to work for Chevron. Gerry did ask me to go with him, but I ended up working for Brian Hart.

"We kept in touch. I painted his house in Purleigh. I was invited to dinner one night and I went straight from work at Brian's to go over there and Ford's European Competition Manager, Mike Kranefuss, unbeknown to me, was also there. He was over on business and was staying in a hotel, so Gerry invited him for dinner. Margaret was cooking. Once I saw that Kranefuss was there, I said, "I'll go." Gerry said, "No, don't go." and Margaret chips in, "You've been invited."

"Another time," I said.

"That was far more important than feeding me and Gerry again, the same sort of thing with Jackie Stewart at Oulton Park a couple of years earlier, he felt guilty."

As was the norm, Gerry was his usual busy self before the start of the season. He was at Hockenheim for the first shakedown of the new Group 2 Cologne-prepared Capri.

All part of the job. Gerry on Ford promotional duties. ***(Ford Motor Company)***

Another Ford training camp gathering, this time 1973. From the left, Fitzpatrick, Mass, Glemser, Heyer, Gerry, team manager Kranefuss, JYS and fitness instructor Traub. ***(Ford Motor Company)***

Reportedly, along with fellow team member Mass, he was astonished at the power that the Kugelfischer-injected V6 engine was now giving. Then he was at Silverstone to sample another Group 2 Capri, this one a Broadspeed example, which had been built to compete in the British Saloon Car Championship (BSCC) for former Ford team-mate Dave Matthews to drive. The outing had two motives. Firstly, a further evaluation of the car after only two hours of running at Goodwood and, secondly, passenger rides for the assembled motoring press on hand for the car's official unveiling. Unfortunately, these had to be cancelled due to a couple of mechanical problems. They missed a treat according to two of the leading journalists of the time who had the pleasure of being alongside Gerry on other occasions.

Jeremy Walton, who had left *Motor Sport* and *Motoring News* to take up a position with Ford handling their Public Relations at Boreham and for the Advanced Vehicles Operation (AVO), recalls one such occasion: "We were travelling back from Silverstone in an engineering development Ford Cortina. Yes, you read that right, one of the ornate Coke Bottle third edition best-sellers from Dagenham. This one carried a 210 horsepower punch from a seriously re-engineered implant of Ford's V6 motor with an early turbo-charging layout.

"The rest of the car (PWC 906K) was largely unmodified, the suspension and brakes were primitive production level. Even the standard steel wheels rested under mundane Dagenham coachwork, although the bonnet did have bumps and scoops to manage airflow and it was the hideous metallic brown of many period Fords. But you could surprise other road users with its 133mph maximum speed.

"Gerry took one look at it resting in my hands and said with a grin, 'Think I'll have a wee drive of that, could take us all night to get home otherwise.' He asked what was under the bonnet and I may have been economical with the truth. I might just have mentioned the V6, but not the extra 80 horses developed by that non-production unit. Oh, and that the chassis was pretty sloppy, and braking required some advance planning if you deployed that nose-heavy power.

"We set off along the lanes and quick B-roads that connect Silverstone with Oxfordshire, which if you wanted an entertaining drive away from main arteries were ideal. The laughter started at the first corner and continued for the next 60 miles which were completed in less than an hour.

"Gerry's best trick was arriving at a traffic light-controlled urban junction and deciding that the brakes really did not need the exertion of a red light stop. So, we turned left through a garage forecourt to join the startled traffic on the adjacent main road at some velocity.

"As you would expect, I also got a driving lesson. One long B-road straight saw the Cortina reach the other side of 110mph. Ahead, an uphill right, one that would usually demand a third gear 70mph scrabble from mere mortals. I slumped a little lower in the plastic seat and looked at Gerry's feet on the pedals and registered the steering inputs. The

First outing in 1973 at Monza in the latest offering from Ford. ***(Josef Mayrhofer)***

view ahead morphed from screen-filling disaster to a 100mph exit, top gear still in place. An easing of the throttle and a determined caress of the unwieldy steering wheel became just another memory.

"My memory is dominated by the monumental speed from such an awkward steed, delivered with the hallmark smoothness of one of Scotland's finest. The lessons of driving so many unlikely vehicles beyond their limits in his earlier motor sporting life had been thoroughly learned by this talented professional."

Next up, Chris Witty, who got to do a lap of a circuit – and some circuit it was! "When I think of Gerry, I remember being strapped in the passenger seat while we did a full lap of the Nürburgring in a works Cologne Capri and were only eight seconds off the class lap record! Now that was a magical lap and an experience I shall always treasure."

All may have been well with the Capri, but that wasn't the case on the Formula Two front. What was it with Gerry and F2? The first outing of the year should have been at the opening round of the European series at Mallory Park in March, but unfortunately his car wasn't finished, so he had to sit it out. With four weeks before the next round at Hockenheim, there was no reason the car wouldn't be ready and, hopefully, a shakedown beforehand would be welcome. It seemed that his campaign was on the back foot already, in what promised to be a classic year of Formula Two.

Gerry with Scheckter, Fitzpatrick and Stewart at Monza finds something amusing. All were driving works Capris. *(Jutta Fausel)*

In what would turn out to be his last column in *Competition Car*, entitled, Birrell on F2, he devoted the entire two pages to his thoughts and predictions for the year ahead. His forecast of Jean-Pierre Jarier and Jochen Mass being the top two contenders turned out to be amazingly accurate, confirming how shrewd and deep-thinking he was not just about his racing, but the whole scene in general. That was something Chris Witty alluded to when paying tribute to him.

The introduction of the new BMW engine in the back of the STP-supported works Marches and selected customer cars brought a serious rival to the established alloy-blocked Hart and BDG powerplants and proved to be a game-changer. And there was unprecedented choice of chassis from March, Chevron, GRD, Surtees, Motul Rondel, Brabham and Elf. A developing tyre war between Goodyear and Firestone. And a real mix of drivers, from the up-and-coming to the established stars who would pit their wits not just against each other, but several graded Formula One stars who would be ineligible for points. Taking all those factors into account, Gerry could ill-afford to be playing catch-up.

His season finally got underway in late March at Monza for the opening round of the ETCC. The season ahead looked all set for a real battle between the Ford and BMW works teams. There was certainly some driving talent on show in both camps. Ford had Jackie Stewart in the line-up sharing with stalwart, Glemser. Established talent Mass was sharing with rising star, Scheckter, while Gerry was partnered with the vastly experienced saloon car exponent John Fitzpatrick, who had rejoined the Ford camp after a brief sojourn at BMW. Their rivals had among their number the likes of Chris Amon, Dieter Quester and Hans Stuck, who had followed former Ford Competition boss Jochen Neerpasch to the Munich-based outfit.

Practice saw all the Ford drivers evenly matched with Stewart emerging as the quickest to claim pole position. Gerry was just over a second adrift but was the most spectacular according to *Autosport*. 'Birrell and Fitzpatrick had setting-up dramas, Gerry managing to lift two inside wheels going through the Parabolica. For the next day harder springs were fitted to the car which helped, but it was still a bit of brute.'

The race proved extremely disappointing. After running in fifth place in the opening laps, Gerry was an early pit visitor with steam coming from under the bonnet. The water system was replenished but to no avail; the head gasket had failed.

Team-mate Fitzpatrick had done very little running in practice and now never got to sample the car in the race. All these years later 'Fitz' doesn't have anything good to say about the Capri but, remembering the time spent with Gerry, he's got nothing but good memories. "Monza was our first time together and the car was absolutely terrible. To be honest, in my opinion, it was pretty terrible all year. In fact, it was almost undriveable. We were just trying to get the best out of the car and improve it. Gerry had done a little testing. I had a few ideas, but it was mainly down to him.

Grahame White discusses things with Gerry, while mechanic Neil Edwards looks on. ***(Unknown)***

"I obviously knew him very well from our many battles in 1971 in saloon cars. We got along very well together with neither of us trying to out-do the other. He had absolutely no side to him at all, didn't pretend to be anything he wasn't. He was always upbeat, never negative. I have only fond memories of him. He was a great guy.

"Plus, we would joke around a lot. There was some rivalry and banter with the Germans. Jochen (Mass) would say something like, 'We may have lost the two heats, but we will win the final.' We all got on extremely well together. It was terrific.

"One of the first things I remember about that season was when we all had to report to the Ford Competition Department in Cologne very early in the year to sign our contracts. I don't think Ford in Britain was actually paying him that much at the time. Saloon car drivers weren't on that much money back then. I get to Cologne and Gerry's there along with Mass and Glemser sitting outside the office of the competition boss, Michael Kranefuss. He calls us in one by one and I'm the first to go in. He shows me the contract and, I mean, it was very good. It was the most money I'd ever been paid. So I go out and Gerry's the next one in. When he comes out he was absolutely over the moon. He came and sat down next to me and says, 'John, I can't believe how much I'm getting paid to do exactly what I would do for nothing.'

"Another perk of the contract was that we were given some special, much-modified, German-registered Capri road cars. We both brought them back to the UK. We would go speeding everywhere and, of course, we'd get stopped by the police. When they saw the German number plates they assumed you were German and just told you to get on your way."

Before his long-awaited and much anticipated first outing in the new Chevron B25 at Hockenheim on 8 April, Gerry attended the pre-Le Mans test the previous weekend with driving partner Hans Heyer. Despite a detached water hose – the same problem as Monza – and still struggling with the car's strange handling characteristics, Gerry showed a good turn of speed to be fastest in his class and ninth quickest overall.

The organisers had decided to hold a four-hour race on Sunday which attracted only 25 entrants. Gerry would take the opening stint and, while running in third place on the second lap, 'Had an enormous triple-spin while experimenting with a nearly-flat curve on the new section of track before the pits,' reported Michael Cotton in *Motoring News*. The spin couldn't have cost much time because Gerry was soon running in second place and would set a fastest lap, some nine seconds faster than his best from the previous year.

Unfortunately, when Heyer had taken over just after half distance, he came into the pits trailing smoke. The performance drew praise from Pete Lyons in *Autosport*. 'The works Capri was driven brilliantly by the pair until sidelined by a broken piston.'

That was the last of the Capri outings for quite a while, which meant Gerry could finally get his hands on his new Chevron and focus on developing and honing it to his liking. That was the part of his job, which involved many of the facets from which he derived the most satisfaction.

Hockenheim proved to be a mixed affair. In practice he suffered three punctures in two laps, losing valuable running time – he'd already only had the briefest of runs at Silverstone beforehand – so to line up just outside the top 10 for the first of the two heats was a good effort.

After dicing with Roger Williamson, Derek Bell, Bob Wollek and Stuck, in and around the lower reaches of the top 10, he would benefit from a couple of retirements to end up in sixth place at the flag.

The second heat saw him going well in the early stages and looking set for a points finish until a locked front wheel while trying to outbrake Bell into one of the chicanes saw him hit a marker cone, resulting in bodywork damage which caused the car to overheat. A visit to the pits for inspection saw him drop down to 18th. Combined with his sixth in heat one, that resulted in a tenth-place finish overall on aggregate.

Back on home soil for the traditional Easter meeting at

A surprising win was on the cards until... *(Chris Walker/Kartpix)*

Thruxton, Gerry almost came away with a win virtually from the back of the grid. His lowly starting position was due to the changeable weather, a down-on-power engine and a fuel problem in the first heat.

The story of a chaotic final, which saw many incidents and multiple changes of lead, was described wonderfully in *Autosport* by Ian Phillips, one of the leading journalists of the period and a lover of all things Formula Two. 'Birrell had come through the field like a rocket and was up to fourth after only 10 laps. On lap 21 Birrell finally made it into second place and two laps later it became first when Coulon disappeared. For a couple of laps, Birrell seemed to establish a small lead but Scheckter and Pescarolo were not giving up and came right back at Gerry and just sat behind him.

'On lap 30, with 20 to go, Birrell, Scheckter, Pescarolo and Beuttler were fighting it out for the lead. The leading battle became split slightly on lap 32 when Scheckter suffered a puncture and spun out of the race. Birrell opened up a small gap as Beuttler pressed his attentions on Pescarolo.

'Birrell was having the F2 race of his life and was the man in charge; he didn't intend to lose it. Beuttler had other ideas, however. Birrell's rather unusual line into the chicane leaves a small and inviting gap for challengers. To make use of it the challenger has to use all the kerb, but the gap is still not big enough to get through. On lap 48 Beuttler tried it, however. It didn't work. The two cars touched and all hell was let loose. Birrell spun and was left in the middle of the chicane exit, Beuttler was out on the grass again, Pescarolo struggled through on the inside and took the lead as Wollek and Mass arrived side by side. Jochen chose the smallest of gaps between the stationary Chevron and the Armco, Bob went down the inside and they met the other side of Birrell. Miraculously they didn't touch and Jochen just took second. Beuttler by this time was rejoining in fourth place right behind Wollek while Birrell got going again in fifth some 20sec down.

'Pescarolo went on to win but arguments will rage for many months about the Birrell/Beuttler incident; it is a pity it happened but it would have been unjust if either had come second after some great driving but third and fourth did not do either justice. Beuttler's placing is currently provisional pending an inquiry.'

The extraordinary race was witnessed by Margaret, making a welcome reappearance on the scene. Although, from what she says, Gerry wasn't that enamoured with the idea. "I was looking after the twins, washing overalls, etc, keeping busy," she recalls. "At one point, Gerry said, 'I've got you trapped now.' I thought, 'Nobody's got me trapped!' I arranged with a local girl who helped me to go to Thruxton. I took the twins

...Beuttler tried an over-ambitious lunge on the final lap. *(John Leck)*

to a hotel and Gerry stayed in another one because he didn't want to be disturbed before he was racing.

"I did that once and realised it took me two weeks to recover and I thought, 'I'll stay at home now.' Which I did."

It would seem that Phillips was being quite prophetic with his 'arguments will rage for months' comment. It took only a matter of hours for them to start after Beuttler was disqualified for dangerous driving (he was reinstated later after an appeal). Reportedly, well after most people had left the circuit, matters became heated in the stewards' room between Grahame White, the Chevron team manager, and Max Mosley of March, representing Gerry and Beuttler, respectively. White pointed out that no protest had been put in by Chevron, although he did ask the stewards to look into the matter thoroughly.

The next two outings were both disappointing and frustrating in equal measure, more so after the strong performance at Thruxton.

At the Nürburgring, he suffered a broken seat mounting in practice on the Friday after a heavy landing, which led to him to quip in his usual dry-humoured way in *Autosport*, 'Now I know how Peter Gethin drives.'

Much more serious was the huge accident he had when he was the first to come across a damp section of the track at Fuchschleite. After clouting the barrier heavily, the car was extensively damaged with no chance of it being repaired for the race. With the next race at Pau on the following weekend, Gerry, Derek Bennett and the rest of the Chevron team flew back to the UK to install his Hart/Ford powerplant into Gethin's car. As Gethin was now busy racing elsewhere, Gerry had become the lone Chevron representative.

As at the Nürburgring, he was delighted with every aspect of the car's behaviour at Pau, his enthusiasm reported constantly by Phillips in *Autosport* and the equally capable Alan Henry in *Motoring News*. It's easy to come over all nostalgic when remembering the excitement of Thursday mornings when you got your hands on the latest issues – it was even better in the '80s when *Motoring News* came out on Wednesday. Two days of excitement!

On this occasion Gerry's enthusiasm was matched by performance and results, both of which had been so hard to come by thus far. A strong qualifying performance in dry conditions earned him a place on the second row for his heat, but the circuit was awash as the heavens opened just before the start. That was manna from heaven for Gerry: a car he raved about and conditions he revelled in. He had a somewhat lonely race, some way back from the leading pair of Vittorio Brambilla and Williamson, but it resulted in a third-place finish. Pau had never been his happy hunting ground, so perhaps he was being cautious to make sure he made the final, where he hoped for the same conditions.

Unfortunately, that wasn't the case, as a gloriously sunny day greeted the 22 starters as Gerry lined up on the third row. A strong start saw him running in the top six until a lengthy pitstop to investigate a distributor problem delayed him for four laps. He rejoined to get some decent race mileage under his belt, and to enjoy himself, and accomplished both. He put on quite a show with a superb display of power-sliding out of the corners. A 10th place finish was scant reward for his efforts, which merited a points finish at the least.

A fine study of Gerry in action at Pau by ace photographer Jutta Fausel. She was a regular on the F2 trail and is fondly remembered. ***(Jutta Fausel)***

ds the Motul of Tim Schenken up the hill at the picturesque Pau. ***(Unknown)***

It should have been back to racing with a roof over his head for the rearranged second round of the ETCC at the Salzburgring. The original race should have been on the same weekend as the Thruxton F2 meeting, so he wouldn't have been present. The irony of the rescheduling was not lost, in light of what happened in Thursday's unofficial practice session. He somehow walked away from an enormous accident, which was no fault of his own, when a tyre deflated while he was taking the flat-in-fifth first corner.

The description of the accident in *Motoring News* gives a graphic example of the magnitude of the accident. 'The Birrell/Larrousse car was being used by all the team to test a new combination of 16in wheels with ultra-low profile Dunlops instead of the 15in rims previously used. Glemser had completed several practice laps in the car and handed over to Birrell, who continued after tyre pressures had been lowered to reduce the effect of doming in the centres with very high pressures.

'Birrell was on what was to be positively his last lap as the last drops of fuel drained from the reserve tank; entering the long, sweeping right-hander at the end of the pits straight, the fastest part of the circuit with 7300rpm showing in fifth, the tail flicked around at the speed of light and Birrell found himself going backwards at 150mph. Enveloped in a cloud

The Bulova watch found at the scene of the Salzburgring accident is now in the safe possession of Alex Shore. ***(Alex Shore)***

of smoke which hid the impending obstacles from his view, the Capri spun round countless times, hit and demolished the Armco with the front left-hand corner, somersaulted end-over-end, landed on top of the barrier on its roof, somersaulted again, landed back on its four wheels on the track, bounced in the air again, flicked on its roof and skated down the circuit upside down for 200 metres.

'A disbelieving Birrell released himself from the harness holding him upside down in a broken seat, shook himself and discovered that he was undamaged apart from one slight bruise. He thought himself even luckier when he observed his battered helmet, a clean cut through both layers of the left sleeve of his overalls and his left hand bereft of glove and Bulova watch, found at the scene of the initial impact along with most of the driver's door panel. The front left-hand wheel was buried in a distorted bulkhead, the rear of the roof flattened by the Armco and every other panel damaged.

'Marks on the track indicated that the left-hand rear tyre had deflated a split second before the crash. The 16in wheels have no safety ledges or bolts and have wells in the machined rims instead of being flat like the extruded 15in variety. When the tyre deflated it slid into the well, leaving the car to run on the rim at that corner, and a narrow rib of magnesium has a negative coefficient of adhesion in a 150mph bend!

"It wasn't as frightening as crashing the Escort at Zandvoort last year: I saw that coming, but this one happened so quickly I didn't have time to be frightened, reflected a surprisingly unshaken Birrell."

It was a massive accident that obviously rendered him a non-starter for the race, and he was very lucky to get off as lightly as he did. While he was reportedly unshaken by it and suffered no injuries of any consequence, you have to wonder how he was mentally. The number of huge accidents was mounting up in both of his chosen categories. They had all been brought about by a failure of some kind, or just bad luck in the case of the Nürburgring F2 shunt, so he wouldn't have been questioning his ability. But he wouldn't have been human if he wasn't thinking along the lines of 'what's next?'.

A major contributing factor in Gerry's survival in the shunt was the modifications made over the winter by Ford's new chief engineer, Thomas Ammerschlager, who would subsequently work for the competition departments of both Audi and BMW. He recalls his first task: "One of my main priorities over the winter had been to reinforce the rollcage, for two reasons: firstly, to make the car stiffer which would improve the handling; and secondly to provide better protection for the driver.

"To calculate the stiffness of the rollcage, we built a scale model from welding wire and tried to bend and twist it. We then removed braces and added new ones until the model was as stiff as possible. In the end, we did such a good job that it exceeded the FIA regulations by far. Jackie Stewart told me that the Capri was the only touring car he felt safe in, and coming from him that was a real statement.

"I am very happy to say that in two high-speed accidents, Gerry's and Dieter Glemser's at the Nürburgring, both drivers were only very slightly injured. To my knowledge, no driver has ever been killed in a race car I designed.

"In my opinion, the tyre deflation was caused by an O-ring seal fitted between the outer rim and the wheel centre not working properly. I don't think that a safety ledge or anything else would have prevented the tyre from leaving the rim because it was a sudden blow-out and not a slow puncture. The 15in rims didn't have safety ledges, either.

"When we arrived at the scene of the accident I remember feeling very happy and relieved that Gerry was OK. He was complaining of sore ribs, but he seemed much more concerned that he couldn't find his watch!"

The timepiece in question was reunited with its owner, much to his delight. It is still in fine working order and is very much a prized possession of Alex Shore, Margaret's son from her second marriage. How Gerry came to have the watch in the first place was cleared up by Jochen Mass when Alex drove him to Donington recently. "I know my granddad had the Bulova for a while, and I was fascinated by it as a kid, which is why I've ended up with it," says Alex. "Mum remembers Gerry telling her that he'd bought it from Jochen and I'd always believed this. Jochen noticed the watch when I was driving and said something like 'I remember those watches,' and I replied that he should do as it was his. He asked what I meant and so I relayed the story I got from mum. He then corrected me and said that actually all the Ford drivers at the time were given them and he thought they had all given them away to a mechanic or other team members and that Gerry must just have kept his.

"I don't think it was necessarily as a prized possession, despite it being engraved with his name, as there are a few photos of him wearing another more traditional chronograph watch and he also had an Omega Chronostop which was designed specifically for racing drivers. Mum still has the Omega."

The next two outings in the Capri, at the Nürburgring 1000km and Le Mans, brought mixed fortunes. At the Nürburgring Gerry was back sharing with Fitzpatrick. The pair lapped very respectably in practice, only a couple of seconds slower than the sister car of Mass and Glemser. The only problem Gerry mentioned to Jeff Hutchinson of *Autosport* was that 'It took all his strength to turn the steering wheel.' The problem was that the steering racks were not standing up to the job due to the vast increase in the car's performance. The Cologne mechanics changed the rubber-mounted racks for stronger metal and Teflon-mounted ones.

"Gerry's so right to say that about the steering being so heavy," says Fitzpatrick. "The Capri was really hard work and to be honest never that good a car. Jochen Neerpasch, who was the competitions boss in '72, had moved to BMW and taken chief engineer Martin Braumgart with him. I never rated his replacement, Thomas Ammerschlager, and that was why the car was so bad.

"Any performance improvements, in my opinion, were down to Gerry's abilities as a test driver. He was bloody good. Plus he was a team player, that's why Ford used him extensively in both their road and rallying development programmes."

In the race the car ran faultlessly, some achievement considering it completed 39 laps of the gruelling, arduous, 14-miles of what is often called 'The Green Hell' and would end up in sixth place and first in class. That was a fine result considering that according to Michael Cotton's report in *Motoring News*, 'Birrell still hadn't settled down properly after his frightful Salzburgring crash.'

"He was a tough guy," offers Glemser. "He seemed OK after the shunt but was quite shaken. I took him to the hospital in Salzburg, where they X-rayed him. In the end he only had some bruises, but the doctors also found something suspicious on his collarbone, a small crack. Gerry told them not to worry, he had broken it a couple of years earlier and never really cared that it hadn't healed properly."

'The Green Hell' was the last place you wanted to be if you were still unsettled, especially with it being on the following weekend. They do say that the best way to overcome your fear is to conquer it immediately, however. And it seemed that Gerry subscribed to that theory, or else he had no choice. Today, there's no way he would have been allowed back behind the wheel so soon after such a high-speed accident without, at the very least, a thorough medical examination. Such different times.

Another change on the co-driver front for Le Mans saw him reunited with Heyer, with whom he had shared the car at the test weekend's four-hour race.

Gerry qualified the car just outside the top 20, right in among his class opposition of the other Capris and BMWs. Disappointingly, he was out within an hour of the start when the distributor rotor arm broke and left him stranded out on the circuit. A replacement was sent out from the pits, but a vital component was missing so the car had to be retired.

Due to his early demise Gerry was drafted into the third works car of the less experienced pairing of Jean Vinatier and Helmuth Koinigg. Again, this would end in retirement after encountering many delays with the fuel pump drivebelts.

Due to the run of consecutive outings in the Capri, Gerry's Formula Two appearances had been affected. Three rounds were missed, which were the races at Kinnekulle (crashing at Salzburgring), Nivelles (Le Mans weekend) and Hockenheim. The Hockenheim race didn't clash with a Group 2 race, but this time he was absent because the Chevron truck had been involved in an accident on the M1 on its way back to Bolton from Nivelles. The resulting damage to both truck and race car was too serious to be repaired in time to make the trip to Germany.

Before his next planned Formula Two outing at Rouen-Les-Essarts, Gerry headed to Castle Combe the weekend before for something far less serious. The meeting was one of the Fordsport Days, which he had competed in before as part of his Ford duties. On this occasion he was entered in a racing drivers versus rally drivers encounter where all participants would be in standard Ford Consul 30-litre GTs. For some strange reason, he was part of the rally drivers' team. Although no stranger to the gravel, he was hardly a rally driver at that stage of his career.

In the early stages he ran in the top six, mixing it with the likes of Roger Clark, Dave Brodie, Barrie 'Whizzo' Williams and Richard Longman. Typical of these encounters, the race ended two laps earlier than planned when Longman and Tony Pond tangled, resulting in both hitting the barriers heavily. How Gerry ended up is not known but he didn't feature in the top six according to *Autosport*.

With the light-hearted event out of the way, it was time to head to France for more serious matters. An outing on the ultra-quick, downright frightening road circuit at Rouen always focused your mind and was never taken lightly. Gerry knew the circuit well and its reputation for inadequate safety standards – even for that era – and of the intransigent attitude of the organising club. Unfortunately, the combination of those two factors would lead to another preventable fatality.

A combination that deserved so much more. ***(Motorsport Images)***

CHAPTER NINE

ROUEN AND THE AFTERMATH

Despite concerns about the venue, the meeting at Rouen was regarded as one of the most popular on the Formula Two schedule. The picturesque 3.4-mile circuit, of which 90 percent was public roads, was a real test of a driver's bravery, skill and commitment.

Since Gerry's last visit in 1971 – he had missed the '72 race through injury – a new permanent section had been introduced so this would be his first on the revised layout. Other significant developments had been made on the safety side, which had always been a concern. The majority of the circuit had been resurfaced and virtually the entire track was lined with Armco barriers, the use of which was still causing serious concerns over their effectiveness – not just at Rouen, but at all the major circuits – amongst the motorsport fraternity. It would be the barriers and their poor installation that would cause controversy and outrage when the meeting got underway on Friday. An accident involving Mike Beuttler – which all parties failed to act upon – gave a foretaste of what was to come the following day.

The accident occurred on the new section of the circuit after official observers reported that a rear tyre deflated and came off the rim when Beuttler was pulling maximum revs in fourth gear when entering an inconsequential curve. The car spun wildly out of control and went straight into and under the barrier. The whole front end was ripped off, including the pedals. In *Autosport* Ian Phillips said, 'How he escaped with just severe bruising to his ankles and shock was hard to believe. For some unaccountable reason, nobody concerned themselves with the alarming way the barrier reacted. The attitude of the supposedly safety-conscious drivers over the weekend was puzzling in the extreme.'

Gerry had been unable to take part in proceedings on Friday when, to begin with, the Chevron transporter had been delayed at Le Havre with customs carnet issues. Then, after sterling work by the team to prepare both his and returning team-mate Gethin's cars for practice, he was denied access to the track by officials who thought the session was about to end. Gethin did manage to get out and set a respectable time in the few laps he was able to complete.

The loss of a full day's running was an added pressure that Gerry could obviously have done without, especially given the presence of Ken Tyrrell who, reportedly, had made the trip specifically to watch him. Unbeknown to all but 'Uncle Ken' and Ford's PR executive Walter Hayes, who was responsible among many things for funding the most successful engine in Formula One history, the Ford Cosworth DFV, Tyrrell's lead driver Jackie Stewart planned to retire at the end of the season. With Gerry's Ford connections and their close alliance with Tyrrell and Stewart, plus Gerry's close friendship with his fellow Scot, the key elements were in place for him to be the perfect replacement alongside Francois Cevert for 1974.

Frustratingly for Gerry, when he finally got out on track he was initially unable to get his hands on the best tyres. "It was always difficult with the tyre companies to get the best quality tyres," recalls Paul Owens who was engineering both Gerry's and Peter's cars. "We managed to get one set of softer, qualifying tyres,"

Owens, who has worked with many drivers, offers an insight into how his two compared. Gethin, by that time, had vast experience of all the major categories, including Formula One, where he had famously won the 1971 Italian Grand Prix and the Victory Race in which Yardley BRM team-mate Jo Siffert had perished, so he was a good benchmark. "I've worked with so many drivers who were good test and development drivers of which, Gerry was one. He was very precise, his feedback was very good and he knew what he wanted. He was always accommodating with the set-up of the car, which you certainly had to be in sports car racing.

"They both worked very well together and it certainly helped me to be able to set up the cars for them with their feedback. I knew more about Peter's driving style, his strengths and weaknesses, having worked with him for two or three years previously. Having done the Springbok series and a couple of F2 races with Gerry, our relationship was maturing. I was learning about him very quickly. There wasn't a great deal of difference between them."

Gerry finally got his hands on the right tyres for the afternoon practice session, once Gethin had completed several laps on them in the morning session. Reportedly, Peter was effusive in his praise, describing them 'as magic' as he urged Gerry to try them. And once they had been fitted, Gerry was immediately among the pacesetters.

But later in the session, while he was plunging downhill towards Six Freres – the third in a series of challenging fifth-gear, 150mph-plus bends – one of the front tyres deflated. With both front wheels locked the car understeered wide, missing the apex and failing to even start taking the corner. With no run-off, the head-on impact with the barrier was instant and sickening in its force. The two-tier Armco barrier, shamefully so poorly secured, lifted up and allowed the car to slip beneath and pass completely through it, inflicting injuries from which poor Gerry stood no chance of surviving. Some reports said he died instantly, others suggest he succumbed on the way to the hospital. Either way, it was irrelevant. The world of motorsport had lost one of its most popular figures in a manner that was sadly characteristic of the times.

One of the first to rush to the scene was Paul Owens. "They stopped the session and we quickly realised that Gerry hadn't come around," he reflects sombrely. "I can remember jumping on a monkey bike and riding down there. Unfortunately, he was in the ambulance and... You know, it was quite a shock for me. I'd never seen anything like that. It was a great sadness, it was a difficult one to comprehend.

"I think it was a marshal who said that it looked like he had a puncture, whether it was a puncture or whether he went straight on because it understeered, we'll never know. There was a recess for a course car or other vehicles and the Armco didn't follow the circuit properly, it kind of jutted out, and the rest is... Such a tragedy."

Of those present that awful day, pertinent recollections are offered by a couple of on-track rivals and two of the leading journalists of the time.

"I was travelling a few hundred yards behind when Gerry went straight on and ripped the Armco up for many yards," recalls Colin Vandervell. "I slowed but could not stop to help because there was no safe place to park the car on the hill. I remember thinking nobody could have survived such a violent accident at those speeds.

"He wasn't a great friend and I can't even remember racing against him before Rouen, but his death had a profound effect. I recall vividly sitting on the grid the following day in my semi-works March/BMW with Emerson and Ronnie in their works Lotuses alongside and thinking, what am I doing here? I decided then and there I would no longer race single-seaters. After the race I told March I would honour my commitments until the end of the season. Max Mosley was very surprised and couldn't understand my decision.

"In my opinion, Rouen was far too dangerous for Formula Two. The cars were too fast for the track."

"I was Colin's team manager," says Andrew Marriott, better known as the legendary ARM of *Motoring News/Motor Sport* fame. "It all sounds very grand, but I was there as unpaid help. I can still remember very clearly Colin coming into the pits. I leant into the car to listen to him and he said that he had just seen something absolutely dreadful. 'I'm not going to practice anymore and got out of the car.'

"In those days you were obviously devastated, especially if it was someone you knew well, but you weren't shocked because it happened so often. I never went down to where Gerry was killed. I just didn't want to go there. In fact, I've only ever been back on one occasion. I've been past loads of times, but never really wanted to go there again. A dreadful place to race, especially F2, one step from F1 in which F1 drivers were competing as well. The French were very intransigent."

Jochen Mass was much more than just a rival, as he was also a close friend. The developing relationship at the Ford training camps had been cemented by their exploits in South Africa. "They were like soul mates," offers Margaret.

"My Surtees had stopped with a minor problem," says Jochen. "I pulled off the track and went to the top of a bank to watch. On one lap Gerry came by slowly trying to cool down his tyres before going for another quick lap. He waved and I waved back, in what turned out to be a symbolic last wave that became goodbye because he crashed soon afterwards. I'll never forget that.

"They stopped the practice and I was towed back to the pits and asked John Surtees why had practice been stopped. He said there had been an accident. I asked who was involved and he said, 'Gerry Birrell.' I said, 'Damn, is he OK?' And he just said, 'No, he's finished,' then turned around and walked away. The way he said it was unbelievable, but he was one of the old guys who had dealt with these things all the time. In our days, it was a little more civilised in a certain way. Only a little bit.

"It was quite a hit in the stomach, you know. I was obviously deeply shocked. Poor Gerry had no chance. It was a bloody puncture at the worst possible place."

In a commendable act of mind over matter, Mass raced to a strong second place the following day. While in that era serious accidents were frequent, the ability to detach yourself undoubtedly made you stronger. But it still can't have been easy. "I was able to rationalise things," he continues. "Nobody forced us to race. You did what you could to minimise risk."

"That was just a horrendous day," recalls Phillips, who of course was covering the race for *Autosport*. "From what I remember the accident was caused by a puncture. The Chevron wasn't a great car compared to the March, but Gerry, as usual, gave it everything. You could never fault his commitment, not at all.

"In single-seaters he would never pull off daring, risky manoeuvres, so he was one of those that you thought it wouldn't happen to him. He was absolutely Mr Consistency.

"He was a smashing guy. Lovely family, very friendly, easy-going, cheerful and always approachable. He was such an easy bloke to like.

Scandalous. ***(Paris Normandie)***

"Serious in terms of his racing, he thought a lot about it. He was mechanically sympathetic and understood cars."

The sorry task of dealing with the aftermath fell to the members of the Chevron team, which numbered five in total, and Brian Hart. The Chevron number was quickly reduced to four when Derek Bennett, the very much hands-on owner of Chevron, "Leapt into his car and left immediately after hearing the news from Paul Owens," according to team mechanic Neil Edwards. The reasons for his swift exit would become apparent a couple of days later.

"We had to pick the car up," continues Edwards. "We just put it straight in the truck and covered it up. When we got back to the factory, which would have been either late Sunday evening or early Monday morning, Derek was there making brackets to fit to all the cars, so we could fit forward-facing roll-stays that ran from the roll-over hoop down to the top of the monocoque. All Chevrons from that day onwards had those stays fitted.

"Derek was a very sensitive man. It affected him. He never mentioned the accident ever again. He prided himself on designing and making safe cars. Gerry was the first – and only – driver to lose his life in a Chevron.

"Some of the other guys offered to help with the car but I said I'd rather do it my own. We took the engine and gearbox out and the rest went in 'The Lodge' which was the name we used for a big hole behind the factory where we put all the damaged cars, bodywork etc... It's now a car park. If only people knew what's under there."

The onerous task of dealing with matters relating to Gerry fell to Chevron's newly-appointed sales and publicity director Grahame White, who had an enormous amount of experience in motorsport. His previous job had been with the British Automobile Racing Club (BARC) where one of his roles was that of the Clerk of the Course at all meetings organised by the club, so he had experience of dealing with

The extensively damaged car. Gerry's helmet hangs on the damaged rear suspension. ***(Paris Normandie)***

issues involving fatalities. But this would be his first on a personal level. "I had to identify Gerry at the hospital," he recalls. "When you are dealing with fatalities there are lots of regulations you have to go through. I stayed on with my wife to visit the Mayor's office, the police station, etc. That was fine because I was prepared to do whatever had to be done. The rest of the team had to get back to England.

"I had to clear his hotel room and tidy up all his bits and pieces. Pack his briefcase/personal belongings... You had to switch into automatic mode and try to cut off emotionally. Strangely, I didn't get emotional until I went to the funeral, then it became very final and real.

"From what I was doing, it meant the family didn't have to come over. I knew Graham and Margaret. I was able to say to them that I would handle everything.

"On the occasions our paths crossed when I was with the BARC or our brief time together at Chevron, Gerry was such a likeable person. Very open, friendly and obviously pretty talented. It was a very, very sad day, but it was no surprise at that time."

The unenviable task of informing Margaret fell to Stuart Turner and Peter Ashcroft after, according to Adam Cooper in his 'Lost Before His Time' feature in *Motor Sport* in 2004, 'Brian Hart had found a phone to call Ashcroft in Essex. Peter and his wife Jean collected Turner and then headed to the Birrell house. Stuart couldn't go in, says Ashcroft. So he stayed in the car with my wife. I had to go and tell Margaret.'

"I knew something awful had happened," recalls Margaret. "Was it fire? He said, 'No' and I thought thank God for that. That was the first thing I said to him. That was the one thing Gerry was frightened of.

"I think Jean Ashcroft was there and Margaret Turner, as well. I remember saying to Jean 'There are some cigarettes for you there,' because Gerry used to bring them back duty-free for them and she said, 'Your needs are greater than mine.' I mean, when you are told something like that you say the craziest things.

"When I had gone to open the door, I'd left the twins in their high-chairs. At the time, I had been feeding them chocolate mousse. When I eventually came back through it was everywhere. I mean, everywhere. I don't know how much they'd actually eaten. It was just unbelievable. It was obviously bath time after that.

"We hadn't eaten, so Peter went out and bought fish and chips. It didn't really hit me until about three o'clock in the morning when my mother and father arrived after jumping in the car and coming straight down from Glasgow. That's when it really hit me.

"Some ridiculous things were going on after that. Iain [Birrell] and Grahame [White] were involved with sorting out his body and there was a post mortem, as far as I can gather, at the hospital in Rouen. Then he was taken to the British Embassy where he was put into a sealed, lead-lined coffin, which could only be flown out of France on an Air France flight, and the only one that landed was on a Thursday at Glasgow Airport. I mean, it was just a nightmare.

"I felt sorry for Grahame because he had to come and see me afterwards. Terrible really. It's an awful thing to have to do. If it's happening to you, you can deal with it, talking to someone else, it's just... Poor guy. I've seen him since. He's a lovely guy, he really is."

Something that didn't register with Margaret at the time was Gerry's unusually philosophical mood before leaving for Rouen. It wasn't until much later after reading comments from Turner and Ashcroft in Cooper's feature in *Motor Sport*, that she cast her mind back.

"Just before Gerry left for Rouen, he was making me pay all the bills – something I had never done – including the life insurance and the disablement policy. I didn't have enough to pay both, so I asked him which one should I pay? He said, 'Use your loaf. I can put a cross against the disablement policy, but the life...' I paid the life insurance.

"Also, I was going to London to meet Daphne, a girl I'd met at relaxation classes and we'd kept in touch, but Gerry was hanging around doing various other things. Not like him, at all. In the end, she got the train to Chelmsford and I went to pick her up. He was just hanging around. It was like he knew what was going to happen, sort of, like a premonition. He never had any history of that sort of thing. Very spooky."

Similar tales are told by the aforementioned Ford men.

"The week before he died we went to Castle Combe together in my car," recalled Ashcroft to Cooper in *Motor Sport*. "It was weird. He almost suggested that it was going to happen. He said that he'd talked to his wife and put his affairs in order – insurance, mortgage, things like that – so if anything happened to him, she knew what it was all about."

"It was quite an extraordinary thing," remembers Turner. "He lived near us and on the Wednesday before he died he phoned and asked if he could pop over. We just had a drink or something. When he'd gone at 10 o'clock in the evening, I can remember saying to my wife, Margaret, 'That was strange.' It was always a joy to see Gerry, but he was almost tidying things up. We'd got four or five ongoing issues and we resolved them. I don't believe in premonitions and I'm not trying to create anything mysterious, but it was an extraordinary experience. My last memory of Gerry was his tidiness and closing all the open issues."

It wasn't only telling Margaret that Turner was involved in, he would make the phone call to another member of the Birrell family. "I got a call from Stuart," recalls Graham. "I didn't know he was racing that weekend, so it was a big shock. Mother was terribly upset."

Another ordeal for Turner was having to address the workforce at Boreham on the Monday morning.

Once Graham had processed the news he took over the mantle of phoning the many mutual friends spread far and wide across the UK. One was Gerry's best man, John Murray: "I was general sales manager at Halesfield Motors in Telford with Mike Leeke at that time. I didn't work on Saturdays but would usually pop in to see how the salesmen were getting on. The phone rang and it was Graham...

"A couple of years later I moved back to work in Scotland. I ended up living close to Graham and Jennifer in Glasgow. One day Graham invited me to their flat on the Great Western Road. I hadn't realised his mum and dad lived in the flat below until Graham went to get them to meet me. His mother, Florence, burst into tears when she saw me. She just broke down. I thought bloody hell, that's a lesson. She obviously thought of Gerry straight away when she saw me.

"Even though he was such a busy guy, we always kept in touch. Never fell out or anything, it was just his world was totally different from mine. He was a very good friend as far as I was concerned. I'm lucky to have known him."

Other key people involved in Gerry's life and career recall quietly and in a reflective, sombre tone how they heard the devastating news.

"I was working for Brian Hart at the time," says John Catt. "He took me to one side on Monday morning and told me. I couldn't believe it."

"I'd dropped him off on Battersea Bridge to go to Rouen," recalls Ronnie Grant. "I'd dropped him off before and we had this ritual when he got out of the car he'd say, 'Make sure you look after Margaret, for me.' And I'd say, 'Of course, I will.' We would both be smiling. His last words on this occasion were, 'I'll see you Monday.'

"I saw the headlines in the newspaper on Sunday when I was working at the garage. When I got home my partner Sheila was in the garden. I poured a very large brandy and said, 'You're going to need this,' and handed her the newspaper. Her face dropped."

Also present was Ronnie's son George. "I used to come home from boarding school for the weekend to spend

Rouen, June 23rd 1973. Because of his behaviour before leaving home, this photo takes on an added poignancy. Gerry looks uncharacteristically serious and annoyed about something, and definitely not his usual effervescent self. *(Jutta Fausel)*

time with Dad. It was a lovely sunny Sunday afternoon. I remember the day, vividly.

"I had no idea what was going on when dad handed the newspaper to Sheila. I picked up the paper. I wasn't a particularly good reader but I understood that he'd died. I couldn't quite comprehend it. Then dad said, 'Gerry's died.' It was the first time I'd experienced bereavement, knowing what it felt like.

"I had only just turned 12, my birthday is on 5 June. The whole day was one of the darkest days I can ever remember. I remember dad being terribly sad. We didn't really talk very much. It was really tough going back to school later that afternoon thinking, 'Oh my goodness, I'll never see Gerry again.' I remember just feeling... It was a tough, tough time."

While those directly affected remember only the feeling of loss, the people whose job was to write about the tragedy – who were equally affected – went into overdrive in their condemnation of the safety standards, the seemingly double standards of certain drivers and those responsible for their enforcement.

The editorial piece in *Autosport* by editor Richard Feast was critical of several issues but it was the similar piece in *Motoring News*, not by editor Mike Cotton, which was usually the case, but Andrew Marriott who was covering the race for *Motor Sport* in between helping Colin Vandervell. That was considerably more forthright and scathing. From the following extracts – which would have been written in the immediate aftermath – you can sense his anger that was understandably still raw and remains so to this day.

'Jochen Rindt, Bert Hawthorne and now Gerry Birrell. All killed in collisions with protective guard rails and, to varying degrees, the mode of installation or construction of those rails has been questioned. In the case of Gerry Birrell's fatal crash, not only was the installation of the guard rail definitely inadequate and ineffective but the whole accident casts considerable doubt on how the safety arrangements are checked, both on behalf of the Grand Prix Drivers' Association (GPDA) and the Commission Sportive Internationale (CSI).

'Intelligent siting of guard rails makes an invaluable contribution to safety, but there's no doubt that an improper barrier can be worse than no barrier at all. Round the circuit at Rouen we found there were sections in which we could physically shake the rail with one hand and by sitting on it could flex it two or three inches. One doesn't have to imagine the consequences if a racing car travelling at 150mph hits that barrier a direct blow. It was all too tragically demonstrated on Saturday.

'Rouen has been sanctioned by the CSI. This means that a representative of the GPDA must have inspected the circuit, reported his satisfaction to the controlling body and they, with their own inspection having been carried out as well, will make the decision to say OK. So how can this happen?

'There must be a certain amount of trust between those requiring the safety work to be carried out and those whose business it is to execute it. If the circuit owners want their tracks passed, then they're under a moral obligation to do the job properly. It's not a question of fiddling an old banger through the MoT test, it's something that will ultimately save or kill somebody. If you're not going to do it properly, say so and don't bother to hold a motor race.

'But what of the inspection? In the case of Rouen, we find it utterly staggering to think that a proper inspection could have been carried without the shortcomings being noticed. And, just in case someone from the GPDA and CSI comes back and says the track was sanctioned with the proviso "that alterations were made by such and such a date," why wasn't it re-checked and found to be wanting?

'The CSI makes stiff rules for the constructors, requiring them to build their cars virtually to aircraft safety standards with deformable structures and safety tanks, yet doesn't seem to be able to control the sanctioning of safety on circuits. What in heavens name is the use of deformable structures when a shoddy old barrier splits in two, slides the car underneath and injures or kills its occupant? Doubtless, there will be much passing of the buck backwards and forwards, but when it finally stops the situation is nothing but a tragi-comedy.

'But the drivers are not without blame either. After Mike Beuttler's accident on Friday, it was obvious that the circuit was lacking; after Birrell's on Saturday it was clear that the place was downright dangerous with the guard rails as they were. Yet the drivers' answer was to put a chicane halfway down the hill; whether they approved of the interpretation that the organisers made of their word "chicane" is another matter, but the fact is they still raced.

'How is it that Emerson Fittipaldi, Ronnie Peterson and other top drivers felt inclined to go out and risk their lives on a circuit as patently dangerous as that when they're usually so consistent in their views of safety?

'They had a tailor-made excuse not to race. And they'd got it for a valid reason. They'd got a golden opportunity to nail down negligent safety work once and for all... and they didn't use it. It's simply not good enough to say "we've got to race" in such circumstances because they'll go on meeting up with other tracks where similar accidents will happen. And more drivers get killed. Guard rails are killers if they are not installed properly.'

How prophetic that last line was. The accidents at Zandvoort involving Roger Williamson or Watkins Glen involving Francois Cevert, only a short while later, and Helmuth Koinigg, the following year, further prove that was the case. Lessons hadn't been learned. But was it that simple? That era is unrecognisable from what we have today on so many levels. The overriding memory is of the continual struggle between the drivers and the organisers to address even the most basic safety measures. The drivers even had a collective force as the GPDA in Formula One, had little power and influence. With that in mind, how much say did Gerry and his rivals have in the lower rungs of the racing ladder? None whatsoever! All they asked for was the best chance of survival should they suffer a mechanical problem or make a driving error. Gerry was denied that chance.

One of the significant points raised in the *MN* editorial piece was that of the lack of a proper, thorough circuit safety inspection. This is confirmed by Mike Doodson, who is known primarily for both his insightful journalism and for being the sports editor of *Motor* magazine for many years. He was present at Rouen in his capacity as the press officer for John Player Team Lotus – whose drivers (Fittipaldi and Peterson) were in attendance to race the new Texaco Star Lotus 74s – and alludes to the fact that the organisers already knew of the guard rail situation and, to their eternal shame, did nothing.

"A few years later I learned something about the background to the accident, from a French colleague," he recalls. "He told me that earlier in the year the circuit had been subject to an CSI inspection following a series of hideous accidents during a previous international race meeting, one of which took the lives of two promising French drivers.

"The CSI's appointed representative, I was told, had been a leading French journalist. The members of the club responsible for the circuit knew very well that it was not up to standard, so before embarking on the inspection they invited him to a slap-up lunch at which his glass was constantly topped up. By the time the tour of the circuit began, he was in no condition to do more than a cursory inspection. The necessary papers were duly signed, enabling the race to take place. Had he done his job, then..."

Damning words from two highly-respected journalists which stir feelings of anguish and despair. Apparent from the memories of those present, whether they were on-track rivals,

Newton Mearns Cemetery 2019. ***(Author)***

team members or journalists, is that they were all united in believing that the outcome of the accident was preventable.

The attitude, and seemingly complete lack of respect for human life, by the part-time organising officials, was abhorrent. One hopes those responsible carried the guilt of their actions, for which there was no excuse, for the rest of their days.

Only a mere six days after the tragedy, on Friday 29, Gerry's funeral service took place at the Glasgow Crematorium in the Maryhill district of the city. The following week's *Motoring News* carried a mention in Track Topics titled, Sad Scenes at Glasgow: 'Hundreds of racing folk from all over Europe flocked to Glasgow last Friday to pay their last respects at Gerry Birrell's funeral. So large was the gathering that far more people than were inside the chapel had to stay outside on the lawn during the service at which Stuart Turner made an extremely deep and emotional address.

'Floral tributes simply swamped the lawn and others present included Helen Stewart, Derek Bennett, Michael Kranefuss, Paul Owens, John Crosslé, John Watson, Brian Hart, Dieter Glemser, Claude Bourgoignie, John Stanton, Rodney Bloor, Peter Ashcroft and Brian Nelson. Doubtless, there were many more familiar faces amongst the vast crowd who turned out to say goodbye to Gerry; a tremendous testimony to his popularity.'

Helen was in attendance representing the Stewart family as Jackie was away racing at the French Grand Prix. But he had played an important part in the immediate aftermath of the tragedy, something he had done on numerous previous occasions and would, sadly, continue to do so, as Margaret recalls. "He rang me not long after the accident and asked if there was anything he could do to help. I asked him to go and speak to Gerry's mum and dad because I felt I couldn't cope with them. There had been a few comments then and on previous occasions. A classic case of opening their mouth without putting the brain in gear.

"I remember we hadn't been going out long and his mum Florence saying to his dad, Jack, that Gerry had brought his girlfriend home. He took his newspaper down from in front of his face and said, 'You're the young lady that keeps my son out all the hours of the night.' I said, 'I'm not allowed out all the hours of the night, you better ask him what he does between Clarkson and Milngavie.' It was pretty cheeky of me. I'm glad in retrospect that I put my foot down, I can tell you. I thought, I'm not having that. He can do it to his kids, but he's not doing it to me.

"One thing they would do, which I thought was bad, was set one off against one another. Graham up against Gerry, with Gerry up against Iain. All three of them were petrified of telling their father they were getting married. At one point, I said to Gerry, 'If you don't do it, I'm going back to America, because what's the point?' I even filled in a form for British Airways. Anyway, that was scuppered. But, as soon as we got married, Graham got married, and then Iain got married.

"When we went south, which was quite a big thing in those days, we lived our own lives and weren't involved with the family as much. They came down a couple of times when the twins were born. We went home, obviously at Christmas time. By choice, we would stay with my parents and Gerry and I would visit his.

"I remember going to see them after the accident and thinking they've lost their son and they would be grieving. There was a Muhammad Ali/Joe Frazier fight on the TV in the kitchen and Florence was shouting at the set, 'Kill him...' It was a weird situation. I thought, 'I'm out of here.'

"Jackie did me a big favour. He was brilliant. They thought it was great when he turned up at their door."

Many present that awful day become quiet, reflective and emotional when asked to think back, even after all these years. Others would sooner not cast their minds back.

Evidence, not that any should be needed, of the impact Gerry made on their lives.

"I was in Oban on one of the rare weekends I wasn't racing," recalls Bill Dryden. "I saw a placard saying 'Scottish racing driver killed' and I thought it could only be one of three, Jackie, Tom (Walkinshaw) or Gerry and all the shops were shut. A man was reading a paper and I went up and said, 'Could I have a look at your paper, please? I've got to find out what's happened.' On the day of his funeral in Maryhill, I'm sitting there thinking to myself, I turned the opportunity down to race in Formula Vee, Gerry took full advantage, so that could have been me.

"Unfortunately we lost a few friends and when it happened.

You felt terrible, but there's something inside you that made you carry on, thinking it wasn't going to you.

"In those days it happened a lot. I mean some days you'd be helping a girl put the car back on the trailer because her boyfriend had been killed."

"I went up with all the other Chevron guys, including Brian Redman," recalls Neil Edwards. "It's the only time I've been to Scotland. Even today when I hear anything about Scotland, my memory goes straight back to that day."

Gerry is buried in Newton Mearns cemetery which is on the south side of Glasgow, close to Clarkston where Margaret grew up. Glasgow Crematorium is approximately 12 miles away on the north side of the city.

"The Birrells bought the stone, which cost £90," remembers Margaret. "I thought '£90 on a stone, and I need the money...' I did take the twins up to let them see where daddy was buried. I gave them a daffodil each, which they used to whip the stone. I never took them back as they didn't understand at two years old.

"The last time I went, which must have been nearly 20 years ago, I couldn't find the gravestone at first. When I did eventually find it, it looked so small. Nowhere near as big as I remember it. When it was new it looked enormous."

The subject of money, or lack of it, raised by Margaret was a matter of concern due to problems with Gerry's insurance. "Because he was killed in a Chevron, he wasn't covered on Ford's insurance," she recalls. "That was how I understood it at the time. Jackie spoke to the powers-that-be at Ford and I ended up with £9000. I'm sure Stuart Turner was also involved in the decision. The theory was that I could go back to work once the twins were at school.

"I gave back the hand-built Capri. Stuart then got me a Cortina estate. Fortunately, Gerry's life insurance of £5000 covered the various outstanding bills."

Only three weeks after the accident Margaret was back at a race meeting when she attended the British Grand Prix at the suggestion of Stuart Turner. "He thought it would be a good time to see everybody without it being difficult, to say thank you for all the support and messages," she says. "When I saw Jody spin in front of the field and the resulting carnage, I thought, 'What am I doing here?' I just wasn't interested any more."

In recognition of his efforts in 1972, Gerry was awarded the Jim Clark Memorial Trophy, which had been introduced two years earlier to recognise the achievements of Scots in either their chosen fields of motoring or motorsport.

He was aware of the accolade, but due to his busy itinerary and that of Jackie Stewart, who was to present the award, they had been unable to arrange a mutually convenient time.

The trophy was finally awarded posthumously in late August to Margaret at a dinner held at the Royal Scottish Automobile Club (RSAC) headquarters in Glasgow.

Unsurprisingly, she remembers very little of the evening but does offer one memory that is still vivid. "I was petrified at

Gerry Birrell

The tragic loss of Gerry Birrell has hit the motor racing world very hard, for the 28-year-old Scot was one of the most likeable and popular personalities involved in the upper levels of the sport. A professional through and through, Gerry managed to combine his serious dedication to motor racing with an easy sense of humour and a genuine interest in other people. Though he was strong, self-reliant and very self-confident, he was never guilty of arrogant or temperamental displays of behaviour in times of stress or at his greatest moments of triumphant elation. These gentlemanly qualities endeared Gerry to everybody who met him or worked with him and in his case more than any other it seems hardly credible that he was snatched from our midst on June 23.

In practice for the European Formula 2 Championship meeting at the controversial circuit of Rouen, Gerry was approaching the very fast, downhill Six Freres corner when, eye-witnesses say, a front tyre deflated suddenly. Although Gerry knew the circuit intimately, nothing could save him from a head-on impact with a metal barrier under which his car passed. Gerry soon succumbed to his injuries.

Born in Milngavie, near Glasgow, in 1944, Gerry left school at 15 to start his motoring career as an apprentice with a BLMC dealer. In this capacity, and as racing mechanic to his older brother Graham, Gerry acquired a first-class knowledge of the technical side of the business which later helped him to become one of the very best racing car test drivers. Soon after his 17th birthday, he began to compete in minor events, sometimes borrowing his brother's car and even using the family Vauxhall saloon which did not make him very popular with his father!

By 1966 he had begun a serious career as a driver, however, and in the following year he launched himself into a series of championship victories, collecting the Scottish Saloon Car Championship, the Scottish National Speed Championship, and the BMRC Trophy in 1967 with the Claud Hamilton Motors Chamois Imp, which Gerry nicknamed the "Chimp." Gerry prepared the car himself and was earning his living as assistant service manager for Hamilton Motors at the same time.

Invited to drive a Formula Vee car at Ingliston late in 1967 Gerry acquitted himself very well by leading for much of the race and finishing 2nd to Nick Brittan, the most successful Vee driver at that time. In 1968 Gerry commuted regularly by air between Glasgow and London to drive Formula Vee at weekends and win the British National Formula Vee Championship.

He made the big move south at the beginning of 1969 with success in Formula Ford, the essential stepping stone, as his goal. Working with C. T Woolers, Gerry suggested that the firm should assemble John Crossle's 16F car for sale in England and run a works car in the European Championship for him. Never a man to follow blindly in the path of others, Gerry also decided to run on cross-ply tyres. With a new and unknown chassis on Avon Wide Safety GT tyres, Gerry embarked on a development programme that produced such good results that his competitors were forced to follow his line. Within weeks everyone in Formula Ford was using the same tyres, but by the end of the year Gerry's homework and driving skill had netted him the European Championship.

The experience and reputation that Gerry gained in that year carried him into Formula 3 with a semi-works Brabham run by John Stanton and Rodney Bloor. No less of an ace in F3, Gerry was rated by *L'Equipe* as the most successful international driver of 1970 in this incredibly competitive branch of the sport. A promising start in Formula 2 was thwarted by a poor chassis at first, though Gerry seemed set to achieve the success he deserved in Formula 2 this year with the works Chevron. Meanwhile, however, he had become a mainstay in the Ford Group 2 Capri team, in which he distinguished himself by being not only the best development driver but also, jointly with Jochen Mass, the most competitive.

As revealed by Stuart Turner, Ford's Director of Motor Sport, plans were in hand to launch Gerry into Formula 1. In a recent statement, Turner said "Gerry Birrell was not just a brilliant racing driver. In him we have lost a very close and dear friend, with whom we enjoyed a long and close association—a consistently cheerful, friendly and co-operative man. As a racing driver, he was one step from Formula 1 in which it was simply a matter of time before he made his debut—certainly by the end of this season."

Our most sincere sympathy is offered to his wife, Margaret, their twin baby daughters, and his family.

Tony Dron

The Obituary by Tony Dron in Motor magazine, 7 July 1973. ***(Author)***

ROYAL SCOTTISH AUTOMOBILE CLUB DINNER

These pictures were taken at a recent dinner in the Royal Scottish Automobile Club on the occasion of a presentation by Jackie Stewart to Mrs. Margaret Birrell—widow of Gerry Birrell—of the Jim Clark Trophy.

Above: Mr. J. Ogilvie, Mrs. M. Birrell, Mr. Jackie Stewart, Major R. Tennant Reid.

Right: Mrs. Helen Stewart, Mrs. Jennifer Birrell, Mr. G. Birrell, Mrs. M. Birrell.

Left: Mr. J. Stewart, Mr. and Mrs. E. Dymock.

Right: R. Tennant Reid, Mrs. J. Hally.

A cutting from Glasgow Illustrated magazine. ***(Margaret Shore)***

having to thank the gathered group. I tried to persuade Jackie to do it but he insisted I did it. He then coached me during dinner on what to say with bullet point references he wrote on the back of a card.

"When the time came, I focused on a light at the back of the room at his suggestion, I couldn't possibly look at anybody."

As you would expect, the entire Birrell family was present, along with Stuart Turner and Peter Ashcroft and their respective wives, who had travelled up from Essex with Margaret.

Gerry was the third recipient of the trophy. The two previous winners had been Jackie Stewart for his two World Championships and Andrew Cowan for his success in the London-Sydney Rally.

The trophy – now titled the Jim Clark Memorial Award – is still awarded every year, and the roll call is a real who's who of Scottish motoring/motorsport. Allan McNish, David Coulthard, Louise Aitken-Walker, Colin McRae, Tom Walkinshaw, Richard Noble OBE and the Franchitti family are the recognisable names, but equally deserving are the likes of Ian Forrest, Lee Mackenzie, Ross Finlay, Robert Reid and perhaps, the most fitting, Ian Scott-Watson.

Understandably things had changed without any direct involvement, but having built up some strong friendships, many of which endure to this day, Margaret wasn't about to cut all ties with the motorsport fraternity.

"I stayed in touch with a small number of racing people," she says. "Annie Hogan, John's wife is Kara's godparent, while I'm godparent to their son Andrew. Peter Hunt, James's brother, who was introduced to me by 'Ping' as 'HP' (his initials backwards. No idea why). He was always a good laugh when 'Ping' and I met him in London, which we tried to do at least twice a year. Sadly, he succumbed to bone cancer in 2015.

"Eventually, after a long time, I went to the British Grand Prix with some of my tennis friends who had wanted to go. Also, I went to the Osterreichring and Zandvoort with Peter Hunt. 'Hogie' would always organise some tickets."

Away from the occasional outing to a race meeting and maintaining her friendships, life slowly returned to some sort of normality for Margaret. Financial pressures meant that she had to return to work. For her to do such a thing, she would require some help which was forthcoming from her mother and father.

"They moved down to help look after the twins when I went back to work part-time in London. I stayed with Ronnie Grant, firstly because Gerry had asked him to look after me (in jest) but he took the responsibility very seriously and, secondly, it was convenient. Eventually, he got fed up with me coming in at all hours of the night due to my work. I think I was driving him nuts. I told him I was fine and not to worry about it, and moved in with one of my girlfriends."

Tragically, as if losing your husband wasn't enough, Margaret was dealt an even bigger blow when Maija succumbed to cancer a month after her eighth birthday in February 1980.

"My boss at the time, Donald Ross, operated at the Middlesex, National Heart and Guy's Hospitals," says Margaret. "He organised for her to be admitted to get to the bottom of what I thought was a stroke. She was in the Middlesex for a week of tests but they couldn't find anything wrong. She was discharged and a week later I realised she was going downhill, so she was admitted again for more tests and by the end of them was taken to the operating theatre to ascertain what the shadows were they had found in her brain.

"She never regained consciousness and the bottom line on her death certificate was intra cerebral deposits of malignant small celled lymphoma. So, in layman's terms, her body was riddled with cancer."

On its own the devastation of losing a child at such a young age is impossible to comprehend, but when combined with Gerry's passing only a mere seven years earlier, the feelings of despair, sadness and anger were overwhelming. How much more could one woman take? Thankfully, apart from the usual detritus of life, Margaret suffered no further loss of that magnitude.

While working at Great Ormond Street Hospital after Maija's passing, she met Darryl Shore, a cardiac surgeon. They were married in December 1981 and had two boys. Alex in 1982 and Andrew in 1984.

Some of her time is taken up with being a grandmother to Andrew's two boys and a girl and spending as much as possible on the golf course.

Now in her eighth decade, she lives alone in the south of England with Kara close by. Having been through so much together they share a bond and a closeness beyond the usual mother/daughter relationship.

As we remember him. The ever-present smile. ***(Jutta Fausel)***

CHAPTER TEN

WHAT MIGHT HAVE BEEN

The reference to the presence of Ken Tyrrell at Rouen was a clear indication that Gerry was in the frame for the team owner's vacant seat for the 1974 season. 'Uncle Ken,' habitually kept an eye on what was happening in the lower formulae, especially if they were one of the support races on the Formula One calendar. But for him to venture to a Formula Two race, which never supported a grand prix, was a rare occurrence.

He was not a lover of change, much preferring a continuation of what appeared to be a winning formula. Loyalty was high up on his list of character attributes. The enforced change brought on by the intended retirement of Jackie Stewart would have seen him looking for a 'JYS Mk2,' if such a thing existed. The closest thing was Gerry.

The close relationship between Jackie and Gerry would have appealed to Ken. He valued Stewart's opinion when it came to drivers, and had hired Francois Cevert on his suggestion. Gerry's lack of Formula One experience would have been a concern but with Stewart staying involved in a consultancy/coaching role, Ken would have relished the benefits of him passing on his vast accumulated experience, hopefully to mould Gerry into something similar. While Gerry was no pushover and had his own strong ideas on what he wanted, initially he would undoubtedly have absorbed all of Jackie's pearls of wisdom. Longer-term, however, you could perhaps have foreseen some problems.

An added dimension was the Ford connection. They would have been keen to keep Gerry on the books, so to place him with a team with they had a close affiliation would have been paramount. That decision would ultimately have been Ken's and Stuart Turner's, who we know was a huge admirer of Gerry's. Turner, like Tyrrell, had a close relationship with Stewart, so would have been receptive to the elder Scot's input. Don't forget that Stewart raced the Capri when his schedule allowed and Gerry was always competitive in identical equipment. You couldn't get a better barometer.

I can't see a way for it not to have happened. All the elements were aligned in perfect symmetry. Unfortunately, and surprisingly, two of the main protagonists involved, Stewart and Turner (Tyrrell died in 2001) seem unwilling to confirm that a deal had been done or that it was even on the cards. Men of such repute will have their reasons.

Other people closely involved with Gerry, including Margaret, seem to think the deal as good as done. Surely, if Gerry's wife says it was going to happen, it would be hard to argue against it.

"It would probably have been Gerry and Francois Cevert at Tyrrell in 1974," offers Margaret. "We had talked about it. I was sworn to secrecy. But it wasn't to be."

"It was on the cards," John Hogan said in Adam Cooper's *Motor Sport* feature. "Stuart Turner had lobbied Ken, and I had also spoken to Ken in a roundabout way. In those days, if you took the right driver, Ford delivered the engines. I remember having a long discussion with Gerry about how much he should get paid!"

"I suspect he would have gone to Tyrrell in '74," offers Andrew Marriott. "I thought Gerry was the complete package and would have been a perfect fit with the team. He had the speed, the contacts, was popular in the paddock, a great person, very well connected. Also, he was unusual for the time in that he had great engineering and technical knowledge. He had everything going for him."

Adding further credence while offering evidence of an agreement, not for the '74 season, but the last two races of the '73 season, is author and journalist Steve Holter: "While I was building the FOM results database, I was going through boxes and boxes of stuff from which I was supposed to be finding what chassis went to what race, and which were used by whom, but it was the other stuff that was a huge distraction!

"I came across a letter of intent in the Tyrrell items that was quite precise. Gerry was to drive in Canada and the USA at the end of 1973, to evaluate test parts for what would have been the 007, in its original form. His flights, accommodation and out-of-pocket expenses would be covered, and he would receive 25 percent of the extra start money (one of the other reasons teams entered three cars at the Glen) and 75% of any prize money, but he was to give up the car without question, should the need arise. There was no reference to the 1974 season, but that letter may have gone astray."

The fact that Tyrrell entered a third car in those two races for Chris Amon adds further credibility to Holter's assertion. Amon only ended up racing in the Canadian Grand Prix, after his car, along with Stewart's, was withdrawn following Cevert's fatal accident in practice for the US Grand Prix.

The loss was a major setback for the Tyrrell team and one from which they never fully recovered. Having to run two inexperienced drivers, South African Jody Scheckter and Frenchman Patrick Depailler, was extremely challenging for both the team and the drivers.

Surprisingly then, given that Scheckter had competed in only five grands prix (Depailler had done two) prior to the 1974 season, he scored two wins and was in with an outside chance of the championship at the final round. Ultimately, an impressive third place in the standings was his reward. It doesn't take much imagination to conclude that with Cevert in the car greater success would have been achieved. Gerry had always been competitive against the South African in Formula Two, the Springbok series and when seen together in the Capris, so it wouldn't be a giant leap to envisage a possible maiden Grand Prix victory for him, especially with Stewart's guiding hand. The latter was something that Scheckter sought to distance himself from as the season progressed.

Jody had calmed down somewhat by that stage, and being one of the first on the scene of Cevert's accident had a profound effect. They had clashed in Canada and there was still a degree of bad feeling in Watkins Glen, but the horror of Cevert's accident changed Jody's whole approach to racing. He was still more of a 'seat of the pants' type of driver, in contrast to the more analytical, studious approach that Gerry had. Both approaches would usually end up with the same result but the more spectacular, aggressive style guaranteed greater headlines and more column inches.

This is undoubtedly a factor when you assess how Gerry is remembered. His smooth, more serene approach is easily overlooked. Even if he won from start-to-finish and by quite a margin, it never seemed to earn the type of headlines generated by the performances of racers such as Peterson, Hunt and Scheckter while they were all climbing the single-seater racing ladder. That is not to disparage the talents of the above. After all, there are two World Champions and one who certainly should have been in that trio. But perception is all.

It was different in saloon car circles where Gerry's spectacular style often overcame deficiencies in the car's performances as he wrung a lap time out of a recalcitrant machine way beyond what was expected. That was why he was regarded as being among the top six or so tintop drivers of that era. But in regard to his single-seater aspirations, it meant very little. Not enough people were looking outside the insular world of formula racing.

To be *über*-critical Gerry probably didn't do enough, especially, in Formula Two, to be bracketed among the likes of the acknowledged lost generation trio of Tom Pryce, Tony Brise and Roger Williamson. Their rise was meteoric, spectacular and headline-grabbing. Gerry's career was more of a slow burn, which again, could skew perception.

The burning question was whether Gerry would have been a success in Formula One? Yes, he would, but... Based upon his performances in the lower formulae, one tends to swing towards a comparison with the likes of Rubens Barrichello, Riccardo Patrese, Patrick Depailler and Jochen Mass. All had their day of days when they looked unbeatable. But also here were too many lacklustre days when, for myriad reasons, they could look anonymous. The likes of Clark, Stewart, Lauda and Prost just didn't have off days. That's what set them apart.

Gerry himself was quoted saying, 'While I keep progressing, I feel I will stay in motor racing. If I ever feel I'm stagnating, stuck on one rung of the ladder, I'll look elsewhere.' You can't imagine him looking outside the motorsport arena for employment, so you can envisage a role within the Ford motorsport hierarchy. Whether or not the Tyrrell or other Formula One opportunities had come his way, you can't help but be drawn to thinking of a management/team owner role. Gerry Birrell Racing with Ford has a ring to it.

Long-term friend Brian Hart in Adam Cooper's *Motor Sport* feature certainly thought so.

"I had the firm opinion that Ford had plans for Gerry. He was so charismatic, he was going to be way up in the Ford hierarchy. He was an incredibly personable guy. Apart from being talented, he was immensely interested, and he took everything in. He knew as much about engines and gearboxes as he did about the chassis. He was a pretty amazing guy."

It would have made perfect sense for Ford to have their own team – after all, they had the perfect, dominant engine of that time – with Gerry running the whole show, answering to Stuart Turner. A potential dream team, if ever there was one.

I'm more inclined to lean towards a more successful career away from the cockpit, than in one. The engineering and mechanical knowledge Gerry could have imparted, not just to his contemporaries, but to the younger generation of up-and-coming drivers and engineers, would have been second-to-none. It is a role he would have relished.

If Gerry was still around today, like Jackie well into his eighth decade, he had enough talent, knowledge and charisma to have left an indelible mark in motorsport circles in whichever role he chose to pursue.

It is only fitting that the final words belong to the lady who was always so loyal, supportive, and enthusiastic. The role of a racing driver's wife in those days should never be under-estimated. "I have no anger towards motor racing, Gerry was racing when we met, so I knew what I was getting involved with," Margaret says in her usual pragmatic way. "You don't stop anyone from doing what they enjoy. He was doing something he enjoyed. The days in Formula Three and Two were enormous fun. We were all a travelling circus. It's better to have had eight years of fun, than years and years of misery.

"Having learnt many new things and had my memory jogged big time throughout the writing process, one thought occurred to me: from his first close shave in his youth when travelling with Bill Dryden right up to the Salzburgring accident the month before Rouen, the number of big, high-speed accidents were mounting up. He was like a cat with nine lives, I guess, with Rouen being the 10th."

Watercolour illustration: Lynne Mitchell

Epilogue: A memorial to Gerry

I first met Gerry in 1968 when we were both contesting the UK Formula Vee Championship. Actually, that is a slight distortion of the truth; the rest of us were contesting the championship but Gerry was normally long gone en route to another win. He was always cheerful, full of fun but utterly focused on his motor racing. He didn't stay long in Formula Vee; having won the championship he was off climbing the motor racing ladder. His untimely and tragic death on the 23 June 1973 when he was practising for an F2 race at Rouen-Les-Essarts is still shrouded in controversy. I remember hearing about the accident on the following Tuesday and being very shaken by the news.

Many years passed by, but he stayed in my head, as memorable people do. The circuit fell out of use and the pits and other permanent buildings on the circuit were bulldozed, erased, then forgotten, as was Gerry and the other five competitors who died there. I felt I needed to do something to remember my friend while I still could and I should do it now to mark the approaching 50th anniversary of his death. The right thing seemed obvious. I would erect a memorial at the spot where he crashed, the very fast and dangerous downhill bend called Les Six Frères.

There is now a small lay-by at the spot so walkers parking there to explore the forest will see the memorial. Fortunately, the Mayor of Orival, the commune in which the circuit lies, was very keen on the proposition and without hesitation gave me the necessary permission. There was also the possibility of an objection from the forestry authority, which the mayor overruled. The project inevitably grew to become a memorial to all six who died there. I felt it would be wrong to ignore the other five competitors. It will be a simple granite stone about 1m 50 in height with all their names, and the dates they died, engraved on it together with a brief explanation about the memorial. Above all though, this is my tribute to Gerry who, had he lived, would very probably have been one of the greats.

I owe an enormous debt of thanks to the following who have so generously contributed to make this possible, it should be finished and erected by the 23 June 2023 and could not have been done without their help and support.
Bob Baillie (VSMA), Ross Baird, Darren Banks, Mar Birrell, Helena Birrell, BARC, Stan Bernard, Graham Birrell, Kara Birrell, Suivi Boote, BRDC, Keith Brown, Christian Burdet, Tim Colman (Chevron Racing Cars), Neil Cochrane, Sandy Denham (SMRC), Bill Dryden, Callum Entwistle, FFSA, Allan Gibson, Ian Grier, Brogan Grier, Graeme Inglis, Robert Kelly, Alex Knox, Andrea Luke, Tim Marshall, Alasdair McCaig (Ecurie Ecosse), Sandy McCracken, Logan Morrison, Ronnie Morrison, Motorsport UK, Iain Nicolson, Mike Sheppard, Margaret Shore, Ian Smillie, Michael Sorensen, George Philip Stewart, Sir Jackie Stewart OBE, Ken Sutherland, Vernon Williamson.

Mike Mitchell
Cailhau, France
April 2022

One of Graham's earliest outings at Charterhall in 1960. He couldn't afford the regulation laminated windscreen. ***(Graham Birrell/Darren Banks archive)***

In action in the Cortina GT at the Rest and Be Thankful hillclimb. ***(Graham Birrell/Darren Banks archive)***

Appendix One: The other racing Birrell – Graham

Inevitably, with Gerry progressing further up the motor racing ladder than Graham his name is the one that is remembered, both for his achievements and his sad demise. But be in no doubt that Graham was equally as talented and had a very successful career in his own right but for a variety of reasons didn't quite reach the level someone of his talent deserved. It certainly wasn't through lack of effort.

Right from the moment he started his career in a low-key sprint at a local airfield in his standard road-going Austin A35, then subsequently moved on to circuit racing, hillclimbs, rallies and sprints, he worked tirelessly to obtain more exotic machinery. He would then modify and develop it – Gerry's domain – to further his career. The financial side was very much down to Graham, something he never shirked from. His upbringing in the affluent middle-class Glasgow suburb of Milngavie instilled the strong work ethic inherited from his father, who was a successful businessman. There was definitely no evidence of a 'silver spoon'.

The first full season in 1960 in an Austin A40 saw him achieve numerous class placings in the vast array of events undertaken. The highlight was first in class at the Rest and be Thankful hillclimb. The next couple of seasons saw him progress from the A40 to something more sporty, a Lotus Eleven powered by a BMC engine. That acquisition enabled him to compete in the usual events on home soil and also to have his first forays south to Oulton Park and Mallory Park. A third place overall at the former was followed by second at the latter.

Those results combined with strong performances/results on home soil were beginning to get Graham noticed. Another factor was that the whole Scottish motorsport scene was a small, close-knit community with the regular combatants competing and socialising as frequently as possible. In some circles Graham was considered to be one of the most promising emerging Scottish talents of that time along with a certain JY Stewart, who was a year older but had less racing experience.

For the 1964 season the Birrell brothers chose a Cortina GT and fitted a suspension kit and cylinder head bought from Wilment, one of the acknowledged performance-enhancing companies of the time. The car handled well but was short on performance compared to the opposition, especially the Lotus Cortinas. It was generally a midfield running car but Graham, and occasionally Gerry, would always be in the mix and near the front if conditions/number of entries were in their favour.

The preference to compete in saloons, rather than single-seaters, was primarily for financial reasons. While still expensive, it was more affordable with the majority of the work being undertaken by Gerry, rather than having to purchase a complete proprietary chassis from one of the many established manufacturers who were based south of the border.

Even though Graham was self-employed, the need to be at work every Monday morning to fund his activities certainly hindered his upward progress compared to many of his contemporaries who included the aforementioned Stewart, Tom Sleigh and Bill Dryden, who had family wealth and/or connections to the motor trade. And while all of them worked in the family business, they could always have the time off to pursue their ambitions further afield. And of course they all had talent, in Stewart's case an abundance of what was necessary to go all the way.

Considering the amount of time and effort invested, the outings in the Cortina were overall a tad disappointing but did enable Graham to claim his first outright circuit victory at Evanton in August. He also made his international rally

The car that Graham is most synonymous with was the Wylie's Escort. ***(Graham Birrell/Darren Banks archive)***

Wringing the neck of the F2 Ecurie Ecosse Brabham in June '69 at Zolder in a non-championship encounter. ***(Graham Birrell/Darren Banks archive)***

debut with an outing on the Scottish with Eric Dymock in a Ford Cortina press car which had been organised by the Scottish journalist.

The following year saw big changes, both on and off track. For the first time, Gerry would have his own race car but would continue his mechanic duties with Graham. He was heavily involved in building Graham's new mount, a Ford Anglia, and again modifying it highly. The main focus was in the engine department and to help on that front Graham had formed an allegiance with George Percival and Peter Dalkin of Perdal Developments, an emerging and highly respected engine tuner/builder who were based in the north-east of England.

A victory was claimed first time out at the first-ever Ingliston meeting in April and he would remain unbeaten in the subsequent meetings at the new Scottish venue. The only blot on Graham's 100 percent record was the meeting in May when he was unable to start his race after Gerry had comprehensively binned the car after a huge engine blow-up.

On the back of Gerry's newly-formed alliance with Claud Hamilton Motors, Graham, who was also friendly with boss Mike Leeke, was seen out in a Singer Chamois at Ingliston and in speed events at Gask Airfield. A couple of third-place finishes at Ingliston were the highlights. He fared better in the rally-spec version of the Chamois, and an impressive second in class on the RAC, with Gerry alongside, was the stand-out result.

Never one to shirk travelling great distances, whether it was to compete in his regular cars or something new, Graham and co-driver Arthur Burton took part in his first overseas rally, the 10,000km Tour of Europe in a Hillman Imp entered by Rootes of Switzerland. Disappointingly, they failed to finish after an accident. The following year, aboard a Cortina GT, a fine second in class was a well-deserved reward for their efforts.

Off track, Graham opened his first shop – run by Gerry – in his home city, selling all the latest 'go-faster' bits and pieces for both road and race, plus the latest helmets, racewear and jackets. Ever the entrepreneur, Graham was always exploring every possible avenue outside of his full-time job that enabled him to keep bankrolling his ever-expanding race programme. The shop, one of the first of its type in the UK, was a roaring success and quickly became the place to be seen for anyone associated with the burgeoning Scottish motor racing scene. Another was opened in another part of Glasgow and with the opening of Ingliston, Graham would cannily take a mobile sales unit along to every meeting to sell his wares.

It was much the same in 1966, but with a slight twist mid-season. At the August Ingliston meeting Graham made his first single-seater appearance for none other than the legendary Scottish team, Ecurie Ecosse. The glory days of the team were a distant memory but despite ever-increasing money troubles, they had managed – with considerable help from several benefactors – to build their first single-seater, the Ecosse-Imp. The neat, well-made, but tiny machine – Graham appearing to be sitting on the car, rather than in it – showed promise on its debut as he came home fifth behind four Brabhams.

Back in his usual domain with a roof over his head, he was very much the man to beat in the over-1200cc saloon class at Ingliston in the further developed Anglia. He scored four outright wins and a second place in the six races he entered – a non-finish at the August meeting spoiling his 100 percent record.

A slightly increased rallying programme, again in a Chamois, resulted in two class runner-up positions on the Scottish and the International Gulf events. Gerry was alongside on both occasions.

Another outing in the rally-spec Chamois was at the Birkett 6-hour relay race at Silverstone as part of a four-car team comprising Gerry, Tony Charnell and Alistair Robertson. The quartet came away surprised and delighted victors.

Showing his willingness to drive almost anything, anytime and anywhere, Graham took the wheel of a Sunbeam Tiger

In the Chevron B19 at Silverstone in May '71. ***(Graham Birrell/Darren Banks archive)***

Graham exposed to the elements in the Ecosse-Imp. ***(Graham Birrell/Darren Banks archive)***

at the August Ingliston meeting. The car was owned by John Melvin, who had run it on that year's Monte Carlo Rally. Unfortunately for Graham, a fuel starvation issue prevented him from showing his and the car's potential.

The meetings at Ingliston must have been hectic, to say the least. On most occasions, Graham would be seen in a minimum of three races out of the eight or nine scheduled. This would increase further in the years ahead. When Gerry was also entered, and on the few occasions, middle brother Iain came out to play, it seemed that a Birrell was entered in every race!

Unusually for Graham, a vastly reduced programme of events was undertaken in 1967 with just half a dozen outings at Ingliston and a singleton outing at Mallory Park on a rare foray south in the Ecosse-Imp. The highlight by far was a victory in one of the two Formula Libre races at the Mallory meeting in October. With Gerry winning the other in another Ecosse-Imp, it was a memorable day for the Birrell brothers. For once the bragging rights were shared, which must have meant the long journey back north of the border was a convivial one.

Arguably, the car most synonymous with Graham is the Escort Twin Cam entered by Wylie's of Glasgow, one of the largest Ford dealers in Scotland. It saw active service throughout the 1968 and 1969 seasons. From over 40 forty races entered, 20 outright victories and seven second places were achieved, together with lap records at Ingliston, Croft, Cadwell Park and Mallory Park.

There were teething and development issues along the way, but overall the car/driver combination became the established benchmark. As in the past, Ingliston proved a happy hunting ground with championship honours in the Hartley Whyte title race. Having clinched the championship with five wins from the five rounds, Graham elected to miss the final round in October and to let his new wife, Jenny, have a go. The former Jenny Nadin was an accomplished pilot in Formula Vee when she had been up against Gerry, Nick Brittan and others. The move into saloon cars showed she had the speed and that she wasn't afraid to mix it with her experienced male rivals, which on occasions included Graham. They were very much the glamour couple of the Scottish racing scene.

On the occasions Graham ventured more often than ever to the northern circuits, Rufforth, Croft and Cadwell Park, and would claim outright and class victories in abundance. Croft, in particular, saw him virtually unbeaten over two seasons. The only blots on his otherwise exemplary copybook were non-finishes due mainly to continual problems with the gearbox.

Never one to be content with just racing one type of machine, Graham competed in a wider range of cars and categories than ever before. The outings in the Ecosse-Imp brought only limited success. Three races in the newly-formed Formula Ford 1600 category in a Crosslé 16F entered by his good friends at Equipe Centro-Scot saw him achieve a fourth-place finish in his first outing at the season-opener at Ingliston in April 1968. A first visit to the hillclimb at Doune saw him out in the Escort and a Lotus Cortina.

By far his most ambitious plan in 1969 was to campaign an ex-Jochen Rindt (Winklemann Racing) Brabham BT23C entered by Ecurie Ecosse in the European Formula Two Championship. They were up against it from the start with a year-old car fighting the works Matras of eventual champion Johnny Servoz-Gavin, Jean-Pierre Beltoise, Henri Pescarolo and on occasions Jackie Stewart; the Tecno of emerging French star Francois Cevert; the works Ferraris of Clay Regazzoni and Derek Bell; the newer Brabham BT30s campaigned by various drivers; and the fact that the European circuits were all new to him. Results were difficult to come by.

Despite all that, a couple of impressive sixth-place finishes at Hockenheim and Monza showed his speed and potential. Unfortunately, an accident in practice for the round at Enna curtailed the campaign.

Never one to be deterred, Graham took the team back for more the following year, this time armed with a new Brabham

BT30. They missed the first rounds when there was a delay with delivery, so the first outing was at the Nürburgring in early May. In those circumstances, 10th place was respectable.

Always one to show his loyalty to Ingliston and the faithful Scottish spectators, Graham took along the old BT23C to the circuit's May meeting. When he unfortunately suffered the biggest accident of his career, he wished he hadn't. While leading the Formula Libre race he came up lap a backmarker at the Esses, they intertwined wheels, and as the car flipped over the barrier it narrowly missed a marshal before ending up just two feet from the spectator enclosure. The car was severely damaged and he emerged shaken, but was saved from serious injury by his seatbelts.

Back on the European trail the results were very disappointing. The only highlight was the Monza Lottery in June. Admittedly there was a depleted entry for the non-championship event, but he beat local ace Tino Brambilla into third place as he finished runner-up to Giovanni Salvati.

The Formula Two programme may well have suffered from Graham's hectic UK schedule. Not only was he still racing the Wylie's Escort at Ingliston but the team contested the British Saloon Car Championship for the first time. Again, the results were disappointing. In between various issues, he managed a season-best fourth-place finish at one of his favourite haunts, Croft.

His schedule reads like that of a professional racing driver but Graham was still working full-time as a manufacturer's agent and was still contributing financially towards his racing. The need to be back at work on Monday morning from faraway places such as Thruxton must have taken its toll.

It was much of the same for 1971, as the Escort programme continued both in Scotland and England but with an ex-Broadspeed Group 2 RS1600 and a Group 5 twin-cam version. This time Graham's European adventures would be with a new team and in a different category. Through his association with Ecurie Ecosse, Graham met Denys Dobbie, a local businessman and former secretary of the Ecurie Ecosse Association. Dobbie had ambitions to be a major player in the Scottish motorsport scene and one of the first steps was to form Dobbie Automobile Racing Team (DART). Graham had driven for them at Ingliston in both a Chevron B8 and B16 towards the end of the 1970 season and had scored first and third-place finishes.

This led to signing for them to contest the increasingly popular European 2-litre Sportscar championship in a Chevron B19 with former Lotus F1 driver John Miles in a second car. The team's first outing was at the BOAC 1000kms at Brands Hatch, the second round of the World Sportscar Championship. Paired together, Graham and John brought their car home an impressive seventh overall and first in class. The opening round of the 2.0-litre series at Paul Ricard saw Graham drive a magnificent race to finish sixth overall despite suffering from badly blistered hands caused by a marathon first stint of over 90 laps. John Miles took over for the remaining 40-plus laps after having some loose bodywork secured. A disappointing outing at Silverstone in the RAC British Sportscar series was followed by a couple of victories back on home soil at Ingliston.

Unfortunately, at the second round of the European series at the Salzburgring in late May, Graham suffered a broken wrist after Vic Elford touched his car coming out of the bottom hairpin and sent it sideways into the guardrail. Once recovered, he returned to the series at Hockenheim in July but an engine failure in the first heat meant a non-finish and rendered him a non-starter in the second.

That was his last outing for the DART team. His relationship with Miles was always lukewarm, to say the least. General disillusionment with the team saw them part on less than amicable terms.

On the Escort front, after a troubled start Graham had his best result – place overall and first in class – at the saloon car encounter supporting the British Grand Prix at Silverstone.

At the end of the season he decided to call it a day. The dangers and the continual financial struggle was just getting too much. In his own words, he 'Was sick of having the phone cut off and not paying the rent.'

It is evident throughout his career that Graham was never daunted by the myriad opportunities that came his way. The thrill of being in control of anything motorised was rarely turned down. When, only a few months into his racing retirement, the opportunity arose to try something he hadn't tried before, how could he resist, the chance to drive from Glasgow to Monte Carlo, then back to Glasgow? What a glamorous sounding idea. But the truth couldn't be further removed from glamorous if you tried.

Take one Chrysler 180 road car, attach an Eccles Topaz caravan, leave Glasgow at midnight on Sunday 20th February 1972, drive 2658 miles, record an average speed of 55.5mph, return to Kelvin Hall, Glasgow on Thursday 24 at 10am in time for the preview of the Scottish Caravan and Mobile Holidays Exhibition, having stopped just once at Fontainebleau for sleep and set a new record in the process. That's exactly what Graham and navigator Kieron Wood accomplished. Unbelievable!

Another wacky opportunity presented itself three years later when he was asked by the *Daily Record*, a leading Scottish newspaper, to road test a three-wheeled invalid car, which at the time was embroiled in controversy surrounding their suitability for use on the public highway. With comments such as , 'I have driven some hairy cars in my career – but that is, without doubt, the most unpleasant vehicle I have ever encountered,' and 'it's a long time since my toes curled up with fear at the wheel. I found it grossly unstable at low speeds. I was acutely aware of how vulnerable you would be in the event of an accident,' it was crystal clear he wasn't a fan.

In among those adventures Graham had made a low-key return to racing at Ingliston in a Rallye Simca 2 entered by

His appetite to try something different led Graham to take part in the Avon Tour of Britain in 1974. ***(Graham Birrell/Darren Banks archive)***

A recent photo of Graham. Still looking great for his age. ***(Alex Shore)***

Halesfield Motors, which was now the domain of Mike Leeke. The association continued the following into 1974 with a more comprehensive programme of events, this time in a Hillman Hunter 1.8 GLS, a far cry from a Chevron B19!

A couple of victories and other top three placings at Ingliston showed he hadn't lost any speed or desire. He even ventured to Kirkistown to try his luck. But the highlight of that period was an outing on the Avon Tour of Britain, a three-day event comprising rally stages and laps of various circuits. It was an ideal event for someone like Graham. He was accompanied to a fine 16th overall by his former Wylie's mechanic Andy Morrison, who remains a good friend.

After another hiatus of a couple of years he returned once again to his former happy hunting ground Ingliston, to contest the Shell Scottish Production Car Championship with an Opel Kadett GT/E. He claimed numerous top three overall finishes and class victories in a pretty standard car.

He had now got the bug again, so the car was lightened and modified by Morrison, and he went on the win the championship.

From then on he dabbled with various drives that came his way from old friends. The chance to contest the Miglia 1000 Historic, which began in Brescia in a Jaguar C-type with the car's owner Campbell McLaren, was the stuff of dreams. Into the Nineties he was reunited with one of the Ecosse Imps owned by Tom McWhirter. Numerous outings in historic races at Ingliston and Knockhill brought a modicum of success.

The last outing before he hung up his helmet for good was at the Coys Historic Festival GT race at Silverstone in 1994 in a Lightweight Jaguar E-Type belonging to Campbell McLaren. They were the first Jaguar home, which made it a fitting end to a long and successful career.

Now in his ninth decade – though he doesn't look it – he still attends the odd meetings closest to his Edinburgh home. The Bo'ness Revival is one such event. He is still a popular figure with many friends, old and new. He is very sociable and knowledgeable, just like in his heyday, when he was present at all the important car club dinner dances and end of season prize presentations. He remains impeccably turned out and cuts the same dashing figure he did in the '60s.

His main passion these days is something more sedate, with golf taking up much of his spare time. He still carries his famous number plate, GA 3, on his road car and makes the trip to Silverstone, as often as time allows, to catch up with old friends at the BRDC, of which he is a proud member.

Shamefully, his racing achievements are easily overlooked, especially with Gerry going on to gain international recognition. But, be in no doubt, that Graham was a force to be reckoned with in whichever machine he was in control of, whether on a circuit or a rally stage. Being Gerry's elder sibling he made connections to further his own career, which also benefited his younger brother. John Crosslé, Brian Hart and Avon Tyres, three of the most prominent names involved in Gerry's early days, all came via Graham. While Gerry would still surely have had the career he had, with or without Graham, the assistance offered by his big brother certainly sped things up and made it an easier climb up the racing ladder.

Graham Birrell should be remembered as one of the leading figures of the Scottish motorsport scene of the '60s and '70s and if things had fallen his way at the right time he could well have had a far more successful career. He certainly wasn't lacking in talent and determination.

Kara getting ready to take part in the Ecurie Ecosse parade in the Ecosse-Imp at the Goodwood Revival. Dario Franchitti offers words of encouragement while the car's owner Vernon Williamson looks on. (Alex Shore)

The trademark helmet and the Birrell eyes. ***(Alan Bowles)***

Appendix Two: The Father I never knew – Kara Birrell

I was four days short of being 17 months old when my father was killed at Rouen, so in essence I never knew him.

I don't remember exactly when I became aware of not having a father, but do recall watching with my twin sister Maija some cine films of him racing in the Springbok series and knowing then he was dead. Maija tragically passed away in February 1980, just after her eighth birthday. She made a very funny comment while watching the film that she thought Jochen Mass was Jesus because he had long hair. I have no idea where that came from, just the sort of crazy thing that enters a child's mind, I guess.

Sadly, back then and even nowadays, I've never really talked at length to Mum about my Dad. I guess, these days we are caught up in the here and now.

As a teenager I would fly up to Scotland on my own, which was petrifying, to stay with my paternal grandparents. I don't remember them coming to visit us. They came down for my sister's funeral but that was about it, really. I went to both of their funerals. Grandad passed first, followed by grandmother. That would have been when I was about 17 or 18 years old.

Sadly, mum fell out with them. I think they blamed her for letting dad carry on racing, especially once he had children. But she didn't want to stop him doing something he loved. They didn't really help financially, but they had the money.

Over the years I have collected photos, race programmes, and other memorabilia. A prized possession is a lovely album of photos compiled by the late journalist Alan Henry. The first page carries a lovely message.

I have a tape recording of dad and was disappointed that he didn't have a really sexy, Sean Connery Scottish accent, which was something I'd always imagined him having. He had this really high-pitched, Glaswegian one. It totally blew my image of him!

In the past few years I've been honoured to drive some of my father's old cars for the documentary being made by Alex. What an amazing but nerve-wracking experience. I was too nervous to be emotional about it all.

I drove the Kent Capri at Donington with Jochen Mass alongside offering advice and instructions, which was daunting. But, even more daunting, was driving the car up the hill at the Festival of Speed at Goodwood. I was so nervous about stalling it in front of so many people. Another nice

Alongside Yvette Fontaine in the replica BP Escort at Brands Hatch in 2018, when they took part in the demonstration to commemorate 50 years of the Escort. ***(Alan Bowles)***

In the Donington pit lane alongside Jochen Mass. What a day! ***(Simon Arron)***

moment was being asked for my autograph. I had to remind them that I was a nobody, to which I got a reply of, 'You're Gerry Birrell's daughter'. Also at Goodwood, this time at the Revival, I drove the Ecosse-Imp belonging to Vernon Williamson.

The other occasion was at Brands Hatch in 2018 when I drove the BP Belgian Escort as part of the 50 years of the Ford Escort celebrations. That was a replica of the original car but I'm in contact with the owner of that, who has offered me a chance to drive it once it's restored. I hope other cars will become available in the future.

I have tried to keep my father's memory alive, believing it to be important that his legacy is remembered. This book will mean he will be remembered forever in writing, which is lovely. I'm looking forward to reading it and discovering many new facts about him.

It's amazing nearly 50 years after his death that people still talk about him. It means a lot.

Note from the Author: The day Kara drove the Capri at Donington was covered in a lengthy feature by the late Simon Arron in the October 2017 issue of *Motor Sport* magazine.

The front cover of the scrapbook compiled by Alan Henry.

What a lovely, touching gesture from the legendary, much-missed AH. ***(Kara Birrell)***

Bibliography

BOOKS

BOREHAM The 40-year story of Ford's Motorsport Dream Factory by Graham Robson (Haynes Publishing, 2004)
CAPRI The Development and Competition History of Ford's European GT Car by Jeremy Walton (Haynes Publishing, 1985 Reprint)
CHEVRON The Derek Bennett Story by David Gordon (DBG Publishing, 2005)
ECURIE ECOSSE A Social History of Motor Racing from the Fifties to the Nineties by Graham Gauld (Graham Gauld PR, 1992)
ECURIE ECOSSE David Murray and the Legendary Scottish Motor Racing Team by Eric Dymock (PJ Publishing, 2007).
ESCORT MK1, 2 & 3 The Development and Competition History by Jeremy Walton (Haynes Publishing, 1985)
FITZ My Life at the Wheel by John Fitzpatrick (Autosports Marketing Associates, 2016)
HIDDEN GLORY The Story of the Crosslé Car Company by Alan 'Plum' Tyndall (Booklink, 2014)
INGLISTON YEARBOOKS – Various years
JAMES HUNT by Maurice Hamilton (McLaren/Blink Publishing, 2016)
JPS Yearbooks 1972 & 1973 edited by Barrie Gill (Queen Anne Press)
KENNY SMITH SCARPBOOK A Celebration of a Kiwi Legend by Michael Clark (Bateman, 2016)
MOTOR RACING DIRECTORY Mike Kettlewell's Guide to British Motor Racing (Kettlewell Transport Information Servies, 1979)
RACES FACES PLACES The Motor Racing Photography of Michael Cooper by Paul Parker (Haynes Publishing, 2009)
SCOTTISH MOTOR RACING AND DRIVERS One Hundred Years of Scotland's Involvement with Motor Racing by Graham Gauld (Havelock Publishing, 2004)
SECOND TO NONE The European Formula Two Story: From Ickx to Thackwell and from Rindt to Streiff by Chris Ellard (W3 Publications, 2017)
TWICE LUCKY My Life in Motorsport by Stuart Turner (Haynes Publishing, 1999)

PERIODICALS

Autocar, Autosport, Auto Tradition, Cars and Car Conversions, Competition Car, Motor, Motoring News, Motor Sport, Motor World, News From the Mews: The Official Journal of the Ecurie Ecosse Association, Scottish Clubman, Top Gear